AMERICA'S

THE FIRST CENTURY

COMMUNITY

BY ALLEN A. WITT,
JAMES L. WATTENBARGER,
JAMES F. GOLLATTSCHECK,
AND JOSEPH E. SUPPIGER

COLLEGES

WITH A FOREWORD BY
EDMUND J. GLEAZER, JR.

Published by the Community College Press, a division of the American Association of Community Colleges
One Dupont Circle, N.W.
Suite 410
Washington, D.C. 20036
(202) 728-0200

ISBN 0-87117-267-4

CONTENTS

FOREWORD

Hundreds of community colleges were established in the 1960s. Many of them are celebrating their silver anniversaries and are using that opportunity to look back, to examine their roots, and to anticipate their future. Recently I spoke to the faculty and administration at a Texas community college where they were doing just that, and I was impressed by their keen interest in the circumstances that brought their institution and 500 others into being. Only a few seemed familiar with the story, but they were eager to learn more. One reason for that is their current need to make decisions about the future mission of their college. They find themselves confronting difficult choices.

They face circumstances as challenging as those that faced the people who opened the college, but they are without the advantage of the broad discussions of community college mission that took place in the earlier days. Typically, citizens of a community voted on the proposition to establish a college and at the same time approved taxes to build the plant and finance operations. Much discussion took place in the community about the nature of the institution they were "buying." After a board was selected, the process of inquiry went on as criteria were established to guide the appointment of a qualified president and suitable faculty. But nothing was more searching in mission definition than planning the campus and physical facilities. The basic question was, What functions will these structures serve? In short, What is the institution to do?

However, when an institution celebrates its twenty-fifth year, there is a likelihood that the process of inquiry into purposes and functions has subsided and the possibility that institutional forms and practices have congealed. I suggested, somewhat facetiously, that to assure vitality they should level their buildings and start all over again. A more practical way, obviously, is to draw upon the valuable experiences of the past in dealing with the issues of the present. Institutions engaged in that essential exercise will welcome a history of the community college for the perspective it provides.

Other developments make this publication timely. Under severe financial pressures many state governments question the kinds of educational programs they will fund as well as the number of students they will support. A current issue that bears directly upon the perception of the community college mission is the California legislative plan, approved in the fall of 1992, that imposed a $50-per-unit fee on community college students who already have a baccalaureate degree. Other students pay one-fifth of this amount. In one district alone (Los Rios) are more than 4,000 students with baccalaureate degrees or higher. The chancellor of the district said that findings of a survey of these students made by the college raised important policy questions. She reported that 40 percent of the respondents were unemployed or working part time. Clearly this is the kind of issue that can only be considered in the light of how the college mission is perceived in an environment of economic stress. Community college history ought to be tapped when such questions are considered.

This is not the first time that under budgetary pressures the difficult problem of priorities has had to be faced. But that fact brings little comfort to those who have to decide what students should be given preference if enrollments must be capped and programs limited. Without question, we are at a point in community college development and in a period of societal change that presses us to consider how these institutions can best continue to provide opportunity for learning. A knowledge of history—of the circumstances and forces that have brought this American institution to its present state—can be a valuable resource in considering future directions. What do we find by looking back that will be useful in confronting the questions of today and tomorrow?

THE CONTINUING SEARCH FOR IDENTITY

There is in community college history a discernible search for institutional identity, that is, for recognition and public understanding in terms of a mission different from and yet in some respects similar to the missions of both of its progenitors, the secondary school and the college. "We are not well understood" is a complaint of long standing. The mixed parentage of our colleges contributed to the problem in the earlier days. The junior college could be another two years of secondary school—an extension of the high school. Or it could be the first two years of college. Other variations were possible. As the institution evolved it leaned toward the college in its structure (organization, facilities, and programs), while pursuing a comprehensive mission more akin to that of the high school.

An example of the problems community colleges faced is provided by the experiences of the American Association of Junior Colleges as it launched a special public information project in 1956. Leading philanthropic foundations announced new grant programs for colleges and universities. No community colleges were included. Junior college leaders were convinced that their institutions were not understood by national leaders, foundations, or business and industry. Moreover, the colleges were not respected and appreciated for their great potential. In a reply to Association overtures a leader in corporate philanthropy said, "We are not interested in junior colleges. And, besides, we do not give to secondary schools."

Further, junior colleges appeared to be supplicants for recognition and acceptance by the universities because no question was more important in determining the quality of a junior college than whether its credits would transfer to the university. To a great extent the universities were determining the curricula of the junior college, although a majority of the junior college students did not transfer.

As these institutions grew in number and comprehensiveness, they were perceived as invaders by established interests in vocational and adult education. Further, measures were frequently taken to protect existing universities and other institutions. A case in point was the action by authorities in the state of Washington in 1959 to ban junior colleges from Seattle and other districts with public four-year institutions.

It was some time before accrediting agencies decided how to treat these new institutions. They were uncertain whether to administer the standards applicable to colleges or to secondary schools. Eventually they found it necessary to view the community college as an institution in its own right.

In many respects the junior college did not look like or behave like a college. Most of the students were commuters. Hardly any of the public institutions had residential facilities. They were open in their admissions, not selective. They were low cost. A high proportion of the faculty were part time. A majority of the students were part time. Conventional academic terminology often did not fit: terms like dropout, attrition, college grad. At the federal level, in times of war and as educational legislation grew in the 1960s, it was often necessary to examine congressional intent in order to determine whether community colleges were included in legislative measures affecting "colleges."

Toward the latter part of the 1970s there was increased public recognition that continuing education, or lifelong education, was replacing the notion of completion of education. Education was viewed more often as concurrent with holding an occupation and the responsibilities of adulthood. However, there were still grievous lapses in the understanding of the community college role. A case in point was the dedication of the new Downtown Center of the San Francisco Community College District in 1979. The facilities were designed to serve 10,000 students, primarily people who worked every day in downtown San Francisco. Speaking at the televised dedication ceremonies, the mayor congratulated the city on having such a fine new facility for "the youngsters" of the city. Many of those "youngsters" were at least the age of the mayor.

Millions of people are served annually by community colleges, and there is one in almost every congressional district. Community colleges are defined and described in legislative language and in accrediting manuals. But still there persists, most notably at the federal and state levels, less than full appreciation of the community college as an institution with an identity of its own. Now the crucial questions are not of college structures but of functions—what functions are appropriate and worthy of support. The necessary continuing examination of community college identity should be guided by the kind of question posed by an educational observer some twenty years ago:

> Is education to be organized around institutions, credit, and credentials...or is education to be organized around learners as an optimal system for distributing knowledge and encouraging its utilization? (Marien, 1972, p. 11).

RELATIONSHIPS OF COMMUNITY AND COLLEGE

As already noted, in the early years of junior college development, the emphasis was on adding two years to the high school program or providing the first two years of college. However, just fifteen years after the first public junior college was established, Dean Alexis Lange of the University of California School of Education and other leaders in educational thought urged the junior colleges to give high priority to programs that would prepare their students for effective participation in community life. Lange called for:

- A junior college department of civic education.

- [An educational goal:] their studies and other activities must be expected to have greatly quickened their communal sympathies and deepened their sense of indissoluble oneness with their fellows...they are possessed of the will to participate vigorously, militantly, if need be, in advancing community welfare.

- [A suggested method:] suitable opportunities for observation at first hand and for direct participation in the civic activities, of one sort or another, of the community maintaining the junior college (Bogue, 1950a, pp. 336–337).

A further step toward community orientation in the building of college programs was evident in the first revision to the statement of purpose in the constitution of the American Association of Junior Colleges (1922b):

> The junior college may, and is likely to, develop a different type of curriculum, suited to the larger and ever changing

civic, social, and vocational needs of the entire community in which the college is located.

The theme of relating to the "needs of the entire community" was made more specific by Byron S. Hollinshead in 1936, and the name "community college" was given to the institution:

> That the junior college should be a community college, meeting community needs; that it should serve to promote a greater social and civic intelligence in the community...that the work of the community college should be closely integrated with the work of the high school and the work of other community institutions (p. 111).

In the pages of this book are reported the ways in which the colleges related to the needs of the community in wartime, depression, drought, and periods of national emergencies. Experience in such times prepared them for the adaptation required in meeting the needs of growing numbers of racial minorities, women, senior citizens, and people with disabilities.

These directions of development were encouraged by the Truman Commission:

> The Community College seeks to become a center of learning for the entire community, with or without the restrictions that surround formal course work in traditional institutions of higher education. It gears its programs and services to the needs and wishes of the people it serves (President's Commission on Higher Education, 1947, vol. 1, pp. 69–70).

The dominant force of the community college, declared the commission, "is its intimate relations to the life of the community it serves" (p. 5).

During the 1960s "intimate relations to the life of the community" brought substantial change in the substance and the methods of teaching and learning. Among the 500 new community colleges were a number of institutions opening for the first time in many of America's major cities, such as Cleveland, Dallas, Newark, Philadelphia, and Seattle. The political unrest of that time, particularly the struggles by minority groups for educational and economic opportunity, swept back and forth across the community college campuses in these big cities. The colleges were in communities caught in the throes of change. New relationships were required with many other community organizations that affected the lives of the citizens, their students: housing organizations, community centers, welfare departments, health agencies, employment offices, and economic development commissions. Educational services were provided on and off the campuses. Many of the larger institutions opened scores of educational centers. The college and community were interfusing both spatially and functionally.

In the late 1970s community college leaders talked more frequently about the "marketing approach." They consulted "customer needs." They asked what educational services the citizens wanted to "buy." And they found themselves facing a plethora of questions. Is the future of our institutions as the first two years in a structure of college and university education or as community-based providers of educational services, perhaps as the hub of a network of community educative agencies and organizations? Where do we put the emphasis, on community or college? Or should they have equal weight? Will this vary from community to community? And beyond all else, how should these institutions respond to the "needs of the entire community" today and tomorrow?

At the time of this writing, communities in the United States are dealing with such problems as racial conflicts among Cuban Americans, African Americans, and Whites in Miami; economic conversion in the Midwest and Texas owing to layoffs in local industries; conflicts between loggers and environmentalists in Oregon; rising disputes, claims, and counterclaims across ethnic, geographical, gender, political, and economic lines in much of America; and mounting numbers of homeless and hungry in the cities. Moreover, America is faced with a wave of immigration that matches that of the early years of the century, with skyrocketing costs of health care and corrections requiring larger shares of public budgets, with a pervasive drug culture, and all of this in a democratic society where citizens argue that they have been pushed out of the political process and that their government and its public officials have failed them.

Are these community needs that require a community college response? They appear to be urgent, complex, and even life-threatening. To judge from the historical relationship of college and community, it is not only appropriate, but essential, to address the educational components of these and other community problems. However, there are obstacles to be dealt with. Some people would say that it is not appropriate for the college to address such needs, that it is more appropriate for other community agencies. Up to this time, state legislators have not generally seemed to perceive the community college mission in this light, nor have they indicated a willingness to provide the necessary support. Basic to dealing with both of these views is a lack of research to assess the value of the economic and social outcomes of such programs. Impact studies must be undertaken to ensure sound judgments about the nature and scope of an institution that is responsive to community needs. Good information is a requisite, but something more is needed. The words of Alexis Lange never seemed more timely and appropriate as when he called for these community institutions to instill "the will to participate vigorously, militantly, if need be, in advancing community welfare" (Bogue, 1950a, pp. 337).

TO EXTEND EDUCATIONAL OPPORTUNITY

A study of community college history shows that a major aim of this evolving institution has been to extend educational opportunity. One of the ways it has done this is to broaden opportunity. In the early 1960s such an objective was viewed as an international need:

> The present expansion in education is not only vastly increasing the number of students; it is also drawing them from many more diverse social origins. This trend should be encouraged further. We should cast our net wider and wider in order to identify, to catch and to bring within the scope of education all available talent, wherever it may be found (Zurayk, 1963, p. 15).

Similar to these recommendations were those made by the Truman Commission some years earlier that gave the community college a major role. The commission called for public education to be made available, tuition-free, to all Americans able and willing to receive it, regardless of race, creed, color, sex, or economic and social status (President's Commission on Higher Education, 1947, vol. V, p. 3).

State plans for community colleges usually stipulated that these institutions be within commuting distance of a majority of the population in a state, be inexpensive for the student, have open admissions, and offer a broad variety of educational programs. Their rapid growth in cities already having universities and four-year colleges gave evidence that these new "opportunity colleges" were drawing a population not served by existing institutions. In fact, that was their charge in California:

> By their history and by their legal mandate California junior colleges are to complement, not mimic, the other segments of higher education.... The junior colleges are particularly charged with providing services and programs not offered by the other institutions and to educate a more heterogeneous student body (Coordinating Council for Higher Education, 1965, p. 3).

Some ten years later the effects of that policy were studied and reported:

> Part-time students now comprise two-thirds of the head count enrollment.... The part-time, older students come with their own objectives relating to educational, career, and personal growth which often are achieved outside degree and certificate programs. They tend to enroll on an intermittent basis, that is, skipping semesters and enrolling in other institutions offering post-secondary programs. Although enrolled in courses offered for credit, they sometimes forego credits and grades on the grounds that they have no need for certification. Many already have baccalaureate and advanced degrees but find courses in their local community colleges

which satisfy a wide range of individual interests.... Thus, continuing education for part-time adult students has become the dominant function of community colleges, with no resultant neglect of the occupational, transfer, and general education functions for more traditional students (Knoell, 1976, p. 8).

To a great extent colleges in other states reported similar developments. People of limited financial means now had a low-cost institution available. For those who could not leave the community to go to college, there was one within commuting distance. And those uncertain about their academic abilities or who wanted programs geared quickly to employment found an environment responsive to those needs. Historically, the community college was based on the assumption that large numbers of people were not being served by existing institutions. The unserved were to be the clientele of these new colleges.

I have heard that theme sounded in numerous ways in my own research and in conversations with community college and citizen leaders: Community colleges should reach out. Go to unserved people. Give priority to those who need the education they did not get at an earlier age. Serve the student with roots in the community. Give those who need it a second chance. Bring people into the mainstream. Serve people hindered by problems of cost and transportation.

A careful study of community college development shows that these institutions have been especially important to people whose educational options are limited by a variety of circumstances. That is a significant factor to consider in any policy discussions about the present and future role of these colleges. From the beginning their call has been to extend educational opportunity.

TO VALUE DIVERSITY

The open-door, close-to-home, low-cost, community-responsive policies of the community college have resulted in a diversity of learners beyond the breadth of any other educational institution. Added to the variety of a typical high school population are differences in age, ethnic neighborhood, and income. In some cities the first genuine interaction among racial and cultural groups takes place when the student reaches the community college.

As these colleges opened their doors all across America, the population that responded was unprecedented in terms of race, lifestyles, economic means, psychological and emotional needs, and educational preparation. By any measure, in terms of previous institutional experience, community colleges were dealing not only with "regular" students but with those that would have to be described as unconventional and nontraditional.

Faculty and administrators found it necessary to accelerate their own learning in order to cope with the needs of their new clientele. And a question became perennial: how to maintain access and at the same time ensure excellence. That challenge remains. Diversity in the community college is a fact. And more diversity is ahead if the counsel of the Truman Commission continues to be heeded: "It gears its programs and services to the needs and wishes of the people it serves—it seeks to become a center of learning for the entire community" (President's Commission on Higher Education, 1947, vol. I, pp. 69–70). Community colleges that follow this admonition will experience more diversity because their communities are becoming more diverse.

It is not appropriate here to examine in detail the changes taking place in American society with regard to race, gender, ethnicity, language, religion, age, and sexual orientation. We can note the enormous, perhaps uncontrollable wave of global migration already taking place from south to north. Community colleges are experiencing the vanguards of this shifting population.

Workplace diversity is already seen by the business world as a bottom-line issue. Executives are telling their managers, who formerly were supposed to be colorblind and to ignore cultural and ethnic differences, now to recognize diversity and to value it. A Conference Board study reports that American business leaders thought that workplace diversity gave their companies a competitive marketplace advantage. According to the report, this attitude represents a fundamental change in the way companies view and deal with the diversity issue. One business leader asserted:

> The goal should be to change people and systems and the way we think about them and the ways in which we deal with them. That's what's meant by cultural change.... We're focusing on changing our systems first and training second (Randle, 1993, p. H2).

Such advice is useful. However, many community colleges have had considerable experience in adapting systems to the needs of people. Their experience can be useful as institutions change to match a changing population. Beyond that, attitude is extremely important. The broad diversity of learners has sometimes been viewed as uncomfortable baggage to be carried by the institution. That diversity needs to be seen as valuable. For example, it serves to open communication and a myriad of relationships with the community. The college that cuts across ethnic lines, socioeconomic classes, educational interests, geographic boundaries, and generations brings people together so that not only their differences, but also their common interests and needs can be acknowledged and valued. Some call this process "community building."

I am grateful to the authors for their invitation to write these pages. Not only did I read the manuscript with interest, I reflected on my own experience and observations of almost fifty years—half of that first hundred years!—in the junior and community college field. What I have described here are persisting themes, as I see them, that may be useful as reference points in the charting of future directions.

The fact that a history is published does not suggest that this is a terminal point for the community college. Its evolution continues. My great concern is that future development be guided by values as worthy as those that have brought these institutions this far.

Edmund J. Gleazer, Jr.
President Emeritus
American Association of Community Colleges

PREFACE

The first question the authors of any history should address—to themselves at the outset and to prospective readers later—is, Why? Why another history? In the case of community colleges, the answer is rather simple. There has never been an analytical history of the national movement that, in this decade, is 100 years old.

Most of the important writings that now form the foundation of the history of community colleges were written as contemporary analyses and only incidentally tie in past events. Landmark books such as Leonard Koos's *The Junior College Movement* (1925), Walter Eells's *The Junior College* (1931), Jesse Bogue's *The Community College* (1950), Leland Medsker's *The Junior College: Progress and Prospect* (1960), and Edmund J. Gleazer's *The Community College: Values, Vision, and Vitality* (1980) were primarily concerned with explaining, defining, and validating the place of community and junior colleges in American higher education in their respective times. This is not to say that there has been a lack of excellent research. Without the considerable research findings amassed in recent years, reported primarily in professional journals and doctoral dissertations, this book would not have been possible. But most research has been directed at individual states or specific functions, programs, or aspects of the community college.

In this book the major intent is to trace the nationwide development of the community college from initial concept to its present position as the largest and fastest-growing sector of American higher education. At each stage we have attempted to relate the development of community colleges to social and economic events and conditions in America and, at times, in the world. In so doing, one exciting fact became evident: community colleges and the socioeconomic development of our nation have been intertwined from the very beginning. Junior and community colleges were created when they were needed, and they have evolved over the years based on specific studies and surveys in their communities, their states, and the nation.

As pointed out in Chapter 1, it is important to have a documented national history of community colleges because so few of these institutions maintain their own histories. Operating on tight budgets with expanding enrollments, they lack the resources to maintain the archives and resident historians that many major universities normally provide. Because community colleges are intensely local in perspective and mission, they often fail to recognize their broader importance to the nation's economic and social progress—in fact to the growth and success of American democracy.

As would be expected in a movement lacking in written history, myths and popular misconceptions have grown apace. We have tried where possible to explore and correct such. For example, popular belief would have it that early junior colleges were developed solely as transfer institutions, with occupational and technical programs developing only after World War II, and with community service coming later and, in the minds of some, to the detriment of "original" missions. The fact is that the earliest junior colleges and systems of junior colleges claimed all three missions from the beginning. Another misconception is that community colleges were rooted in a populist movement and always opposed by elitists. In an interesting relationship, populists *and* elitists in higher education were both responsible for the growth of junior and community colleges. Populists wanted to provide access to higher education for the masses, whereas elitists hoped to purify higher education by providing separate institutions for the teaching of lower-division students.

It is not surprising that the only sector of higher education to be called a movement would have its giants. Among the colorful leaders of the movement we find iconoclasts, explorers, robber barons, inventors, visionaries, politicians, evangelists, and, most of all, true believers. But just as the history of the movement is not well known, neither are its early leaders.

For example, to many George Zook is not a well-known name; yet his promotion of junior and community colleges throughout his professional career merits him a place in the forefront of those responsible for the growth and development of America's community colleges. As a representative of the U.S. Bureau of Education, he was responsible for the first national meeting of junior college leaders. As president of the American Council on Education, he supported the growth and recognition of two-year colleges. As chair of the Truman Commission, he, more than any other individual, was responsible for the development of the national system of public community colleges.

We are indebted to too many individuals, past and present, to try to acknowledge all of the many contributions that have made this book possible. We hope that for many, accurate quotations, citations, and inclusion in the bibliography will suffice to recognize their accomplishments and contributions. We must acknowledge the leadership and scholarship of Leonard Koos, Walter Eells, Jesse Bogue, and Leland Medsker, without whose writings a book such as this would have been nearly impossible. The support, encouragement, and assistance of Edmund Gleazer, Dale Parnell, and David Pierce also have been invaluable.

Certainly there will be those who will feel we have missed one or more key points in this history or slighted individuals who made significant contributions. To those readers we apologize. A great deal has happened to two-year colleges in the past hundred years and many people have played important roles in their evolution. Obviously, it would have been impossible to include every event and mention every person involved. We hope our work will inspire others to continue to research and publish the history of these important institutions.

It may appear to some readers that this history of community colleges gives undue attention to national associations, particularly the one now known as the American Association of Community Colleges. It becomes apparent, however, as one looks carefully at the movement that at every point in history these associations have reflected the interests, the concerns, the status, and the leadership of the colleges they represent. It would have been impossible to report on the history of these institutions without giving attention to the ways in which they organized themselves at the national level and the people they chose to represent them as they struggled for recognition.

Finally, some may think we write with too much excitement to be impartial observers. It is true that we are guilty of pride. An early statement in this book says, "The fuel for the junior college movement was America's expanding democracy." If this sounds excited and prideful, it is exactly such excitement and pride that we have found within the community college movement and wish to communicate to the reader.

Allen A. Witt
James L. Wattenbarger
James F. Gollattscheck
Joseph E. Suppiger

CHAPTER 1

THE EVOLUTION OF AN IDEA

This junior college idea has been conceived; it was born... [but] we are not quite sure of its parentage.

—Doak Campbell

The American community college movement is the most important higher education innovation of the twentieth century. It was born in the American heartland before the turn of the century and spread rapidly throughout the expanding West. As growing populations demanded educational opportunity, two-year colleges sprang up in all fifty states. A century later, there is a community college within a short drive of most Americans.

THE HISTORICAL CONTEXT

The fuel for the junior college movement was America's expanding democracy. As historians have pointed out, democracy is contagious. Once the door to full citizenship is open, more and more people demand to be admitted. Accordingly, from time to time this nation of immigrants has expanded the limits of democracy. Rights and privileges that had been limited to male landowners have been extended to the middle class, the poor, former slaves, women, and Native Americans. At times the progress was agonizingly slow, but it always continued. Over two centuries the rights of citizenship have been extended to every American.

One of these expansions of basic rights—the abolitionist movement of the nineteenth century—set the stage for the Civil War. After the war's end the concept of equal protection under the law was written into the Constitution with the 13th, 14th, and 15th Amendments. Over the course of the twentieth century, women's suffrage and the civil rights and women's rights movements refined and expanded the nation's view of democracy. The concept of equal rights was broadened to include equal opportunity—the right of all citizens to test their potential. With these expansions of democracy came demands for public education. Proponents elevated education to the status of a right. They argued that without the right to an education, other rights—such as free expression—had little meaning.

Although most other rights were enshrined in the Constitution, public education began as a grassroots movement for equal opportunity. Average citizens demanded that their children be taught to read, write, and cipher. As early as the 1640s, Puritan settlements sponsored tax-supported "grammar schools" (Zoglin, 1976, pp. 1–2). The idea grew slowly, and by the mid-nineteenth century grammar schools were a common part of American life. Eventually, compulsory schooling and child labor laws brought this basic education to the children of every social class. To many Americans the right to an education became as essential as the right to vote.

A rising tide of grammar school graduates created a demand for public junior high schools and high schools. By the Civil War there were already several hundred public high schools. In 1874 the decision in *Charles E. Stuart v. School District No. 1 of the Village of Kalamazoo* established the ability of local governments to fund secondary education, and the high school movement exploded. Over the next thirty years high school enrollments increased by nearly 600 percent.

The new high schools churned out tens of thousands of graduates. Unfortunately, America's elite colleges were usually too expensive or exclusive to meet the needs of these new graduates. The federal government stepped in, funding a series of state universities through federal land grants. These universities, however, were far away from the small towns and farms where most Americans lived. While land grant universities opened college doors to thousands, they did not touch the average high school graduate. Then, in the 1890s, there began developments that would bring about the last major link in American public education, the two-year college.

THE UNIVERSITY OF THE COMMON MAN

The two-year college made higher education available to the surging tide of high school graduates. Whereas universities fought to remain exclusive, junior colleges measured their success by inclusion. Admission did not require wealth or unusual intelligence. Students could take college classes near their homes, without moving to some distant city. Older students could work and support a family while earning their degrees. By reaching out to the average citizen, these "people's colleges" allowed a generation of Americans to achieve a goal that would have been unthinkable to their parents— a college diploma.

Whereas universities molded students to fit their classical curricula, two-year colleges adapted to meet the needs of a changing nation. They created vocational, technical, and preprofessional programs to train skilled workers, from nurses to keep people healthy, to mechanics to keep people mobile. Nearly every facet of American life, it seems, has been touched by the pervasive influence of two-year colleges.

All of the nation's great four-year universities and colleges combined have not affected the average citizen as profoundly as has the neighborhood community college. In fact, nearly one-half of all American adults will eventually take a course at a community college. The community college has truly become the university of the common man.

The rapid growth of the community college movement is well documented; however, there is much confusion about its origins.

Most community colleges have no archivists, no document vaults like those at many major universities. They have no wealthy alumni associations to publish the college history. Two-year colleges operate on tight budgets in the face of expanding enrollments. Consequently, few good histories of individual colleges, much less of the national movement, exist.

As any seasoned traveler knows, to determine how far one has come, one must know where one started. The same is true of academic institutions. As the community college movement begins its second century, it is important to understand where it came from and what it has achieved.

This chapter traces the junior college idea back to its beginnings, to an era when higher education was limited to a wealthy few. For most Americans of that era, college was a faraway dream. A century later, college is accessible to nearly every high school graduate. To students with average intelligence and motivation, educational options are virtually unlimited. The availability and variety of modern higher education are largely due to the pioneering efforts of America's two-year colleges.

An Unexpected Synthesis

The history of a civilization is not a series of isolated ideas and occurrences. It is an unbroken chain of sequentially related thought and action, with each link dependent on the one before it. Great historical movements are not created, but synthesized from ideas and movements of the past.

This concept of historical synthesis is particularly evident in the junior college movement. An examination of the ideas and individuals involved in the early junior colleges reveals two separate movements: the elitist and the democratic or populist (Zoglin, 1976, p. 4).

The populists insisted on educational opportunity for all citizens. Having created public grammar schools, junior high schools, and then high schools, by the 1880s populist leaders were demanding greater public access to colleges and universities. The elitists, on the other hand, were generally university scholars who wanted to maintain the exclusive nature of their institutions. These academicians were seeking a way to divert the rising tide of high school graduates. Although the two groups seemed incompatible, it was their union that eventually spawned the community college movement. This uneasy synthesis is best understood through an examination of the development of higher education in early American society.

Colleges have been a part of America since the founding of Harvard College in 1636. These elite institutions allowed the local gentry to get a classical education—in Greek, Latin, mathematics, and other disciplines—without having to return to England. The purpose of these colleges was to prepare young men for the professions and a place at the top of colonial society.

The early colleges were not universities in the German tradition of scholarship and research. Disciplines such as engineering and science were not considered appropriate for English gentlemen. Instead, the colleges adopted the British model of rote learning, a system that had changed little since medieval times. Students were molded by exposure to great ideas. Professors acted primarily as tutors. The result was a graduate who was prepared for life in the colonial upper classes and for little else.

After the American Revolution these liberal arts colleges multiplied. As the nation pushed westward, hundreds of isolated towns built their own colleges, many of which were church-sponsored schools that served the added function of training ministers. These private institutions perpetuated European civilization in the great American wilderness. Like their colonial predecessors, they shunned technology and science. Because of the colleges' size and isolation, academic standards were often low and libraries small. The first attempts at accreditation were still decades away.

By the mid-nineteenth century progress had overtaken the small college. With the coming of the railroad and the telegraph, once isolated towns now communicated more closely with major cities. America was entering a period of massive industrial growth. In this new era a classical education was no longer sufficient. The new industries demanded scientists, engineers, and business people.

A new breed of university emerged to meet the needs of an industrial society. Leading eastern colleges expanded their curricula and became true universities. Industrialists such as Leland Stanford and John D. Rockefeller founded their own research universities. More importantly, Congress passed the Morrill Act of 1862, which provided grants of federal land that could be sold to create state universities or to support existing state universities where appropriate. These land grant universities were to be dedicated to the mechanical sciences and agriculture.

Many leaders of these new institutions looked to the German university as a model. In the German system the professor was primarily a scholar and researcher, and students chose a specialized course of study rather than a generalized classical curriculum. This interest in German education led to the establishment of the Ph.D. degree and inevitably to the modern research university.

Higher education in America, no longer the exclusive province of gentlemen, sought to enroll the intellectually inclined: individuals from all social classes, with a flair for science, business, or the law. Scholarships allowed the gifted ones to study at the most prominent universities. Many graduates stayed on as faculty members and scholars, raising the university standards of research and scholarship. Despite these changes, however, universities served only a tiny percentage of the population. The average American lacked the wealth or the extraordinary academic ability needed to attend. Most university scholars preferred it that way. In the 1880s the university faculty remained a very select club.

During these same years high schools were becoming commonplace in American cities and towns. The trickle of high school graduates became a torrent that threatened to overwhelm the university system. University enrollments rose from 52,000 in 1870 to 238,000 at the turn of the century (Zoglin, 1976, pp. 2, 3).

With high school graduates seeking easier access to higher education, university elitists looked desperately for a way to divert them elsewhere. These conflicting demands led to the creation of two new institutions: the six-year high school and the two-year college. The six-year high school, mainly funded by local school systems, was formed by extending the secondary school curriculum to cover the first two years of college. Similarly, the two-year college was formed by eliminating the last two years from the curriculum of some small private colleges. These new institutions gave advanced training to high school graduates without flooding the universities. In so doing, they pleased both the university elitists and the new college freshmen. By the early years of the twentieth century, both six-year high schools and "decapitated" colleges were commonly called junior colleges.

THE GROWTH OF AN IDEA

The idea of the two-year college is not unique to this century. Nor was it born in the democratic aspirations of citizens for higher education. In fact, many of the first theorists to favor the concept were elitists who wanted to keep a growing number of high school students out of major universities. These elitists viewed the university as a place of scholarship, research, and specialization. Like many modern research professors, they dreaded the idea of teaching general education courses to freshmen and sophomores. They argued that the first two years of college were actually an extension of high school and that the "tutoring" of these years had no place in a research university.

The elitists pointed to the German system, in which students remained in a secondary school—called the gymnasium—until about twenty years of age. This prolonged high school completed the student's general education. Most gymnasium graduates needed no further education; those few who proceeded to the university were well qualified and ready to specialize. As a consequence, the German system had gained a worldwide reputation for research and scholarship.

The earliest elitist plan for creating two-year colleges was published just after the American Revolution. Doak Campbell, secretary of the American Association of Junior Colleges, cited it at the Association's 1929 convention.

I call your attention to a notable book in American education which was written at the suggestion of Thomas Jefferson, by DuPont de Nemours. This book, *National Education*, was writ-

ten at the beginning of the last century. In it the author out-
lines quite in detail...a secondary school which he calls a
"college", and which rather closely fulfills the description of a
junior college (Campbell, 1929, p. 13).

Pierre-Samuel du Pont de Nemours proposed an institution that
would fall between the secondary school and the university.
Although none of the later American elitists referred to du Pont's
book, their ideas were remarkably similar to his.

Campbell implied that du Pont's book may have led to the junior
college movement. The facts, however, dispute this assertion. Du
Pont's manuscript was written in French and was not available in
America. By the time an acceptable English edition emerged, in the
1920s, the junior college movement was already well under way
(Du Pont de Nemours, 1923).

The first serious proposal for separating the lower division of the
university curriculum came seventy years after the du Pont book, in
1851. Henry Tappan blasted American higher education. "In this
country," he said, "we have no universities. Whatever may be the
names by which we choose to call our institutions of learning, still
they are not universities" (Diener, 1986, p. 27).

Tappan proposed radical changes in the "deficient" American
university. His plan required students to complete their general
education in a college before being admitted to a university. These
colleges would "guard the entrance of the universities" (p. 24). Students who entered the university would be fully prepared to conduct scholarship and research. Like many other elitists, Tappan patterned his proposal after the German system:

> Collegial tuition [general education] in the German Universi-
> ties does not exist, because wholly unnecessary, the student
> being fully prepared at the Gymnasium before he is permitted
> to enter the university. Without the Gymnasium, the Univer-
> sity would be little worth.... The Gymnasia are really the
> Colleges. The education they furnish is more thorough, we
> believe, than what is obtained at the Colleges of either Eng-
> land or of our own country (pp. 25–26).

Tappan was not diplomatic, however. In attacking the entire American system of higher education—he referred to colleges and universities as mere secondary "academies"—he angered many of his peers.

In 1852 Tappan was named president of the University of Michigan. His proposals, however, were never successfully implemented there or elsewhere. Eventually Tappan "was fired for his elitist attitudes" (Ratcliff, 1987a, p. 9). Some scholars have attempted to link Tappan to an innovative University of Michigan curriculum plan adopted in 1882—two decades after his departure. There is, however, no known historical support for this claim.

In 1859 a trustee of the University of Georgia, William Mitchell, proposed a plan for separating the freshman and sophomore years from the university. In this case the issue was discipline. According to Diener (1986, p. 29), "Too many young boys not sufficiently prepared for the rigors of scholarly study had enrolled in the University." Their parents and the university felt that these young Georgians needed more supervision. To solve the problem Mitchell proposed that the university create a boarding school that would provide both a secondary and early postsecondary (freshman and sophomore years of college) education. Students "would be watched over night and day till fully prepared for the Junior Class" (p. 30). Graduates of the academy would then be admitted without examination to the university's upper division. The Georgia proposal was tabled and eventually abandoned during the Civil War.

William Watts Folwell proposed a similar system at the University of Minnesota. Like Tappan, Folwell, who had studied at the University of Berlin in 1860 and "attended several recitations at the local Gymnasium" (Buck, 1933, p. 200), was impressed by the prolonged secondary education. In 1870, the year after he was appointed president of the University of Minnesota, Folwell proposed a sweeping reorganization plan patterned after the German system. His innovative design became known as the Minnesota Plan.

Like many universities of the time, the University of Minnesota operated a preparatory department. This department was essentially a high school that prepared students for admission to the university. Folwell's plan would have extended the preparatory curriculum to include the freshman and sophomore years (Buck, 1933). The extended high school was to be renamed the Collegiate Department (p. 206). It would not grant a degree, but graduates would receive a "certificate of fitness," allowing them to enter the university. The board of regents adopted Folwell's plan unanimously. Unfortunately, "about half of the faculty members were opposed to the plan" (Gerber, 1971, p. 53). Their strident opposition prevented the Minnesota Plan from being implemented. Folwell's plan was retained as university policy for fifteen years, though never carried out, and was finally dropped from board policy in 1885. Had it been adopted, the Minnesota plan would have created America's first six-year high school.

Although it ultimately failed, Folwell's plan created considerable attention among other university presidents. After reviewing the Minnesota Plan, President Charles Eliot of Harvard wrote, "Your notion of relegating the studies of the Freshman and Sophomore years of the common American college to a secondary department squares with our practice and hopes" (Buck, 1933, pp. 210–211).

Folwell's ideas also influenced William Rainey Harper, founding president of the University of Chicago. Early in his career Harper was given a copy of the Folwell plan and "expressed his high approval and appreciation of the principles involved." Those principles included the idea of removing "the first two years of college work" from all American universities (Gerber, 1971, p. 52). The ideas fit with Harper's own plan for the "great university."

Unlike Tappan and Folwell, Harper put these new ideas into action. Harper successfully separated his university's upper and lower divisions and campaigned for the establishment of six-year high schools and two-year colleges. His achievements were the true beginning of the junior college movement. As Ratcliff (1986) noted, "Tappan and Folwell expressed ideas similar to Harper a generation earlier, but it was Harper who had the resources and ambition to try to transform the American education system" (p. 12).

Other prominent educators whose ideas foreshadowed the junior college movement include Charles A. Joy and John Burgess of Columbia College; R.H. Jesse of the University of Missouri;

Henry Barnard, U.S. commissioner of education; David Starr Jordan of Stanford (Diener, 1986); and Edmund James of the University of Illinois (Colvert & Littlefield, 1961).

EARLY PROTOTYPES

There is considerable disagreement among educators about the actual starting date of the junior college movement, much of which is due to isolated reports of early two-year colleges. Clearly, several private two-year institutions existed before the 1890s; however, there is no evidence to connect these institutions with the junior college movement.

The best documented of these early institutions are Lasell Female Seminary (Stanley, 1965) and New Ebenezer College. Lasell was established in 1851 at Newton, Massachusetts, as Auburndale Female Seminary, and renamed the following year for its founder, Edward Lasell, who had died of typhoid fever. The institution became Lasell Junior College in 1932.

From the beginning Lasell offered "the last two years of high school and the first two years of college" (Lasell College, 1991, p. 9). During the 1940s it dropped the high school unit and concentrated entirely on junior college studies. Lasell remained a two-year college until it added bachelor's degree programs in 1989. It continues to operate under the name Lasell College.

Lasell claims to be America's oldest junior college. The claim is not wholly justified. According to an early catalog, the seminary was designed to produce "first-rate...women, full of practical knowledge for daily living and versed in the classics as well" (Lasell College, 1991, p. 9). It would seem that the seminary was more of a finishing school for women than a two-year college.

New Ebenezer College was formed by the New Ebenezer Baptist Association of Central Georgia (Alderman, 1985). Planning for the college began in the fall of 1884, and the first enrollment was held on January 10, 1887. The original college included a preparatory school and two years of college work. According to the first catalog, its purpose was "to prepare pupils for business or for the

Junior Class in universities" (p. 27). In 1917 New Ebenezer became a branch of the Georgia State College of Agriculture and Mechanical Arts (p. 28). Ten years later the college was renamed Middle Georgia Agricultural and Mechanical College, then simply Middle Georgia College. During the 1930s it was taken over by the newly created University System of Georgia. Today it remains a two-year unit of the university system.

The historical details of other early colleges are sketchy. They include Monticello Seminary, Illinois, founded in 1835 (Stanley, 1965); YMCA College, Illinois, 1885 (Ratcliff, 1987b); Sinclair Community College, Ohio, 1887 (Ponitz, 1989); American International College, Massachusetts, 1894 (Ratcliff, 1987b); and a college that operated in Greeley, Colorado, during the 1880s (Zoglin, 1976). Most were small and their two-year programs were short-lived. According to a study by the American Council on Education (1967), there were only eight two-year colleges at the turn of the century, with a total enrollment of approximately 100. As Koos (1925) noted:

> A small number [of two-year colleges] were reported to have been existent before or at the opening of the century, but it is unlikely that they were established with anything like a consciousness of the relationship of such establishment to a junior-college movement (p. 8).

Although there is no evidence to connect these small schools to a national movement, such early experiments, like the proposals of Folwell, Tappan, and Mitchell, at least indicate a gradual trend. Clearly, educators nationwide were realizing the essential difference between the upper and lower divisions of the university curriculum. Small colleges were discovering that they could meet some important community needs without including the upper division.

CHAPTER 2

BIRTH OF A MOVEMENT

I have a plan which is at the same time unique and comprehensive, which I am persuaded will revolutionize University study in our country.

— William Rainey Harper

After a century of discussion and false starts, the junior college movement finally began to move forward. The birthplace of this new movement was the University of Chicago. Its founder was William Rainey Harper, the university's first president.

Harper's innovations were not new ideas. Henry Tappan had proposed similar changes at the University of Michigan, as had William Folwell at the University of Minnesota, but their ideas had been rejected. Harper, on the other hand, had virtual free rein over the University of Chicago. He had founded the university with a $2 million gift from his friend John D. Rockefeller and had hand-picked the faculty. Harper was also one of the great scholars of his day and a rising power in higher education. His national stature and institutional influence gave him wide leeway to pursue innovations.

In 1892 Harper divided the upper and lower divisions at the University of Chicago. Initially, the lower-division departments were referred to as the "Academic Colleges," to indicate their similarity to high schools and academies (University of Chicago, 1892); the upper-division departments were known as the "University Colleges" or "Senior Colleges" (Storr, 1966, p. 113). In 1895 Harper coined a new name for lower-division departments: he called them junior colleges, "for want of a better name" (Campbell, 1929). In 1899 Harper created the associate degree for graduates of the junior colleges. Two years later one of Harper's affiliated schools formed America's first six-year high school.

THE HARPER PLAN

In 1890 Harper was offered the presidency of the new University of Chicago. After meeting with the trustees, and on the long train trip back to Yale University, Harper sketched out the basic plan for his new university. This plan included the innovations that gave birth to the junior college movement. Harper's friend and biographer Thomas Goodspeed (1928) described the fruitful trip:

> On his journey back to New Haven, after his election to the presidency, and five months before he accepted the position, he began to work on an educational plan.... So rapidly did his mind operate that before the end of the journey the broad outlines had been sketched. As he himself wrote to Mr. Rockefeller as soon as he reached home: "On my way from Chicago the whole thing outlined itself in my mind.... I have a plan which is at the same time unique and comprehensive, which I am persuaded will revolutionize University study in our country" (pp. 110–111).

The University of Chicago became a proving ground for innovations that would indeed revolutionize American higher education. Goodspeed (Reed, 1971) described the new university that awaited the 142 junior college students who enrolled in the fall of 1892:

What they found was a new model American University... which divided the traditional four collegiate years into two equal parts—the first to be known as the junior college or academic college, where the spirit would be collegiate and preparatory (p. 43).

Harper's plan for the junior college went far beyond dividing the upper and lower divisions. His long-range goal was to develop a system of free-standing two-year colleges, "affiliated" with the university. These affiliated institutions would take over the training of freshmen and sophomores, allowing the university to concentrate on advanced studies and research. Storr (1966) described this plan:

At the first meeting of the Faculty of Arts, Literature and Science, Harper expressed the hope that the work of the lower colleges might be removed from the campus. That statement but echoed the Official Bulletin, No. 2, proposing that such work should be accomplished largely through affiliated colleges: "This will permit the University in Chicago to devote its energies mainly to the university colleges [upper division] and to strictly university work." If the faculty had made the fulfillment of Harper's expectations its chief business...anything resembling the old-fashioned four year college program would have disappeared (p. 117).

Harper's ideas were not limited to the University of Chicago. He developed a nationwide plan for creating junior colleges. His strategy was threefold. The first part involved small liberal arts colleges. In the 1890s hundreds of these colleges were failing, and those that remained could not compete with expanding universities. Harper proposed modifying these floundering colleges into junior colleges.

Along the same lines, Harper encouraged new colleges to limit their curricula to two years. In 1896 he helped found the Lewis Institute in Chicago, and in the following year, the Bradley Polytechnic Institute in Peoria. Both of these two-year colleges became affiliates of the University of Chicago (Colvert & Littlefield, 1961; Griffith, 1976; Hardin, 1976, p. 22).

The third part of Harper's strategy involved the "development of high schools into junior colleges" (Diener, 1986, p. 57). He encouraged a network of secondary schools to affiliate with his university. Later these affiliates formed America's first six-year high schools. Acting as a kind of accrediting agency for these schools (University of Chicago, 1898), the university approved their courses and accepted their graduates into the upper division. Harper held great hope for the six-year high school. He predicted that "at least 40 percent of those finishing the first four years would continue to the end of the sophomore year" (Diener, 1986, p. 58).

Harper hit the lecture circuit, extolling his innovations from New York to California. With a corps of professors, university presidents, and public school officials, this educational evangelist spread the gospel of the junior college throughout the nation. Zoglin (1976) explained the role of Harper and other educators as champions of junior colleges:

> Thus did the elitist forces seeking to close the universities to the masses and the democratic forces seeking to open higher education to them join together to promote the community colleges. And promote them they did! Harper *et al* set about helping found community colleges, guaranteeing the transferability of their courses, spreading the word about their advantages, and even persuading state legislatures to pass laws encouraging their growth.... At the very least, their contributions were those of midwife (p. 4).

FATHER OF AN INNOVATION

William Rainey Harper founded the greatest democratic movement in the history of American higher education. Junior colleges would open college classrooms to millions who otherwise would have been denied a higher education. Harper himself, however, was a product of the old elite universities of the nineteenth century. A Yale professor with a round face and thick glasses, Harper was the image of the serious scholar. His friend Thomas Goodspeed (1928) recalled:

He was looked upon at Yale as a man who needed no sleep. The students thought the light burned all night in his study in North College. Professor T.D. Seymour told how he had often been driven by wakefulness to rise and go to his own study on the campus at 4 o'clock in the morning, and said that he usually encountered Dr. Harper leaving his study after a night with the books (p. 107).

At Yale, Harper built a reputation as one of the great classical and biblical scholars of the day. His books on biblical interpretation and his translations of ancient literature are still considered classics. By 1888 he held three professorships. In that year John D. Rockefeller decided to fund a new college in Chicago.

Rockefeller, a devout Baptist, was persuaded by Thomas Goodspeed, of Chicago's Union Theological Seminary, to combine his new college with the seminary. Harper, also a Baptist and a friend of Goodspeed's, helped to shape the plans for Rockefeller's college. In February 1891 Harper resigned from Yale and accepted the presidency of the new institution. By that time Rockefeller's proposed college was being called the University of Chicago. With millions of dollars from Rockefeller and other businessmen, Harper became the robber baron of higher education, raiding the nation's leading universities to assemble his faculty. Historian Frederick Rudolph (1962) described the unprecedented academic raid:

> When he was finished [Harper] had collected eight former college or seminary presidents.... He had relieved Yale of five professors; he had swooped down on Clark University...and flown off with a majority of the academic staff.... The day that Harper arrived in Worcester sixteen faculty and student biologists were engaged in study; twelve of them followed him to Chicago. The president of the University of Wisconsin was happy to accept the chairmanship of the department of Geology.... With a budget for a faculty of eighty, he hired for the first year a faculty of a hundred twenty. (pp. 350–351).

The new president also used his endowment to buy an entire 200,000-volume library from a German university and ship it to

17

Chicago. When the university began classes in October 1892, its 328 undergraduates and 210 graduate students were presented with one of the world's finest universities.

The unique character and reputation of William Rainey Harper made him the perfect mediator between the elitist forces of the large universities and the democratic forces of the public schools. To the elitist, Harper was a scholar of unquestioned credentials. At the tender age of fourteen he graduated from college, delivering the commencement address in Hebrew. At nineteen he earned a Ph.D. from Yale in Semitic languages. At thirty-five he was installed as president of the University of Chicago (Diener, 1986, p. 49). A noted biblical scholar as well as an expert in ancient languages, his translations and commentaries from Latin, Greek, and Hebrew made him one of the most noted intellects of his day.

To public school officials, however, Harper was a helpful fellow educator (University of Chicago, 1901). His writings expressed a deep concern for the work of the public schools. Rather than snub them, he convinced the public schools to affiliate with the university. With publications such as the School Review and a faculty that included John Dewey, Harper's university became a leading light in the field of secondary education.

Ratcliff (1986) explained Harper's enduring contribution to the philosophy and structure of American education:

> Harper saw a unified school system in which there was a smooth transition from elementary to secondary to higher education. [He believed that] the last years of secondary school and the first years of college were periods of personal exploration and citizen development. It was best not to confuse university studies (research, advanced studies in a specialized subject) with the general education which was prerequisite to it.... The logic behind the organizational distinctiveness of the community college should be recalled, and should remind us of the true gift of William Rainey Harper to the community college movement (p. 17).

If Harper had lived for another decade, he might have been universally recognized as father of the two-year college. Unfortunately, he did not live to see the movement reach full bloom. Harper died in 1906 at the age of forty-nine. By that time the movement had developed its own momentum. The following year California passed its milestone "upward extension" law. Even without its founder, the junior college movement rolled steadily forward.

THE SIX-YEAR HIGH SCHOOL

In present-day America educational divisions are relatively clear. A child enters kindergarten at about five years of age and, barring withdrawal or retention, graduates from high school thirteen years later. The length and composition of the secondary curriculum is relatively standard nationwide. Accrediting agencies assure this uniformity. Employers and universities demand it.

Today it would be unthinkable for a school district unilaterally to lengthen its course of study. A century ago, however, this practice was common. High schools were then a new development, the length of their curricula still fluid. During the nineteenth century the average high school curriculum had grown from two years to four years. Koos (1925) found that expanding high schools had pushed the college entrance age forward by fully two years:

> In the half-century beginning about 1830 and ending with 1880 the median age for this institution [Harvard] advanced from sixteen years and seven months to eighteen years and seven months.... The typical Harvard freshman of a century ago was fully two years younger than the freshman of the more recent period (p. 192).

By the turn of the century, there was an increasing demand for the high school curriculum to expand even further. Local educators and parents, raising the issue of articulation with colleges and universities, wanted postdiploma courses equaling grades thirteen and fourteen ("Proceedings," 1904). Yet few students were willing to take postdiploma classes at their high school if those courses did not count toward a college degree. On the other hand, if a transfer system could be established, many students would opt for courses

19

at their local high school over the inconvenience and expense of attending a faraway university (McLane, 1913).

The University of Chicago already had an articulation system in place through its Board of Affiliating and Co-operating Schools. Harper had formed this network of high schools to provide feeder schools for the university. The Board of Affiliations, as it was known, served as a kind of accrediting agency. To be accepted as an affiliate, an institution had to have its curriculum approved by the board. With such approval the high schools were assured their graduates would be accepted into the university.

The university's Board of Affiliations worked closely with the university's lower division, called the junior colleges. Before the turn of the century, several affiliated schools asked for permission to offer lower division courses on their campuses. The first such proposal is reported in the board's minutes of October 15, 1897:

> [Dean John Grant, of the Harvard School of Chicago] moved that courses in the work of the Junior Colleges may be given at the Affiliated Schools provided (1) that every such course shall be approved by the Departmental Examiner or other proper person in the proper Department of the university, and (2) that the final examination of such cases shall be set by the direction of that instructor in the University by whom such course is usually given in the University (University of Chicago, 1897).

The board passed both of Grant's motions, but reversed itself three months later because of a negative committee report. A similar proposal was presented to the board in January 1899. This time the motion was passed on the first reading.

The new motion allowed students who gained more than the required units in high school to receive college credit for their work. An accompanying motion required that a student remain in the high school longer than four years to receive college credit. These two motions created the basis for the six-year high school. Almost immediately, affiliated high schools began offering college courses—primarily Latin and mathematics. This new idea caught on quickly in the small towns around Chicago. As public demand grew, school boards approved a fifth and sixth year of high school instruction. The first six-year high school began in 1901 in nearby Joliet, Illinois.

Joliet High School, formed in 1849 as part of the school system of the city of Joliet, affiliated with the University of Chicago through the guidance of J. Stanley Brown. Appointed principal in 1893, Brown, who was a personal friend of William Rainey Harper's (Ratcliff, 1986, p. 12), became a supporter of Harper's junior college scheme and a leader on the Board of Affiliations (Hardin, 1976, pp. 22–23).

Brown showed an early interest in offering postdiploma courses. In 1896 he corresponded with several university professors about the idea of granting advanced credit for such courses. A Latin professor from the University of Michigan replied:

> The University is glad to give some advanced credit for work done in this way. It encourages the student and reduces the amount of required work to be done in the college course, so that the student has more time for the heavy...courses of the senior year (Fretwell, 1954, p. 13).

In 1899 Joliet voters approved the creation of a separate high school district and elected Brown as superintendent. The voters also approved a $100,000 bond issue for the construction of a new high school building to accommodate 1,400 students. The moment seemed ideal for Brown to put into practice his experiment with the six-year high school (Fretwell, 1954, p. 10).

At a Joliet school board meeting in December 1900, Brown announced his intention to offer postdiploma courses. He predicted that five students would enroll in advanced courses in February. A month later Brown reported "the enrollment of one additional postgraduate student," bringing the total to six (pp. 11–12). These students were offered a two-year curriculum, preparing them to enter the university as juniors. The University of Chicago, the University of Illinois, and Northwestern University accepted their coursework (Hardin, 1976).

In his opening address at the dedication of Joliet's new high school building in April 1901, Brown praised the early success of the postdiploma program:

The result has been to keep in school those who were otherwise inclined to think their education was ended when they received their diplomas (Fretwell, 1954, p. 12).

According to some early researchers, Joliet's six-year high school began in 1902. Their misconception is based on a motion, passed by the high school board on December 3, 1902, authorizing free tuition for postdiploma students. In reality, the motion simply legitimized a practice that had been in place for nearly two years. Thomas Deam, a longtime Joliet faculty member, explained:

> [At the end of 1902] the number of post-graduate students was becoming large enough to add materially to the cost of running the institution, and the superintendent desired official approval for allowing post-graduate students to attend the high school without paying tuition (Fretwell, 1954, p. 12).

In Joliet's early years, Brown avoided using the term junior college. Instead, he referred to the new section as the "postgraduate department." As one of Brown's faculty members, I.D. Yaggy, later explained, this choice was influenced by local politics:

> [He] was very much afraid that the taxpayers might object to using high school funds for college work if it were publicized too much (Fretwell, 1954, p. 15).

The construction of a second building in 1913 provided a separate library and offices for the postgraduate department, which became known as Joliet Junior College three years later, when it was also officially recognized by the North Central Association of Colleges and Secondary Schools. Despite these changes, however, Joliet Junior College remained essentially an advanced department of the high school. Although the junior college had its own dean, it was governed by the high school board and superintendent. By 1920 its enrollment had risen to ninety students (Fretwell, 1954, pp. 10–20).

The second six-year high school was established at Goshen, Indiana. Goshen High School began its postdiploma courses in the fall of 1904, with seven students paying a tuition of $30 a year. The

Board of Affiliations of the University of Chicago encouraged and accredited the school. Goshen's superintendent explained the reasons for switching to the new curriculum:

> The six years' work offered by the Goshen High School is a result of real demand.... [In the past] a number of parents kept their children at home the year after graduation because they thought them too young to be sent away from home. During the year out of school the boys usually found work...and the girls developed other ambitions. The plan for extending the course was projected to satisfy cravings of the first class...and to correct the mistaken tendencies of the second. (Diener, 1986, p. 62).

In 1906 J. Stanley Brown of Joliet announced that a graduate of his six-year high school had completed her college degree. Quoted in the *School Review,* the announcement, along with the editor's comments, is the first published record in which six-year high schools are referred to as a movement.

> ... "Miss_____is the first of our students to complete our six-year high-school course and to graduate from college in two years. She could not have attended college four years following her graduation from high school because of financial conditions. In her case is shown the completion of what Dr. Harper worked for...."

> ...the movement toward the secondary school affording, in addition to the regular four-year course, two additional years of "preparation for life," and articulating directly with the university...is slowly but steadily progressing. ("Editorial Notes," 1906, p. 609).

A committee, headed by Brown, assessed the movement's progress for a 1903 educational conference in Chicago ("Proceedings," 1904). The committee found that Harper's idea had spread rapidly and built strong public support, that parents and students throughout the Midwest were demanding local access to higher education:

All over this state you may find, if you investigate, that within the past five years high schools…have increased the work to five or six years. These movements have gone on, are going on, without any blare of trumpets…. The demands of the people that our educational schemes be systematized and made to do service are bringing about these changes (p. 20).

The following year Brown reported that high schools in Illinois (Philadelphia), Michigan (Muskegon and Saginaw), and Missouri (Saint Joseph), as well as "eighteen other semi-public institutions" were "working out" six-year high school plans (Eells, 1931, p. 55). There is no apparent record of how many of these plans were carried through.

The Goshen experiment was relatively short-lived, having been abandoned several years later after the Mennonite church opened a four-year college in the area (Frye, 1992, p. 131). Joliet Junior College continues to operate. It is widely recognized as the oldest public junior college in America.

DECAPITATION IN TEXAS

While Harper was building his junior college strategy, a group of Texas educators was making similar plans. Following the reorganization of the Baptist colleges of Texas in 1897, under a plan devised by Reverend J.M. Carroll and the American Baptist Education Society, three institutions became two-year schools. The reorganization "decapitated" the upper division from Decatur Baptist College, Howard Payne College, and Rusk Baptist College, transforming them into two-year institutions. They were not initially called junior colleges.

Eells (1931) gave Harper credit for influencing this reorganization:

While the decapitation of small colleges was never widely realized under the leadership of the University of Chicago, it was accomplished in two states, Texas and Missouri, in somewhat systematic form. Perhaps Harper's influence was a strong factor in causing such action (p. 63).

Over the next two decades several other Texas colleges submitted to decapitation. In 1908 Burleson College joined the statewide Baptist system as a junior college. It was followed by Wayland Baptist College in 1913 and the College of Marshall in 1917. In that year the Methodist Episcopal Church South reclassified four of its institutions as junior colleges (Eells, 1931, p. 151).

THE MICHIGAN CONTROVERSY

Some early scholars place the beginning of the junior college movement at the University of Michigan. This notion was fostered by Alexis Lange, a Michigan graduate and early leader in the California junior college movement. The claim first appeared in a master's thesis by Arthur Gray, one of Lange's students at the University of California (Ratcliff, 1987a).

Gray's thesis indicated that the University of Michigan had separated the upper and lower divisions in 1882 and conducted the first junior college experiment at a Saginaw high school in 1895. According to Gray, these events were sparked by the ideas put forth by former University of Michigan president Henry Tappan. These unsubstantiated claims were repeated by Walter Eells in his 1931 book, *The Junior College*, and have been quoted by scholars ever since. There is no apparent historical basis for these claims, other than Gray's thesis. Despite their frequent repetition, Gray's statements probably were not accurate.

The University of Michigan did adopt a plan of instruction in 1882, called the University System, but it had no connection with the ideas of Tappan, who had been dismissed as president two decades before (Ratcliff, 1987b). The University System was designed primarily to allow superior students to spend more of their time in independent study and reading. Although it recognized the distinction between the general work of the lower division and the specialized work of the junior and senior years, the University System did not encourage the development of six-year high schools. The plan was abandoned in 1901, largely because independent study courses were too demanding on the faculty (Eells, 1931, p. 46; Ratcliff, 1987b).

25

Likewise, there is no corroborating evidence to support the existence of a junior college in Saginaw. Eells (1931) stated that the University of Michigan accepted one year of work done at Saginaw's East Side High School, beginning in 1895, but eventually the program was discontinued. Eight students from this experiment eventually graduated from the university (p. 53). Stating that the experiment happened "possibly at Saginaw," Eells himself seemed uncertain. Although Eells did not cite a source, his information seems to have come from Gray's thesis.

James Ratcliff (1987b) conducted a thorough investigation of the Saginaw claim. His research uncovered a report by the Saginaw superintendent of high school enrollment between 1891 and 1896. The report showed no students enrolled beyond the twelfth grade.

Ratcliff also examined reports of school board meetings from 1894 to 1896 by the Saginaw Evening News. These exhaustive reports discussed everything from storm windows to curriculum. They did not, however, mention any college work in high school. After examining the records, Ratcliff concluded that "Saginaw Junior College never existed" (1987a, p. 9).

There is one likely explanation for the Saginaw confusion. In the 1890s universities commonly granted college credit to well-prepared high school graduates (Ratcliff, 1987b). Usually, these students were required to take an examination, just as modern students take the College Level Examination Program (CLEP) tests. In a sense, these students received credit for knowledge that they acquired in high school. Such may have been the case with those eight students from Saginaw.

If the Saginaw experiment took place, it was an isolated event soon abandoned. It was clearly not the beginning of a national movement. Apparently, Michigan's next (or first) public junior college was founded in 1914, long after the junior college movement was under way.

Gray's assertion that Lange carried the movement to California has more validity. Certainly, Lange was exposed to the ideas of Henry Tappan and took them with him to Berkeley. Lange, however, was only one of many California proponents of the junior college, of which David Starr Jordan, president of Stanford University, was probably the most important. Jordan's exposure to the junior college idea came through his friendship with William Rainey Harper.

THE CRITICS SPEAK

The junior college movement caused a revolution in the traditional world of higher education. And like any revolution, it had its critics. Critics claimed that junior colleges lacked collegiate standards, that they should be more exclusive—more like the universities. They complained about the noncollege subjects, such as vocational courses, being taught. Some of the earliest critics were presidents of small liberal arts colleges, which were already suffering from low enrollments. The rise of inexpensive junior colleges threatened to cut even deeper into their enrollments.

The findings of a survey conducted in the early 1900s revealed overall distrust on the part of presidents of small colleges toward the junior college idea. College presidents in Indiana, Iowa, Minnesota, and Wisconsin not only disagreed with the six-year high school, they viewed it as a threat to American society ("Proceedings," 1904). One of the presidents seemed to speak for the entire group when he wrote:

> ...I note the probable harm that would come to the American college, if the proposed plan were to be carried out. The college has largely trained the leaders and makers of public opinions who have given shape to our institutions and national life. These men of the past were all well trained in the old traditional prescribed course....
>
> It seems to me that your proposed change is likely to deprive many men of the two best years of the college course, and greatly to limit, if not to destroy, the most excellent work of the American college, and so in short to do more harm than good (p. 22).

The earliest scholarly criticism of six-year high schools came in a 1905 issue of the *Educational Review*. The author, Julius Sachs, attacked the "scheme" that he had heard discussed at the University of Chicago. Sachs (1905), a secondary educator, saw the six-year high school as a plot by elitists to free themselves of their freshmen and sophomores:

> [No] greater danger besets the secondary teacher than the blind hope that he can at some time or other, or through some peculiar circumstances, supplant the work of the early college years. I believe we are as far removed from that as is conceivable at the present moment....
>
> If our schools are not so constituted that they can effectively assume the burden of two college years, then any attempt to do so is a case of usurpation fraught with danger to the usurper, as well as to the institution it endeavors partially to supplant.
>
> The judgment of college officers who have been favorable to this plan cannot be accorded much weight, partially because they do not know sufficiently well the normal attainments of our secondary teachers, and the peculiar conditions of our secondary schools; mainly, however, because they are desirous of freeing the college curriculum of instruction that is analogous to secondary teaching (p. 488).

Critics saw the junior college movement as a great threat to the traditional American college. In many ways, they were correct. With the technical and social changes sweeping America, the age of educating only cultured gentlemen was at an end. Junior colleges were designed to meet the needs of the average citizen in a changing world.

CHAPTER 3

SPREADING THE GOSPEL (1892–1919)

I took the opportunity of this meeting to lay before those assembled our plan for the degree of associate.

— William Rainey Harper

For its first eighteen years, the junior college movement was centered in the Midwest. At least thirteen junior colleges and six-year high schools, virtually all of which were connected in some way with the University of Chicago, had been founded by 1910 (Fretwell, 1954, p. 148). The first junior colleges were the lower division colleges of the University of Chicago. These colleges, separated from the upper division in 1892, began granting degrees after 1899. The Bradley Polytechnic Institute and the Lewis Institute, both private two-year technical colleges based in Chicago, followed in 1896.

In 1901 John Million organized Hardin College, a Baptist junior college in Missouri (American Association of Junior Colleges, 1922a). In the same year Joliet High School increased its curriculum to six years. In 1904 six-year high schools were established in Goshen, Indiana, and Detroit, Michigan (Blocker, Plummer & Richardson, 1965, p. 25). Soon public and private junior colleges were springing up throughout Illinois and surrounding states.

Many small religious colleges took William Rainey Harper's advice and eliminated their junior and senior years. This trend was particularly strong in Missouri, Texas, and the Deep South. Between 1900 and 1916 more than half of the nation's junior colleges were religiously affiliated (Brint & Karabel, 1989, p. 29).

The Board of Affiliations of the University of Chicago remained the primary vehicle for spreading the movement, reaching out to schools throughout the Midwest. In November 1903 a conference of affiliated schools attracted about 385 educators. This group represented fifty-six schools and institutes in Illinois, Indiana, Iowa, Michigan, Missouri, Ohio, and Wisconsin. A major topic at this conference was "to extend the work of the secondary school to include the first two years of college." Superintendent J. Stanley Brown of Joliet gave a glowing report on the success and growth of the movement.

The *School Review*, published by the University of Chicago Press, became a cheerleader for the movement. This journal carried the latest news from fledgling junior colleges, in addition to conference reports from the Board of Affiliations. Most of the early published accounts of two-year colleges were printed in the *School Review*.

In 1896 the *School Review* became the official journal of the North Central Association of Colleges and Secondary Schools. When the association held its 1903 annual meeting at the University of Chicago, the university used the occasion to push the six-year high school scheme (Sachs, 1905, p. 488).

All the while Harper did his utmost to sell the junior college idea, delivering speeches to such groups as the National Educational Council (Harper, 1902) and the Association of American Universities (Harper, 1903), visiting campuses, even using his influence with educational leaders to get them to come to Chicago. Some of these educators, such as David Starr Jordan of Stanford and Benjamin Ide Wheeler of the University of California, played important roles in spreading the movement.

MISSOURI: ACCREDITATION AND UNION

Missouri became an early leader in the establishment of private junior colleges. R.H. Jesse, president of the University of Missouri from 1891 to 1908, was a strong supporter of these colleges. He and his close friend William Rainey Harper shared the view that the freshman and sophomore college years were a part of secondary education. In 1896 Jesse told a meeting of the North Central Association of Colleges and Secondary Schools:

> The first two years of college are really secondary in character. I always think of the high school and academy as covering the lower secondary period and the freshman and sophomore years of college as covering the upper secondary period (Carpenter, 1962, p. 477).

It was Jesse's successor, Ross Hill, who brought these ideas into reality. In the early years of the century, Missouri had a large number of church-related four-year colleges and women's finishing schools. Hill campaigned to transform these institutions into junior colleges. In return the university would accredit the schools and accept their graduates. Stratton D. Brooks, a later University of Missouri president, recounted this effort:

> In Missouri we had a lot of colleges that were trying to be four-year colleges.... In 1911 we began our cooperation with these colleges, persuading several alleged four-year colleges that their own interest and honesty in education required them to devote all their resources to two years.... The results in those colleges have been very satisfactory to them. They have actually increased their attendance (Eells, 1931, p. 64).

The university accredited most of these early junior colleges. Beginning in 1913, university faculty made annual inspections of junior colleges and submitted reports to the university's Committee on Accrediting Junior Colleges for the improvement of teaching, administration, libraries, and facilities, which were followed "willingly and promptly." Graduates of accredited colleges were allowed to "enter the university without examination and continue their work on the same basis with students who came up through the freshman and sophomore classes" at the university (Coursault, 1915, p. 59).

The Missouri Junior College Union, formed in 1914 to help colleges solve their administrative problems, was America's first statewide association of junior colleges. Its founding members were Christian College, Cottey College, Hardin College, Howard-Payne College, Lindenwood Junior College, Stephens College, and William Woods College (Coursault, 1915, p. 61).

Cottey College, like most of Missouri's early junior colleges, was a women-only institution. William Woods College had been founded in 1870 as the women's counterpart of a nearby men's school. Stephens College and Christian College in Columbia and Lindenwood Junior College in St. Charles also began as women's finishing schools.

All of the accredited colleges were private institutions until 1916, when Kansas City Junior College was accepted. A second public institution, St. Joseph Junior College, was accredited the following year.

ONWARD TO CALIFORNIA

California was fertile ground for the junior college movement. Unlike eastern states, California did not have an extensive system of small four-year colleges. Its two large universities were clustered in the San Francisco Bay area. Although there were a few small colleges in other areas, most California towns had no access to higher education. Even the populous San Joaquin Valley was 200 miles from the nearest college (McLane, 1913, p. 163). The lack of a small-college system created a grassroots demand for advanced courses at California high schools.

In California, as in other parts of the country, both the democratic and elitist forces supported the growth of junior colleges. Stanford and the University of California-Berkeley, both elitist institutions, had enacted restrictive admission requirements before the turn of the century (Brint & Karabel, 1989, p. 47). The presidents of these schools viewed the freshman and sophomore years as a part of elementary education and sought to separate them from the work of the university (McLane, 1913). At the same time, the democratic forces that represented the rural counties were demanding postdiploma courses. These opposing groups would eventually come to terms, and in the process foster the rapid growth of junior colleges.

There has been considerable debate about how the junior college idea came to California. Recently discovered evidence indicates that it came from the University of Chicago. In a letter dated March 3, 1900, William Rainey Harper stated that he was working with three California colleges that "were ready" to drop their upper divisions and become junior colleges:

> I took the opportunity of this meeting to lay before those assembled our plan for the degree of associate.... You can understand that I was greatly surprised to find, first, that many of them had already heard indirectly concerning it.... President Jordan of Leland Stanford and President Wheeler of the University of California informed the gentlemen that already five colleges in California were ready to come down to the grade of junior college in accordance with this proposition. With three of these colleges I myself had been at work. Those who were most enthusiastic over it were the Presidents Jordan and Wheeler (p. 2).

Two years later the University of California-Berkeley adopted a reorganization plan that mirrored Harper's concept at the University of Chicago. The plan created a wall between the upper and lower divisions. Students were required to complete their general education courses during their freshman and sophomore years, and at the end of these courses, they were granted a version of the associate degree, called a "junior certificate." President Benjamin Ide Wheeler explained the reason for this reorganization:

> The new plan proposes a clear line of demarcation between the elementary work as normally done in the first two years and the advanced work belonging to the last two years....

[This policy] creates between what will be virtually a lower college and upper college a marked distinction which it is intended and expected shall express itself in sharp differentiation of methods both of teaching and study (California State Department of Education, 1928, p. 6).

President David Starr Jordan of Stanford became the most important figure in the early California junior college movement. His "dynamic articles and addresses urging the amputation" of the university's lower division "made the public sit up and take notice" (Lange, 1915, p. 120).

Jordan was infected with the junior college idea by Harper. The two friends kept up an extensive correspondence from 1893 until 1905. Both were founders of the Association of American Universities and shared membership on several other educational and religious boards. Jordan visited the University of Chicago on several occasions. Harper visited Jordan's campus in 1899 (Harper, 1899). He probably traveled to Stanford again in 1902 and 1903. Ratcliff (1987a) described Harper's effect on Jordan:

[Jordan] and William Rainey Harper had discussed the merits of encouraging small colleges to restrict their curriculum to the first two years.... His interchanges with Harper in the Association of American Universities reinforced his notion that proper university education should begin with the junior year (p. 9).

Jordan and Harper frequently exchanged their views on the budding junior college movement. In a 1902 report to the U.S. commissioner of education, Harper stated:

President Jordan, of the Leland Stanford Junior University, has suggested to me that among the various important movements of the year is the disposition of small colleges to become junior colleges.... Within my own observation, many facts pointing to this direction have occurred (Eells, 1931, p. 61).

Intending to eliminate freshman and sophomore instruction at Stanford, Jordan saw junior colleges as a vehicle to free the university of this "elementary" function:

I am looking forward as you know to the time when the large high schools of the state in conjunction with the small colleges will relieve the two great universities from the expense and from the necessity of giving instruction of the first two college years. The instruction of these two years is of necessity elementary and of the same general nature as the work of the high school itself (McLane, 1913, p. 166).

Another early supporter of junior colleges in California was Alexis Lange. Lange had heard about Henry Tappan's ideas while studying at the University of Michigan. After joining the English faculty at the University of California, he supported efforts to separate the lower division from the university, and from 1909 began advocating six-year high schools. Lange later chaired the university's education department and became dean of faculties. Through his writings and speeches, Lange helped gain rapid academic acceptance for junior colleges (Ratcliff, 1987a).

SIX-YEAR HIGH SCHOOLS IN CALIFORNIA

A California law adopted in 1907 allowed high schools to offer "postgraduate" classes. Many historians have described this law as the beginning of the California junior college system. The historical record, however, does not support this view. Both extended high schools and two-year colleges appear to have existed before the 1907 law. Walter Eells, a former Stanford professor, stated that California high schools were offering postdiploma courses before the law was passed and that the law "simply legalized" the practice (Ratcliff, 1987a, p. 13). Harper noted in 1900 that five California colleges were already preparing to convert to junior colleges (Harper, 1900). These institutions may have converted before 1907.

Whether or not the 1907 law began California's junior college movement, it undoubtedly gave it a boost. There was a pent-up demand for colleges in the state, and this law opened the floodgates. Offering no funding or other state support for junior colleges, it simply allowed local school boards to offer postdiploma courses and to charge tuition for nondistrict students. The text of the law read:

> The board of trustees of any city, district, union, joint union or county high school may prescribe post-graduate courses of study for the graduates of such high school, or other high schools, which courses of study shall approximate the studies prescribed in the first two years of university courses. The board of trustees of any city, district, union, joint union or county high school wherein the post-graduate courses of study are taught may charge tuition for pupils living without the boundaries of the district wherein such courses are taught (California State Department of Education, 1928, p. 7).

Educators continue to debate the origin of this so-called Upward Extension Law. State senator Anthony Caminetti, a rural legislator who became one the most important figures in the history of California education, wrote the bill.

Caminetti was a longstanding proponent of local education. During the 1880s he had sponsored the Caminetti Act authorizing California's public high schools. As a populist, he distrusted the elitist university presidents. During the 1907 legislative session he worked to reduce university influence in the state's board of education. Some scholars argue that the populist Caminetti therefore could not have been influenced by the elitists at Berkeley and Stanford (Ratcliff, 1987a).

Other junior college historians insist that the 1907 Upward Extension Law must have been influenced by the university leaders. Eells (1931) credited Lange and Jordan with influencing Caminetti, but admitted that there was no evidence. Lange (1915) credited Jordan with prodding "schoolmen into taking the initiative" (p. 120). The California Department of Education (1928) also credited Lange, describing him as "father of the California junior college idea" (p. 1). None of these authors, however, can provide a definite link between university leaders and Caminetti.

In reality, Caminetti was probably influenced by both the elitists and the populists. As chair of the senate education committee, he was in frequent contact with the presidents of the University of California-Berkeley and Stanford University. Jordan, who served on the California Education Commission, and Wheeler, who served on the California Board of Education, were enthusiastic about junior colleges. Certainly, these presidents had mentioned the idea to education officials in their home state—including Caminetti. It is hard to believe otherwise.

However Caminetti got the idea, his motives for sponsoring the law were undoubtedly populist (Ratcliff, 1987a). The senator represented a rural county (Amador) that was served neither by Berkeley nor by Stanford, both of which resisted increases in their student bodies (McLane, 1913). Caminetti's law was designed to offer higher education to all Californians.

The University of California at Berkeley reacted quickly to the Upward Extension Law. Beginning in 1907 the university accepted advanced high school courses for undergraduate credit. Students in most curricula could complete all of their English and mathematics credits at an extended high school (California State Department of Education, 1928, p. 8).

In 1909 the legislature passed a second junior college bill. Unlike the Upward Extension Law, this bill provided for state funding to help high schools create junior college programs. Unfortunately, it never went into effect. The governor vetoed the bill because of its potential costs. State funding for California's junior colleges would not arrive for another eight years.

The first use of the Upward Extension Law was at Fresno High School. Fresno's superintendent, Charles McLane, sent out a questionnaire in June 1910 to gauge public support for a proposed junior college. All 200 replies were favorable. The universities of Stanford and Berkeley, on request, helped Fresno choose the principal and instructors for the junior college (McLane, 1913, p. 164).

The following fall Fresno High School began offering college-level instruction in English, mathematics, history, Latin, economics, modern languages, and "technical work." Berkeley agreed to accept coursework completed at Fresno "as if the work had been done at the University of California and without the necessity of any further examinations" (McLane, 1913, p. 168).

Within five years Fresno's postdiploma student body had risen from fifteen to 115. Courses were free to residents of the school district; nonresidents paid a tuition charge of $4 a month.

A 1910 report explained the success of the junior college. The factors it described—proximity and cost—echo throughout America's junior college movement and continue today as major rationales for community colleges:

> There is no institution of higher education within two hundred miles of Fresno where students may continue their studies beyond the regular high school courses. Many of our high school graduates are but seventeen or eighteen years of age and parents are frequently loath to send these young people so far from home. Many who desire to continue their studies cannot afford the expense necessary to college attendance where the items of room and board mean so much (McLane, 1913, p. 164).

Fresno High School's principal, A.C. Olney, transferred to Santa Barbara High School in 1911 and there established the state's second six-year high school (California State Department of Education, 1928). The following year junior colleges opened in Hollywood and Los Angeles.

In the fall of 1913, Bakersfield, Fullerton, and Long Beach founded junior colleges. Over the next four years, Azusa, Placer, Sacramento, Santa Ana, and five other cities added high school extensions (Eells, 1931, p. 96). By the fall of 1917, the state had sixteen junior colleges. The largest of these, and probably the largest public junior college in America, was Los Angeles City High School, with 520 students. In a single decade California had created the most extensive junior college system in the nation (California State Department of Education, 1928).

In 1917 the California legislature passed the Ballard Act, providing state and county support for junior colleges. Under the act school districts were required to have taxable property valued at $3 million before new public junior colleges could be organized. The state would fund junior colleges on a per-student basis, using the same funding formula as for high schools.

The Ballard Act sparked the growth of additional junior colleges. This expansion was slowed by World War I, but rapidly regained momentum after the 1918 armistice. By the end of that year, the state had twenty-one high school extensions (Diener, 1986, pp. 77–78). The following year California's legislature appointed a special committee, headed by Senator H.C. Jones, to study higher education in California. The committee proposed additional state funding for junior colleges as an alternative to expanding the University of California (Eells, 1931, p. 100).

Jones's report formed the framework of the District Junior College Law, passed two years later. Not only boosting the California junior college movement, this law became the model for public college districts nationwide.

THE COMPREHENSIVE JUNIOR COLLEGE

Many educators believe that there is an inherent difference between early junior colleges and today's community colleges. According to their view, the early junior colleges were limited to academic courses, whereas modern community colleges offer terminal degrees, vocational education, and other community services.

This supposed dichotomy is not supported by fact. From the very beginning, junior colleges had a terminal function. William Rainey Harper in 1898 stated that many students were likely to terminate their education after completing junior college in order to seek positions as teachers or to go into business. These students could leave college "honorably" with an associate degree (Diener, 1986, p. 57). Angell (1915) reported that some junior colleges were anxious to "specialize particularly in industrial, engineering, and vocational directions, with its main interest centered on young people who will not go beyond the instruction it offers" (p. 295).

The first California junior college at Fresno provided "practical courses in agriculture," including instruction in dairy farming and citrus, peach, and apricot growing (Fields, 1962, p. 31). The California junior college regulations of 1921 included a provision for "courses of instruction designed to prepare persons for agriculture, industry, commerce, home-making, and other vocations and such other courses of instruction as may be deemed necessary..." (Ricciardi, 1928, p. 55).

By the early 1920s the official definition of a junior college, according to the American Association of Junior Colleges (1922b), included a broad scope of community and vocational education: "The junior college may, and is likely to, develop a different type of curriculum, suited to the larger and ever changing civic, social and vocational needs of the entire community in which the college is located" (p. 2).

The person who most clearly defined the dual nature of the junior college curriculum was Leonard V. Koos. While summarizing the research that would later be included in his book *The Junior College Movement*, Koos (1922) described possible conflicts between the terminal and transfer functions:

> The problem of the junior-college curriculum is one of great complexity and even greater moment. This problem is...that of serving adequately the needs of students who will continue their training on higher levels...and those who will not, cannot, and should not go on to these higher levels... (p. 70).

Recognizing that the junior college served both functions, vocational and terminal, was important to elitists, who wanted to keep students who were "not really fitted" out of the university (Diener, 1986, p. 57). It was also important to populists, who wanted advanced career training for the average citizen. Although expanded after World War II, both functions had their roots in the early junior colleges of the Midwest and California.

A NATIONAL STUDY

The first national study of junior colleges was conducted in 1918 by Floyd McDowell, the dean of Graceland College, a small two-year institution in Lamoni, Iowa, that six years before had eliminated its upper division owing to McDowell's persuasion (Higdon, 1989). McDowell conducted the study in fulfillment of his doctoral dissertation at the State University of Iowa. It is the first known dissertation on the subject and amounts to a nationwide examination of the junior college phenomenon.

McDowell found that thirty-nine public high schools had lengthened their curricula to become junior colleges. Most of these were in California. At least ninety-three church colleges and small liberal arts colleges had decreased their curricula to two years. Most of these conversions were in Missouri and Texas. Teacher training schools (normal schools) in ten states had extended their curricula to become junior colleges (Diener, 1986, pp. 77–78).

McDowell surveyed seventy-four junior colleges, all connected with a high school or academy. The public colleges, he found, experienced a 168 percent enrollment jump between 1915 and 1917, while their graduates increased by 211 percent during the same period.

Most of the colleges studied did not award a degree. Nearly three quarters of the public junior college graduates went on to a university. McDowell found that 17 percent of the work offered by public junior colleges was vocational.

McDowell also explored the reasons why junior colleges were prospering. Asking twenty-one junior college administrators to list the most important purposes of their colleges (Brunner, 1970), he ranked their responses accordingly:

1. To keep children at home (parents desire)
2. To provide a completion school for those who cannot go any further
3. To secure college work near home (students desire)
4. To meet specific local needs
5. To compensate for geographical remoteness from a standard college or university, tied with
6. To meet the entrance requirements for professional schools
7. To provide vocational training more advanced than high school work, tied with
8. To compensate for financial difficulty in maintaining a four-year course
9. To provide additional opportunities for teacher training

10. To secure the segregation of the sexes, tied with
11. To provide opportunities for higher education under church control (p. 30).

At the time of McDowell's study, the Association of Colleges and Secondary Schools of the Southern States and the North Central Association of Colleges and Secondary Schools had already established junior college accreditation standards. Junior colleges were also accredited by the universities or education departments of Arkansas, California, Idaho, Indiana, Illinois, Iowa, Kansas, Michigan, Minnesota, Missouri, Texas, Washington, and West Virginia (Diener, 1986, pp. 79–80).

CHAPTER 4

THE SOARING TWENTIES (1920-1929)

Going to college has become the great American

habit. The junior college should be the "people's

college" and be available to all.

— Walter C. Eells

J unior college enrollments declined during the First World War. Some colleges were forced to close their doors while their students fought on the battlefields of Europe (Eells, 1931, pp. 98–101). Following the 1918 armistice, a postwar recession set in, temporarily slowing the growth of new colleges.

The decline was short-lived, however. By 1920 American industry was booming, with automobile manufacturing and mass production of consumer goods leading the way. Corporate stock and real estate prices skyrocketed.

The Roaring Twenties were not prosperous for American farmers, though. As farm revenues dropped steadily, many farm workers settled in nearby towns, while others swelled the populations of major cities (Frye, 1992, p. 22). The industrial boom and the rural exodus created a new demand for low-cost higher education.

ANATOMY OF A BOOM

By 1920 public education had become an accepted part of American life. More than 80 percent of school-age children were enrolled in public schools, and most would graduate from high school. At the time few jobs required more than a high school diploma, but change was already in the wind. As the decade progressed the number of white-collar and technical jobs increased dramatically, with the higher-paying occupations often requiring postsecondary training. As a consequence, the middle class began to view college as the road to success.

The profile of the college student was also changing. Many students were working their way through school, studying for a specific occupation. Some were already married and had a family. An increasing number enrolled in the inexpensive public junior colleges springing up around the country. As Eells (1931) saw it:

> Going to college has become the great American habit. The junior college should be the "people's college" and be available to all. It should provide collegiate opportunities for the mass of high school graduates who can't, won't or shouldn't become university students (p. 192).

The junior college movement had gained nationwide acceptance. In the 1920s America was still a nation of small towns. The local college served as a focal point for these towns, a place of community pride, where concerts, plays, art exhibits, lectures, and countless other activities could be held. More importantly, the local college made higher education accessible and affordable to the average citizen. Although the term community college had not yet been coined, it was common to refer to junior colleges in general as democracy's colleges.

Establishing a junior college placed financial burdens on many small towns. Through construction contracts, increased salaries, and state funding, however, such costs were repaid. Junior colleges attracted students from the surrounding countryside, boosting the local economy (Eells, 1931, p. 196). In fact, in many towns the college became a major employer, expanding the tax base and bringing new, mainly educated people into the community. For these reasons, local chambers of commerce and civic boosters were often responsible for creating new junior colleges. As Pedersen (1988) noted:

> In a surprising number of cases, a chamber of commerce assumed the responsibility of familiarizing the larger community with the aims and purposes of the junior college, providing a forum for outside popularizers of the movement and nurturing support for the concept until the local school board was willing to act (p. 45).

The peak year for new junior colleges was 1927. In that year alone thirty-two new colleges were established (Greenleaf, 1936, p. 43). By the end of the decade junior colleges enrolled more than 55,000 students (Campbell, 1936a, p. 109).

THE CURRICULUM OF THE 1920S

The most popular junior college curriculum was clearly university transfer. Junior colleges arranged their curricula to dovetail with those of nearby state universities, and to a great extent copied the university undergraduate program. A 1928 study of fifteen public junior colleges found that most courses were in science, foreign languages, and social sciences (Whitney, 1928, pp. 126–127).

Adult and continuing education were also a part of these early colleges. A California educator declared that "the new junior college will take over the functions of the old liberal arts college and will extend the benefits of such college training to adults in their hours of leisure" (Cooper, 1928, p. 36). These leisure courses ranged from the fine arts to automobile mechanics, and through them the junior college reached out to every facet of the community.

Today nearly every community college offers a wide variety of degrees and certificates. In the 1920s, however, such was not the case. Whitney (1928) reported that only about 16 percent of the public junior colleges offered an associate of arts degree, and about 48 percent granted no degree at all (p. 213).

THE JUNIOR COLLEGE STUDENT

Junior college students of the 1920s were younger than those of later decades; most students were recent high school graduates (Whitney, 1928, p. 29). The junior college became a haven for students who could not afford or did not meet the admission standards of a university. As Lillard (1929) explained:

> Many a student in high school has an off-year, fails to find himself, gets into courses for which he is not well prepared, is hindered by illness or home duties, falls in love, spends too much time in student activities or in earning his way, and so fails to meet arbitrary university standards (p. 70).

A 1929 study of junior college catalogs added other reasons for choosing a two-year school, including:

> ...to obtain individual attention, to economize in terms of both time and expense, to enjoy smaller classes, to maintain the influence of their homes, and to secure occupational training (Campbell, 1930, p. 17).

Many junior college graduates who transferred to the university made better grades than their university peers. In 1926 Walter Eells studied the eighty junior college transfer students at Stanford University. He found that 30 percent of this group graduated with honors—double the level of native university students (Eells, 1931, pp. 173–177).

Eells's study showed that junior college students were performing well, even in the elitist halls of Stanford. Other studies showed that junior college transfers were doing as well as university natives at the universities of Southern California, Minnesota, Colorado, and Iowa, and the universities of California at Berkeley and Los Angeles (Brint & Karabel, 1989, p. 45; Hill, 1936). Other studies over seven decades have consistently shown that junior college graduates transferring to a four-year baccalaureate program continue to match or outperform native university students (Wyman, 1935; Hill, 1936; Bird, 1956; Knoell & Medsker, 1966; Kintzer & Wattenbarger, 1985; Illinois Community College Board, 1986; Knoell, 1990; Bender, 1990).

Most university leaders welcomed the growth of two-year colleges. As the demand for higher education increased, universities fought to remain exclusive enclaves of scholarship and research. Junior colleges released public pressure like a steam valve, providing timely relief to the four-year institutions. As Henry Tappan had predicted in 1851, junior colleges began to "guard the entrance" to American universities (Diener, 1986, p. 24). Consequently, university presidents and deans became vocal supporters of the junior college movement.

FROM PRIVATE TO PUBLIC

During the first three decades of the movement most junior colleges were private liberal arts colleges that had dropped their upper division. Texas led in private enrollment, followed by Missouri and North Carolina. (Eells, 1931, p. 24). Most private junior colleges were affiliated with the Methodist, Baptist, Catholic, and Lutheran churches. The largest non-church sponsor of private junior colleges, the Young Men's Christian Association, was responsible for five junior colleges, primarily in Ohio (p. 27).

In 1921 only 26 percent of America's junior colleges were public institutions, but the shift was under way (Frye, 1992, p. 88). The following year California's District Junior College Law gave the movement a boost. A 1922 study found that about a third of America's 207 junior colleges were public institutions, and these seventy were among the youngest, largest, and healthiest of American junior colleges (Koos, 1924, pp. 41–42), enrolling half of all two-year college students. Among four-year colleges and universities, public enrollment would not surpass that of private until after World War II (Frye, 1992, p. 89).

Between 1922 and 1927, public junior college enrollment jumped 217 percent (Eells, 1931, p. 69), primarily reflecting growth in three states: California, with thirty-one public junior colleges; Iowa, with nineteen; and Texas, with seventeen. By the fall of 1927 there were 146 such institutions in the United States (Whitney, 1928).

Most public junior colleges of the late 1920s were municipal institutions supported by local school districts. Many of these held classes in local high schools. There were also a few state junior colleges and two-year university branches. The fastest growing type of public college, however, was the district junior college.

The district junior college originated in California. Supported by property taxes from a junior college taxing district, and often supplemented by state funds, district junior colleges were controlled by a local board. Their students paid little or no tuition (Whitney, 1928, p. 9). Of the more than 39,000 students enrolled at public junior colleges by 1930, nearly 34 percent attended the district junior colleges of California (Eells, 1931, pp. 25–33).

The eastern states were slower to develop public junior colleges (Eells, 1931, p. 24). In the Northeast, where small liberal arts colleges still prospered, only one public junior college, Springfield Junior College in Massachusetts, existed. Vermont, Rhode Island, and New Hampshire had no junior colleges of any type. In the Deep South most junior colleges were private church-related institutions, many of which were former women's finishing schools (Greenleaf, 1936, pp. 45–48, 56–71).

THE GROWTH OF VOCATIONAL EDUCATION

During this decade, junior college leaders placed an increasing emphasis on vocational education. In 1924 Leonard V. Koos, the greatest booster of vocational programs, surveyed university deans to find out if some professions could be taught at two-year colleges. In engineering alone, the deans cited forty-three occupations that could be shifted to the junior college level (Koos, 1924, p. 108). These "semiprofessions" became the framework of a national effort to expand junior college vocational programs.

Koos also studied the catalogs of early junior colleges. His findings revealed that vocational, terminal education was frequently identified as a primary college mission, and that fully 50 percent of the junior colleges were already providing "occupational training of junior-college grade" (p. 124). Most of these vocational programs, commonly in agriculture, commerce, engineering, home economics, and industrial arts (Whitney, 1928, p. 127), awarded a diploma or certificate rather than an associate degree.

The fastest growing vocational programs were at public junior colleges. At the forefront were the district junior colleges of California. In 1928 Nicholas Ricciardi, of the California State Department of Education, reported that Riverside Junior College had been developing terminal vocational courses "for the last five years," and that of the 328 students currently enrolled, fifty were in terminal vocational programs (1928, p. 58). Junior colleges in Sacramento and Santa Ana offered similar programs.

Vocational programs were a boon to local industry. Junior colleges quickly learned to adapt to the needs of area employers, efficiently altering existing programs and developing new ones to serve industry. Towns with junior colleges became more competitive in attracting industry. Because of the college programs' inherent job training function, local business people became leading supporters of their local junior college.

AN ALTERNATIVE PLAN

Most American junior colleges were organized as the final link in the 6-3-3-2 or 6-2-4-2 system of public education, capping an already existing primary and secondary education system. Some educational theorists, however, proposed a reorganized public education system. The most popular of these plans, the 6-4-4 system, included six years of elementary education, four years of middle school (grades seven through ten), and a four-year junior college (grades eleven through fourteen).

Early in their careers Alexis Lange of Berkeley and David Starr Jordan of Stanford espoused the 6-4-4 plan. In the 1920s several leaders of the junior college movement, including George Zook of the U.S. Bureau of Education, Frederick Eby of the University of Texas, and William Proctor of Stanford, endorsed it.

The greatest 6-4-4 advocate was Leonard Koos, prolific author, researcher, and later editor of the *Junior College Journal*. Koos began advocating the system in the 1920s and never let up (Koos, 1946): as late as the 1960s he was still encouraging states to adopt it (Conger & Schultz, 1970). He believed that the plan was superior for five reasons:

- The span of grades 11 through 14 is more psychologically homogeneous than any other possible grouping.
- The first two years of university work are essentially secondary in nature and should be articulated with grades 11 and 12.
- The four-year college attracts a better faculty than the traditional high school and thus enables gifted high school students to progress more rapidly.
- A four-year unit is more economical than a two-year unit.
- Occupational education is enhanced by a four-year integrated program (Conger & Schultz, 1970, p. 30).

Several junior colleges were organized as four-year institutions under the 6-4-4 plan, including Hillsboro Junior College in Texas, and Pasadena and Ventura junior colleges in California. The 6-4-4 plan reached its zenith in 1946, with about two dozen 6-4-4 systems nationwide (Sexon & Harbeson, 1946). A decade later few of these systems remained (Conger & Schultz, 1970, p. 31).

The 6-4-4 plan worked well in theory. In practice, however, it never proved popular. By the 1920s the high school was an established American institution, and the high school diploma the terminal degree for most students. Few cities were willing to tamper with their high school to create a four-year junior college (Diener, 1986, pp. 99–115; Eells, 1931, pp. 327–328). However, after years of lying dormant, the 6-4-4 idea would resurface in the tech-prep movement of the 1980s.

CHAPTER 5

STATUS REPORT (1929)

The community college movement began the great transformation into a learning society.

— Clark Kerr

The 1920s was a period of spectacular growth for America's junior colleges. By the decade's end there were 450 colleges in the nation enrolling nearly 70,000 students. This growth was highly concentrated. Nearly a third of the national enrollment came from California and Texas. Only two other states—Illinois and Missouri—had more than 2,500 students. Most states had fewer than ten junior colleges, and five states had none at all (Eells, 1931, p. 24).

Walter Eells examined the status of junior colleges in each state for his landmark book *The Junior College* (1931). He found that in America there was no nationwide pattern for developing junior colleges, that, instead, colleges were being created in a haphazard fashion based on a host of local factors.

The findings of Eells and several of his contemporaries are presented below. Taken together, these observations show a rapidly expanding system of two-year colleges, the vast majority of which were private institutions still sharing facilities with local high schools. Few colleges had enrollments that numbered in the thousands. Most, in fact, were struggling with a few dozen students. As the nation entered the Great Depression, their future seemed uncertain.

CALIFORNIA: THE DISTRICT COLLEGE

California developed America's largest system of public junior colleges. The state had twenty-one public junior colleges by 1921, compared with only four private institutions. Most of these public colleges were still affiliated with local high schools (Eells, 1931). In that year the California legislature passed a new law creating district junior colleges.

The District Junior College Law of 1921 amended the Ballard Act of four years before. It allowed for the creation of districts to fund and administer junior colleges. These districts could be formed by a single local high school district, by two or more contiguous high school districts, or in any part of a county that was not covered by a high school district (Eells, 1931, p. 103).

Each public junior college district was required to have an assessed real estate valuation of $10 million, a population of 15,000, and an average daily high school attendance of 400. The state would provide each district with an annual appropriation of $2,000 plus $100 for each student enrolled. This state funding covered 40 percent of the estimated instructional costs. The remaining costs were paid for by the district.

With the establishment of college district boards of education, for the first time free-standing institutions of higher education were controlled by the electorate, not by an academic elite. This combination of local control and public funding allowed junior colleges to adapt rapidly to the needs of their districts. Local control also contributed to the rise of vocational education, adult education, evening classes, and other innovations that distinguish today's comprehensive community college (Eells, 1931, pp. 101–102).

Although locally controlled, district junior colleges could affiliate with the University of California. The 1921 law allowed the university to inspect affiliated junior colleges and dictate their teacher qualifications. Nevertheless, few junior colleges were actually affiliated with the university. Instead, articulation was usually accomplished by "friendly advice" (p. 104).

The new law had an immediate effect, with three junior college districts forming within the year. Modesto Junior College was approved by the state as a district junior college on September 22, 1921. Eight days later, Riverside Junior College, formerly a high school extension, reorganized under the district plan. Two months later the high school extension at Sacramento became a college district (Cooper, 1928).

The next year brought four new college districts, in Chaffey, Fullerton, San Mateo, and Santa Ana. Financially well-supported, these districts grew rapidly. Most conferred the associate of arts degree and various certificates (Eells, 1931, p. 102).

Pasadena organized California's eighth junior college district in 1924. Established in the buildings of a defunct private college founded in 1888, the institution did not have to build new facilities, and so got off to a running start. It soon became one of the largest colleges in the state.

All of California's district junior colleges created before 1924 survived the Depression and remained robust into the mid-1930s (Greenleaf, 1936, pp. 56–57). Many of them are still thriving.

Over the next five years, colleges were formed in Compton, Glendale, Long Beach, San Jose, and Santa Rosa (Eells, 1931, pp. 106–107). By 1928 California had thirty-one public junior colleges, fourteen of them district colleges (Whitney, 1928, pp. 13–16).

Once the district law was passed, few high schools added junior college programs. To receive state funding, many of the existing high school extensions reorganized as college districts. This trend increased after 1929, as extensions struggled to survive the Depression. In this way the six-year high school was gradually supplanted by the free-standing district junior college (Eells, 1931, pp. 106–107). The 1921 law also provided for teacher training schools (called normal schools) to operate junior college programs at the request of local high schools. Six of California's seven state normal schools received contracts from high school districts to offer junior college instruction, but over the next six years half of the normal schools dropped their junior college component. The provision that allowed this arrangement was repealed in 1927.

California also experimented with other types of two-year institutions, such as the California Polytechnic Institute, a state junior college at San Luis Obispo. At various times counties also operated junior colleges (Eells, 1931, pp. 102–105).

Private junior colleges, many of them church-related, could not compete with the state-subsidized public colleges. As several private colleges clung to existence, enrollment rapidly decreased. At the end of the decade there were only fifteen of these institutions with a combined graduating class of sixty-seven.

California developed several junior college associations during the 1920s. The Southern California Junior College Association was formed in 1925, followed three years later by the Northern California Junior College Association. Both of these groups, which met semiannually, primarily served administrators. The Federation of California Junior College Associations, formed in 1929, coordinated the work of the regional associations. In the same year the Central California Junior College Association was established. This organization included students and faculty as well as administrators.

The legislature passed another junior college law in 1929. Developed by advocates of tax control, the new law raised the financial requirements for establishing a junior college district by 150 percent and required that a college reach an average daily attendance of 200 by the end of its second year. This law slowed, but could not stop, the growth of new junior college districts.

California's district system was the most important junior college innovation of the decade, proving remarkably responsive to the needs of individual communities. Other states moved quickly to pass similar legislation. The district college was destined to became the model for most of America's public junior colleges.

Texas: Going Public

Before 1920 there was only one public junior college in Texas. By the decade's end, however, public junior college enrollment had surpassed that of private institutions (Eells, 1931, p. 24). Private junior colleges in Texas reached their peak in 1929, with twenty-eight institutions enrolling 4,131 students—the largest private enrollment in the nation. Most of these colleges were church-related. All were segregated—seven of them for African Americans only (p. 27).

Texas's first public two-year college was operated by the state. In 1917 the legislature took over John Tarleton College and created the Grubbs Vocational School. Managed by Texas Agricultural & Mechanical College, this two-year institution provided agricultural training in the western part of the state (p. 150).

The first locally controlled junior college in Texas was founded in El Paso in 1920. This municipal junior college later became the University of Texas at El Paso. In 1924 Gainesville College, later renamed Cooke County College, was founded. It is the oldest continuously operating public junior college in Texas (Hill College, 1986).

The state's first junior college district was created in 1923 in Hillsboro. For many years the Hill Junior College District operated a four-year program, including the final two years of high school and two years of college (Eells, 1931, p. 149), but later dropped its high school offerings.

The University of Texas also experimented with junior colleges. In 1925 the university offered junior college courses in the evening at a San Antonio high school, attracting 300 students. A ruling by the state attorney general, however, forced the university to withdraw its support, and the college was continued as a municipal institution (Eells, 1931, p. 151).

After 1925 Texas shifted heavily toward public junior colleges. By 1929 there were nineteen public junior colleges with an enrollment of 4,788. Nationally, Texas ranked second, behind California, in public junior college enrollment (Eells, 1931, p. 24). Only five of Texas's public colleges had their own buildings; the remainder were housed in local high schools.

In 1929 Texas passed a strong junior college district law, akin to the California law of 1921. The General School Law allowed local districts to establish public junior colleges if they had property assessed at a minimum of $12 million and an average daily high school attendance of 400 students.

Texans of the 1920s had a strong sense of county identity. For this reason the idea of locally controlled college districts caught on quickly. Before the end of the decade all of the state's municipal junior colleges had reorganized as college districts (Eells, 1931, pp. 149–150). The Texas Junior College Association was also founded during this period (p. 81).

State funding of two-year colleges in Texas was slow in coming, for the most part owing to the opposition of Frederick Eby (Eells, 1931, pp. 82–83), a leading junior college theorist and author of the influential book *The Development of Education in Texas* (1925). Eby, a professor at the University of Texas, insisted on four-year junior colleges, like the one at Hillsboro, believing that the future of public education lay in a 6-4-4 plan. Eby (1937) argued against financing two-year experiments that did not conform to his plan.

ILLINOIS: THE LARGEST JUNIOR COLLEGE

Illinois ranked third, behind California and Texas, in public junior college enrollment. Most of the state's 4,776 public junior college students attended Crane Junior College in the booming city of Chicago (Eells, 1931, p. 24). Crane traced its roots to 1911, when twenty young men enrolled in free postdiploma classes at Crane Technical High School. With the combination of college-level classes offered at this school and at Land and Senn high schools in 1917, Crane Junior College was formed. By 1929 Crane was the largest public junior college in America, enrolling more than 4,000 students.

Despite Crane's initial success, its future looked bleak. Rapid growth, it seemed, had resulted in declining academic standards. Finding fault with Crane's "teaching load, internal organization, inadequacy of physical plant and facilities, class sizes, library, lack of adequate records [and] general tone" (Fretwell, 1954, p. 27), in April 1930 the North Central Association of Colleges and Secondary Schools withdrew its accreditation. Accreditation was eventually restored, but Crane continued to suffer from overcrowding and underfunding until July 12, 1933, when the school board and Mayor Edward Kelly closed the school as a cost-cutting measure.

The protests began almost immediately. Students, parents, and civic leaders decried the loss of this popular institution. Robert M. Hutchins, then president of the University of Chicago, became a vocal supporter of Crane. In a newspaper article Hutchins lashed out at the school board:

> The board is not making an honest effort to save money because it flouted the Superintendent and ignored other experts who would have been glad to advise it.... The economic and social condition of Chicago will be worse for twenty-five years because of what this Board of Education has done.... The abolition of Crane Junior College is one of the most serious crimes of the Board of Education (Fretwell, 1954, p. 34).

Local civic groups, organized into the Citizens Save Our Schools Committee, rallied 25,000 angry taxpayers in protest. Finally, in March 1934, the mayor compromised by supporting a move to replace Crane with a three-branch system known as Chicago Junior College (Fretwell, 1954, pp. 22–39).

Illinois had six other, much smaller public junior colleges. Most of these began as six-year high schools, such as Joliet Junior College, whose pioneering principal, J. Stanley Brown, became a founding member of the American Association of Junior Colleges (Reid, 1928). Because these schools were not sanctioned or funded by state law until 1937 (Fretwell, 1954), they had to rely on local school boards for support and direction. The University of Chicago, the University of Illinois, and other institutions accepted the graduates of these colleges without examination (Eells, 1931, p. 130).

To assure high standards, the University of Illinois developed detailed guidelines for accrediting public junior colleges. Each college was required to have at least fifty students, with classes capped at thirty, and an annual minimum budget of $10,000. At least 75 percent of the faculty had to possess a master's degree (Eells, 1931, p. 176). Accredited colleges were also required to have a 5,000-volume library and six academic departments, with the library, laboratories, and study rooms kept separate from high school facilities. The university suggested that "a separate floor" or "a distinct wing" of the high school be set aside for the junior college (p. 428).

Illinois also developed twelve private junior colleges. The total 1929 enrollment of these private colleges stood at 1,747 (p. 24).

MISSOURI: A DECADE OF EXPANSION

Missouri's first junior colleges were primarily church-related, private institutions accredited by the University of Missouri (Reid, 1928). The university inspected the colleges and, through its "Circular of Information to Accredited Junior Colleges" (Carpenter, 1962), suggested the equipment, facilities, and record-keeping methods (Eells, 1931, pp. 381, 438). By 1929 Missouri was second to Texas in private junior college enrollment, with sixteen institutions enrolling 3,307 students (pp. 24, 27).

Missouri's first public junior college was St. Joseph Junior College, established in 1914, followed the next year by Kansas City College. Over the next twelve years at least three more public colleges came into being—all created locally, without state approval or support. In 1927 the state legalized its public junior colleges. The legislature passed a bill allowing any district with an accredited high school to offer junior college courses. Unlike California and Texas, Missouri did not require a local election in order to establish a junior college (Eells, 1931, p. 141). The state contributed $100 a year for each teacher with a salary above $1,000; in practice this amounted to about $1 per junior college student (p. 540).

Despite the minimal state support, the number and size of public junior colleges grew rapidly. By the decade's end Missouri had twenty-three public junior colleges with a total enrollment of 5,554 (p. 24). The largest of these, Kansas City College, was the third largest public junior college in the nation, with a 1928–29 enrollment of 1,744.

NORTH CAROLINA: A LEGAL CHALLENGE

North Carolina had the nation's third highest private junior college enrollment, with fifteen colleges enrolling 2,133 students by the end of the decade (Eells, 1931, p. 24). These were primarily church-related institutions, connected with the Baptist, Methodist, and Presbyterian denominations.

North Carolina's major universities were concentrated in the north-central portion of the state. As in California, this geographic concentration created a demand for higher education in the distant rural counties (p. 144). The expense and inconvenience of studying in Chapel Hill, Durham, or Raleigh helped to foster public and private junior colleges in the state's western mountains.

North Carolina's first public junior college was founded at Asheville in 1926. A year later Buncombe County Junior College opened in the nearby town of Biltmore. By the end of the decade North Carolina had three public junior colleges with a total of 306 students (p. 24).

The state's public junior colleges were nearly forced to close in 1930 after the state attorney general issued a ruling forbidding the Asheville Board of Education from funding junior college classes. The state supreme court overturned the ruling the following August.

Although North Carolina adopted no junior college laws during the 1920s, the North Carolina College Conference, in 1927, set standards for colleges in which teachers were trained. The standards required a minimum teaching staff of five part-time faculty members holding at least a bachelor's degree (a year of graduate work was preferred). These standards, administered by the state education department, were applied to many junior colleges (p. 144).

IOWA: JUNIOR COLLEGE EPIDEMIC

Iowa's first junior college was established in 1918 in Mason City. Over the next decade the state experienced an epidemic of junior colleges, producing in 1927 alone thirteen colleges—a national record. By 1930 twenty-five junior colleges were in operation, and five more had been approved. It appeared that every county seat in Iowa, no matter how small, was destined to have its own junior college (Eells, 1931, pp. 132–133).

Unfortunately, there were few students to fill the classrooms. By the end of the decade, the average Iowa junior college had only sixty-six students—one-fourth as many as its California counterpart (p. 24). Most colleges were public institutions formed haphazardly by local communities without any state authorization, funding, or standards. Many of them offered only one year of instruction.

A professor at the State University of Iowa described the condition of junior colleges in the state:

> Since Mason City launched the experiment in 1919, it has extended to other centers, until now almost a third of our counties have within their boundaries a public junior college. This movement has developed in typical Iowa fashion without much direction and with practically no legal control.... We have 28 public junior colleges, about seven of which come near meeting the minimum requirements now laid upon communities in California (p. 132).

The Iowa legislature, in 1923, attempted to slow the growth of new colleges by passing a law requiring public junior colleges to charge a tuition that "fully covered the cost of maintenance of such school" (p. 132). As the law applied only to towns of more than 20,000 residents, and only two Iowa towns fit this category, the rest of the state continued to build colleges.

In 1927 the legislature passed a more effective law, requiring a districtwide election and approval by the state education department before a new public junior college could be established. The education department was to regulate the curricula of these schools (p. 133). Statewide standards for new public junior colleges, set the following year, required a minimum enrollment of twenty-five students in order to establish a one-year college and fifty students for a two-year school. Once again, all costs were to be covered by tuition.

The state standards succeeded in slowing the pace of new college formation. Still, Iowa finished the decade with the nation's second largest number of public junior colleges and tenth largest enrollment (p. 24). Iowa's first junior college organization—the Junior College Section of the Iowa Teachers Association—was also established during this decade (p. 81).

KANSAS: AN ORDERLY EXPANSION

Kansas's junior colleges, in contrast to Iowa's public colleges, which grew haphazardly, were created and controlled by state legislation. The first Kansas junior college law, enacted in 1917, set rules for establishing a public junior college. Proposed by the citizens of Holton after their own private junior college had failed, the law required the district to hold an election and to levy taxes to support the college, and empowered the state board of education to set the curricula and inspect the institution. Shortly after the law was passed, Holton established the first public junior college in Kansas. Over the next two years public junior colleges were founded at Fort Scott, Garden City, and Marysville.

The University of Kansas conducted feasibility studies for colleges in Atchison, Chanute, and Hutchinson. Colleges in Arkansas City, Coffeeville, Independence, Iola, and Parsons soon appeared (Eells, 1931, pp. 134–135).

Because none of the state's public colleges charged tuition, local taxpayers bore all operating costs (p. 512). Two pieces of legislation introduced in the 1920s attempted to relieve this burden. In 1925 and 1929 the state legislature considered bills to fund public junior colleges at $100 per student and $800 per instructor. Both were defeated. As the decade closed, Kansas had not yet provided state support for junior colleges (p. 541).

In 1929 Kansas had 2,232 students in nineteen junior colleges. The vast majority were enrolled in public institutions. A professional organization—the Kansas Public Junior College Association—was established during the decade (p. 81).

MICHIGAN: TAPPAN FINALLY SUCCEEDS

Michigan's first public junior college was probably Grand Rapids Junior College, founded in 1914. However, Detroit Junior College, thought to have been founded the following year, may have existed as early as 1913 as a one-year college (Eells, 1931, p. 138).

The Michigan legislature passed its first public junior college law in 1917. Initiated by the city of Detroit to ensure that its junior college had a "legal basis" (p. 138), the law allowed cities of more than 30,000 residents to establish a junior college. As public junior colleges increased in popularity, the population requirement was lowered, dropping to 25,000 in 1923 and 18,000 in 1929. Michigan's junior college laws did not require an election or state permission in order to form a college.

The University of Michigan accredited many of the state's early junior colleges. The university's inspection committees gave advice and set standards for accreditation. Graduates of accredited colleges were accepted as juniors at the university.

Near the end of the decade the University of Michigan finally separated its lower division, calling it the University College. This move had been proposed seventy years before by elitist president Henry Tappan. The University College granted a diploma after the sophomore year (p. 138).

By 1929 Michigan's junior colleges enrolled 2,046 students, over 95 percent of whom attended the state's nine public institutions. Michigan's two private junior colleges had only ninety-seven students. The Michigan Association of Junior Colleges was also founded during this decade.

ARKANSAS: A RECORD DONATION

Arkansas's first two-year colleges were founded by the state government. They included three agricultural and mechanical colleges and a polytechnic college, the earliest of which was formed in 1909 (Eells, 1931, p. 126).

Most of Arkansas's other junior colleges were municipal institutions, organized in the late 1920s. One of the largest, in Little Rock, in 1927 received a $2 million bequest from a private donor. This is the first known instance of a major bequest to a two-year college (p. 127).

By the end of the decade Arkansas had twelve junior colleges with 1,956 students. Over two-thirds of these students attended the state's seven public junior colleges (p. 24), most of which were housed in local public school facilities. Their costs were presumably covered by tuition (p. 127). Arkansas had no junior college law to provide a legal standing for its colleges. The state attorney general, however, ruled that it was legal for public schools to operate such institutions.

OKLAHOMA: A SLOW START

Oklahoma's first two-year college was probably a church-related women's school called Oklahoma Presbyterian College for Girls. Little is known about this early institution (Eells, 1931, p. 146), which may have been more of a women's finishing school than a junior college.

The state's first public junior college was the University Preparatory School and Junior College. Founded as a technical school in 1902, within two years the institution began offering college vocational and transfer curricula, though its primary focus remained vocational programs. In 1914 the college changed its name to the Oklahoma Institute of Technology (Ratcliff, 1986, p. 15). Oklahoma's second public junior college was founded in 1920 at Muskogee. Three years later the legislature authorized a state junior college called Oklahoma Military College. Other state colleges followed in 1924 and 1927.

By the end of the decade Oklahoma had fourteen junior colleges with 1,744 students. More than 90 percent of these students attended the eleven state and municipal colleges. Oklahoma's private junior colleges had only 153 students (Eells, 1931, p. 24). The Oklahoma Association of Junior Colleges was also formed during this decade.

Like Arkansas, Oklahoma had no general legislation authorizing junior colleges. State-operated colleges were authorized on a case-by-case basis, with the tacit understanding that one should be established in eastern Oklahoma for each one established in western Oklahoma (Eells, 1931, p. 146).

THE NORTHEASTERN STATES

The Northeast was a latecomer to the junior college movement, largely owing to the extensive system of small private colleges already in place. These liberal arts colleges provided local access to higher education and slowed the public demand for junior colleges. In fact, many of the area's first junior colleges were reorganized private colleges. The original British colonies of the Northeast, where the word *public* was equated with *second-rate*, were bastions of private education (Zook, 1946). Consequently, only one public junior college existed in the entire area in 1929: Springfield Junior College in Springfield, Massachusetts.

Springfield Junior College, actually a one-year extension of Central High School, began offering classes in the fall of 1918 (Ratcliff, 1987b). An articulation agreement allowed its students to transfer to nearby Wesleyan University (Ratcliff, 1986). Despite local newspaper reports of the success of California colleges, the college attracted an enrollment of only thirty-five students by 1929. Another public college had been organized at Newark, New Jersey, in 1918, but was closed four years later.

Only two northeastern states—Pennsylvania and New York—had more than 700 junior college students in 1929 (Eells, 1931, p. 24). Pennsylvania's largest junior colleges were actually branches of private universities. In 1927 Pennsylvania passed special legislation allowing school districts to lease facilities to private universities for "junior college purposes" (p. 147). In that same year the University of Pittsburgh opened a junior college at Johnstown and almost overnight enrolled 141 students. The following year the university opened junior colleges at Erie and Uniontown. By 1929 Pennsylvania had 1,000 students at nine private junior colleges (p. 24).

New York's junior colleges were primarily outgrowths of women's finishing schools. In addition, Columbia University founded Seth Low Junior College in Brooklyn, and the prestigious Sarah Lawrence College opened as a two-year college in 1926. The State University of New York set the standards for these private colleges, requiring, at a minimum, four full-time instructors, 4,000 library books, and an endowment of $250,000. In 1929 New York had eleven private junior colleges enrolling 1,087 students.

The state also operated six technical and agricultural institutes. These small two-year colleges, all founded before 1913, offered little academic work, concentrating primarily on terminal vocational programs (Medsker, 1960, pp. 248–256).

At the end of the decade, Massachusetts had 627 junior college students. The smaller northeastern states had far fewer, and Vermont, Delaware, and Rhode Island had no junior colleges at all (Eells, 1931, p. 24).

OTHER SOUTHERN STATES

During the six years ending in 1928, the number of public junior colleges in the South rose by a phenomenal 1,125 percent, with forty-nine colleges in place. Most southern states had no legislation to legitimize their junior colleges. The exception was Mississippi, where the state legislature established an orderly method for creating public junior colleges (Medsker, 1960, p. 245).

Mississippi's first junior college law was adopted in 1922. Six years later the legislature passed a more detailed law setting standards similar to those of regional accrediting agencies for faculty, curricula, facilities, libraries, and graduation. An established system of inspection and control enforced these standards (Eells, 1931, p. 139). The 1928 law also brought into being a commission to plan the state's junior college system. After examining the tax base, probable enrollment, transportation, and existing colleges in various parts of the state (p. 140), the Legalized Commission on Junior Colleges grouped all counties not served by higher education institutions into thirteen zones. These zones formed the basis of the Mississippi junior college system (pp. 152–153).

A major impetus for this projected structure came from the state supervisor of agricultural high schools, Knox M. Broom, who helped develop the criteria used as a basis for the state plan. Broom, a graduate of the University of Chicago, where he learned from Leonard Koos about junior colleges, used his graduate work to develop a type of 6-4-4 plan for agricultural high schools. He supported the 1922 and 1928 laws that made it possible to extend the agricultural high school upward to include two years of college (Todd, 1962).

Even before the enabling legislation, Mississippi had a growing number of public and private junior colleges. The early private institutions included Hillman College (1910), Presbyterian-sponsored Mississippi Synodical College (1916), Gulf Park College (1921), and Methodist-sponsored Whitworth College (1928) (p. 141). The public junior colleges grew out of agricultural high schools. In 1922 agricultural schools in Pearl River County and Hinds County became the first to offer college classes (p. 142).

At the end of the decade Mississippi had eighteen junior colleges with a total of 1,396 students (Eells, 1931, p. 24). In 1930 the state legislature approved a blanket appropriation of $170,000 to fund these colleges.

Virginia's so-called junior colleges, many of which had been in existence since Reconstruction, were primarily private finishing schools for women. These institutions usually included a two-year college, a high school, and a special school of art and music. One state official likened the campus atmosphere to "a sort of three-ring educational circus" (Eells, 1931, p. 155).

The state's first junior college standards were adopted in 1913 by the Virginia Association of Schools for Girls. Most of the junior colleges for women reorganized to meet these standards. By the end of the decade Virginia had twelve junior colleges (eleven for women) with a total of 1,586 students (p. 155).

Kentucky's 16 private junior colleges had an enrollment of 1,557 in 1929 (p. 24). Most of these had been founded during the 1920s and were accredited by the Association of Kentucky Colleges and Universities. The state's only public junior college was a segregated institution for African Americans (p. 135).

Tennessee also developed a system of private, church-related colleges. The largest of these, Ward-Belmont, Inc., a women's finishing school, had nearly 500 students in its junior college program by the end of the decade (p. 148). At that time Tennessee had thirteen junior colleges and a total of 1,680 students (p. 24).

Tennessee Polytechnic Institute had organized as a public junior college in 1915, but it soon expanded to four years. The state's second public junior college, a branch of the University of Tennessee located in Martin, was the state's only public junior college as of 1929 (p. 148).

Georgia developed state, municipal, and private junior colleges. Its two state colleges, in Cochran and Douglas, were nominally branches of the University of Georgia. In reality, however, they operated as independent institutions. Each had its own board of trustees and received a separate appropriation from the legislature. The state's first municipal junior colleges were formed by the county school boards in Augusta and Waynesboro in the mid-1920s (p. 129). Georgia's most popular type of junior college was private and church related. By 1929 Georgia had nine private junior colleges, enrolling about 55 percent of the state's 1,435 junior college students (p. 24).

There was a smattering of junior colleges in Alabama, Florida, Louisiana, Maryland, South Carolina, West Virginia, and the District of Columbia. None of these states had more than 700 junior college students. In Florida and West Virginia most students attended public junior colleges. In the other states they primarily attended private institutions (p. 24).

OTHER MIDWESTERN STATES

After California, the junior college movement's greatest strength was in the Midwest, with Arkansas, Iowa, Illinois, Kansas, Michigan, Missouri, and Oklahoma leading the way. In addition to these, three other states had enrollments of more than 700 students.

Ohio developed five private junior colleges during the 1920s. Most of these were sponsored by Young Men's Christian Association (YMCA) branches in major cities. Ohio's first YMCA junior college was organized in 1925 in Columbus, followed two years later by YMCA colleges in Youngstown and Cleveland (Eells, 1931, p. 145).

Junior college laws introduced in the Ohio legislature during the 1927 and 1929 sessions, similar in content to the California Upward Extension Law of 1907, would have permitted local school boards to create junior college programs, but both bills failed to pass. At the end of the decade all of Ohio's 1,724 junior college students attended private institutions (p. 24).

Minnesota developed a strong public junior college system. The first public college was established in Rochester in 1915. Hibbing and Eveleth organized junior colleges three years later. These colleges were legalized by a 1925 junior college bill allowing for the creation of additional junior colleges if approved by a three-fourths vote of the district (p. 139).

In 1927 the Minnesota legislature passed a second junior college law, which made it easier to establish new colleges. Under this law any city of 50,000 or more residents could organize a college by a majority vote of the school board. At the end of the decade Minnesota had eleven junior colleges enrolling 1,403 students. Only three of these institutions were private (p. 24).

Most of Nebraska's junior colleges were private, church-related institutions. The Lutheran church operated three, and the Catholic church four. In addition, the cities of McCook and Norfolk operated public municipal colleges. Of the 805 students enrolled in Nebraska junior colleges in 1929, 646 were in private institutions (pp. 24, 142).

The states of Indiana, South Dakota, North Dakota, and Wisconsin had fewer than 400 junior college students at the end of the decade.

OTHER WESTERN STATES

California and Texas had the largest junior college enrollments in the nation. In the other western states, however, enrollments were much lower. Wyoming and Nevada had no junior colleges. Of the rest, only Utah and Idaho had more than 600 junior college students.

Half of Utah's junior colleges—Weber, Snow, and Dixie colleges—were controlled by the Church of Jesus Christ of Latter-Day Saints (Mormon Church). A fourth church-related junior college, Westminster College in Salt Lake City, was operated by six protestant denominations. Utah had one public junior college, a branch of the state agricultural college located in Cedar City.

In 1929 the Mormon church backed away from operating junior colleges, withdrawing all subsidies from the three Mormon colleges then in place. This move encouraged the state legislature to provide public funding for junior colleges.

Idaho had only one public and one private junior college, but both had high enrollments. Idaho Technical Institute, organized in 1915 and reconstituted as a branch of the University of Idaho in 1927, at the end of the decade had 667 students (Eells, 1931, p. 130).

Ricks College in Rexburg, Idaho, supported by the Mormon church until 1929, was the largest of five Mormon institutions established in Arizona, Idaho, and Utah. For the 1927–28 academic year Ricks had 354 students and received a $47,400 subsidy from the church.

CHAPTER 6

ASSOCIATIONS AND ACCREDITATION

The junior colleges are practically the only large

body of people concerned with a definite type of

education which so far have not held any

national conferences.

— George Zook

In 1890 William Rainey Harper predicted that the junior college idea would revolutionize higher education in America (Goodspeed, 1928, pp. 110–111). Three decades later that prediction was coming true. The movement that originated in the Great Plains found fertile ground in the southwestern and western states. By 1920 junior colleges were also expanding in the Deep South. In that year these far-flung colleges held their first national meeting and founded the American Association of Junior Colleges.

FOUNDING A NATIONAL ASSOCIATION

The first national meeting of junior college leaders was organized by the U.S. Bureau of Education (Eells, 1931). The idea came from George Zook, the bureau's higher education specialist. Zook, who had joined the bureau in February 1920, spent several months reading reports and bulletins to acquaint himself with the job. One publication that caught his attention was a bulletin titled *The Junior College* by Floyd M. McDowell. Rutledge (1951) explained Zook's reaction:

> Of all the educational groups studied, here was one which represented a large group of institutions but for which there was no organization. Zook began a correspondence with some of the presidents of junior colleges and it was decided to call a conference in the summer of 1920 (pp. 18–19).

Philander Claxton, the U.S. commissioner of education, was also enthusiastic about a national junior college conference. Fearing an educational crisis as the nation's two million high school students began to demand higher education, Claxton supported junior colleges for reasons of economy. He hoped that financially troubled small colleges would convert to junior colleges. He explained his plan to the conference:

> All the 307 colleges [in the nation] having incomes of less than $50,000...should cease to try to do more than two or three years of work.... Most of them would find themselves with two or three times their present number of students.... In addition, they would have the consciousness of serving their country and the world more effectively than they can now do (Diener, 1986, pp. 87–88).

Claxton believed that a well-publicized national conference would encourage additional four-year colleges to drop their upper divisions. It was probably Claxton who chose St. Louis as the site; the commissioner had several close friends in Missouri, including James Wood, president of Stephens College, and Martha Reid, dean of William Woods College.

Reid and Wood organized the conference on the Missouri end. Wood, a leading advocate of the 6-4-4 education system, chaired the conference and served as the first president of the American Association of Junior Colleges (AAJC) (Eells, 1931, p. 81). Reid acted as secretary for the conference and became the first secretary of AAJC. Their colleges had been leaders in the Missouri College Union, the nation's first statewide junior college association, founded six years before.

The conference took place on June 30 and July 1, 1920. In his opening address Zook explained the bureau's reasons for calling the conference, and his hopes for a national association:

> During the last twenty years, there have been formed a large number of national educational associations.... The junior colleges are practically the only large body of people concerned with a definite type of education which so far have not held any national conferences. It, therefore, occurred to the Commissioner of Education to call a meeting of representatives from the junior colleges of the country for a full and frank discussion of their mutual interests and problems. This, in brief, is the occasion for this conference (Eells, 1931, p. 75).

Only thirty-four delegates, mainly from private, religious-oriented colleges, attended the two-day conference. Of the nation's 165 junior colleges, only twenty-two were represented (Campbell, 1936a, p. 109). Many educators refused to attend, doubting that "the junior college had a future sufficiently important to justify a conference" (Zook, 1946, p. 411). California, the fastest growing junior college state, had no official representation, although records of the proceedings show that Merton E. Hill from California spoke at the conference (Rutledge, 1951, p. 19).

Two delegates in attendance had participated in the early junior college movement at the University of Chicago: John Million, founder and current president of Hardin College in Missouri, and J. Stanley Brown, founder of Joliet Junior College in Illinois and current president of Northern Illinois State Normal School (Reid, 1928).

The delegates at this first meeting represented vastly different institutions. Between those representing the private, church-related college, with its primary emphasis on classical studies, and those representing the larger, public college, with its much broader mission, there was wide disagreement on the function and future of the junior college. Some delegates came from high school extensions. They viewed the junior college as a part of secondary education. When Commissioner Claxton spoke of junior colleges as a branch of higher education, this group thought that he was ill informed.

Other delegates came from colleges without degree programs. When Wood spoke of two-year degrees, these delegates argued that junior colleges should not grant a degree. Some delegates thought that Wood was talking about baccalaureate degrees. The confusion was cleared up by H.G. Noffsinger of Virginia Intermont College, who reminded the skeptics of the associate degree as created by Harper (Eells, 1931).

Only a handful of the delegates came from public junior colleges. Some of these delegates emphasized the role of vocational education and specialized technology in the junior college curriculum. They also stressed the community service function of junior colleges. David MacKenzie, dean of Detroit Junior College, argued:

> It is a great mistake to limit the scope of the junior college.... The junior college in large cities is going to appeal to thousands when it offers courses of this [vocational] character and particularly courses in the evening. This, I believe, is going to be the saving grace of democracy (Eells, 1931, p. 236).

In addition to the junior college delegates, the conference attracted representatives from the University of Minnesota, Washington University at St. Louis, and the University of Missouri. The educational director of the *New York Evening Post* also attended.

Despite the disagreements, the delegates succeeded in creating a national organization: the American Association of Junior Colleges (AAJC). The name would be retained until 1972, when the organization became the American Association of Community and Junior Colleges (AACJC). In 1992, in an effort to unify the diverse membership of community, technical, and junior colleges, the organization would again change its name, this time to the American Association of Community Colleges (AACC).

David MacKenzie, dean of Detroit Junior College, was elected to replace Wood as Association president in 1921. MacKenzie represented one of America's largest public colleges, with more than 1,000 students. T.W. Raymond, the "lady principal" of Mississippi Synodical College, was elected vice president. Martha Reid became secretary (Eells, 1931, pp. 75–76).

The fledgling Association appointed a standards committee to set the basic ground rules concerning admission, graduation, curriculum, and length of study. Another committee faced the controversial issue of whether the AAJC should accredit its member colleges. As the conference ended each institution was levied a $5 fee to plan and publicize the first annual convention—a grand total of $170.

After the sweltering St. Louis conference, the Association decided to hold its meetings in the winter, and the first regular AAJC meeting took place February 16–17, 1921, in Chicago. Attendance at this conference increased dramatically, with at least seventy junior colleges represented—more than a third of the two-year colleges in America (Campbell, 1936a, p. 109). Thirty of those were members of the Association (Brick, 1964, pp. 62–63).

The primary accomplishment of the Chicago meeting was the adoption of a constitution. According to the constitution, the Association existed primarily to set national standards for junior colleges:

> The object of this Association shall be to define the Junior College by creating standards and curricula, thus determining its position structurally in all of its types (endowed, municipal and state) in order to make a genuine contribution to the work of education (American Association of Junior Colleges, 1921).

Every standardized junior college in the nation was entitled to become an active member. Each member college could appoint one voting representative. Educators could become associate members but could not vote.

The constitution continued the elected office of president and expanded the secretary position to secretary-treasurer (Rutledge, 1951). In addition, it created a senior vice president and vice presidents for each state. State vice presidents were elected at the

Chicago meeting ("Texan," 1921). The senior vice president position, however, was probably never filled. Both positions were eventually written out of the constitution (Brick, 1964, pp. 39–40).

The constitution created a committee structure, built around six standing and three temporary committees. The most influential of these, the six-member executive committee, became the governing board of the organization, which established policy and arranged for the annual meetings. The Association president served as an ex officio member. During the 1920s the executive committee was usually dominated by presidents of the older, private junior colleges.

The other standing committees dealt with publicity, finance, credentials, curriculum, and standards. The temporary committees handled nominations, auditing, and resolutions. Although the constitution spoke of standards, no set of standards was adopted. Its own work incomplete, the standards committee was continued for another year.

At the Chicago meeting AAJC members elected George Winfield, president of Wesley College in Greenville, Texas, to succeed MacKenzie as president. At the time Winfield served on the executive board of the Texas State Teachers Association and the standards committee for Texas high schools. His college was one of the largest private junior colleges in the nation, with an enrollment of nearly 500 ("College Head," 1922). AAJC members also reelected Martha Reid as secretary.

In the days before airlines and superhighways, cross-country travel was a long and expensive undertaking. Few junior college presidents could afford more than one trip per year. For this reason the first few AAJC conventions were held at the approximate time and place as meetings of the National Education Association and regional accrediting associations, to enable AAJC members to participate in other conventions.

The strategy also attracted leading university educators to the AAJC convention. During the Association's first decade nearly a third of all convention speakers were representatives of four-year institutions. The Association continued to meet in conjunction with other associations until 1929 (Rutledge, 1951, p. 201).

THE MEMPHIS SESSION

By the time of its second annual session, AAJC was drawing national attention. The *Memphis News Scimitar* ("College Head," 1922), reporting that the "junior college movement is sweeping the country," relayed the Association's expectations:

> Between 75 and 100 of the leading educators, including representatives of a number of the great universities, are expected to attend. The place of the junior college in the American system of education will be the theme of the convention.

Winfield proved to be an optimistic spokesperson for the movement. His exaggerated statements were quoted in newspapers in Texas, Tennessee, and New Jersey ("High Schools," 1922). He told a reporter for the Newark *Evening News* that the junior college had become as essential a part of the public education system as the high school ("Educator," 1922).

Winfield took his talent for overstatement even further with the Memphis newspaper ("High Schools," 1922), claiming that "more than 200 junior colleges are members of the association." The actual membership was only forty-one schools (Brick, 1964, pp. 62–63). Winfield said that junior colleges were on the verge of entirely eliminating the university lower division:

> Within 10 years I predict every university of standing will require students to complete work equivalent to the junior college course before they can enter ("Educator," 1922).

The claim that several "great universities" would be represented was not an exaggeration. The chancellors of Vanderbilt University and the University of Mississippi and the president of Texas A & M attended, as well as deans and faculty from the University of Chicago, the Carnegie Institute of Technology, the University of Minnesota, Stanford University, and the University of California. The new U.S. commissioner of education, John J. Tigert, was scheduled to speak but sent George Zook in his place.

The most memorable of the university speakers was T.N. Powers, chancellor of "Ole Miss." This southern educator believed that the junior college could save young students from the "evil" of flapper dancing that was sweeping the nation. His arguments seem almost comical today, but at the time they were viewed as a positive reason for the growth of junior colleges:

> Modern degenerate dances which are thrust upon young university students constitute the paramount educational evil of the day and, by the same token, they are the most powerful arguments in favor of the junior college.... I am afraid that the college heads of the country, including myself, have been cowardly in facing this degenerate dance evil.... The junior college will minimize this evil by allowing the student to remain at home two years longer ("Says Modern Dance," 1922).

James Wood, who had chaired the first national conference, was elected Association president. He served in the office for two years. Louis Plummer of Fullerton Junior College in California was chosen vice president, and Doak Campbell of Central College, Arkansas, secretary. Over the next two decades Campbell became one of the most influential leaders of AAJC.

NATIONAL STANDARDS

Before the Memphis meeting adjourned, the committee on standards presented the results of its two-year study. The committee decided that AAJC should not accredit junior colleges, that the function should be performed by either a state university, a state education department, or one of the five existing regional accrediting associations.

Although the committee decided not to accredit, it did set specific guidelines for admission and graduation. Unless the junior college had an accredited preparatory program, the committee deemed, only graduates of accredited high schools were to be admitted. Graduation would require students to complete sixty semester hours or thirty-four year-hours, or work equivalent to two years of college study.

Newts /922

More importantly, the committee presented the first nationwide definition of a junior college. This definition legitimized the comprehensive junior college curriculum, including community service and vocational and recreational courses (Barton, 1928), and spelled out all the components of the modern community college.

> The junior college is an institution offering two years of instruction strictly of collegiate grade. This curriculum may include those courses usually offered in the first two years of the four year college; in which case these courses must be identical, in scope and thoroness [sic], with corresponding courses of the standard four year college. The junior college may, and is likely to, develop a different type of curriculum, suited to the larger and ever changing civic, social and vocational needs of the entire community in which the college is located. It is understood that in this case also all the work offered shall conform to collegiate standards (American Association of Junior Colleges, 1922b).

Not unintentionally, the definition omitted the words *higher education*. Many junior colleges had started as high school extensions, and their representative leaders felt very strongly that the junior college should not be separate in its funding and administration from the parent high school. In effect, they regarded junior college education as secondary, not higher education. And they feared a hasty, expensive, and unwanted separation.

These standards went far toward unifying the organization and giving it both purpose and momentum, but at a heavy cost. Many of the weaker junior colleges, too small to meet the minimum standards for financial support, number of departments, and library volumes, and too impoverished to afford the minimum faculty loads and class sizes, dropped out or never joined the Association. Others kept their membership and battled to relax the standards. Throughout the 1920s heated debates over standards stirred every Association convention.

Ironically, several colleges forced out of the Association were pioneers of the junior college movement. Many of these were former four-year colleges that had followed Harper's advice and eliminated their upper divisions. Now these private colleges found themselves in a precarious position. They were shunned by both the stronger two-year colleges of AAJC and the four-year institutions that dominated the accrediting agencies. Without official recognition and unable to attract students and funding, many had ceased to exist before the end of the Depression.

Some members wanted AAJC to become an accrediting agency. This issue would have caused further division in the Association, and would probably have split the junior college movement, had not the regional accrediting agencies and state education departments quickly stepped forward to accredit junior colleges. While AAJC continued to set and revise its membership standards, it never jumped into the treacherous waters of accreditation (Brick, 1964, p. 35).

BECOMING TRULY NATIONAL

For the next seven years AAJC continued to meet in the Midwest and South. Three additional conventions were held in Chicago, as well as meetings in Cleveland, Cincinnati, Jackson, and Fort Worth (Walker, 1926). Finally, in 1929, AAJC held a convention in the Northeast. By convening there, in Atlantic City, Association members hoped to spur the slow pace of junior college growth in that region.

In 1930 the Association met in Berkeley, California. By that time California had more junior college students than any other state in the nation, accounting for nearly a tenth of the active AAJC members (Brick, 1964, pp. 62–63). With the Atlantic City and Berkeley conventions, the Association moved out of its base in the Midwest and "became national in fact as well as name" (Eells, 1931, p. 75).

One sticky problem in the early years of this organization was intercollegiate sports. To deter student athletes from switching colleges, many universities imposed a rule barring transferees from intercollegiate sports for one year (Rutledge, 1951). At its 1926 convention the AAJC approved a resolution requesting the Big Ten conference to exclude junior college graduates from the one-year rule. The conference responded by amending the rule to exclude any "student who has been out of school a year or more or a graduate of a junior college" (p. 40).

During its first decade AAJC grew from twenty-two founding colleges to 210 active members and fifteen associates. States with the largest membership were Texas, with thirty-one, and California, with twenty. Georgia, Iowa, Kansas, Michigan, North Carolina, Oklahoma, and Pennsylvania each had more than five members. Despite this impressive growth, less than half of the nation's 450 junior colleges had joined the Association (Eells, 1931, pp. 24–25).

THE JUNIOR COLLEGE JOURNAL

At the fourth annual AAJC meeting, F.A. Branch of Georgia proposed that the Association sponsor a quarterly or monthly publication to "show what the Junior College stands for" (Rutledge, 1951, p. 147). Although there was some interest, the Association lacked the membership or finances to support such a journal, and the idea was tabled for five years. Finally, in 1929 Stanford University offered to cover the costs of a publication. The Association accepted the offer, and the first edition of the *Junior College Journal* was published in October 1930.

The *Junior College Journal* was originally produced by the Stanford University Press, with clerical and editorial support provided by the university. It lost over $2,000 in its first year of publication, and over the next twenty years, it would show only one annual profit (Rutledge, 1951, p. 169).

From the very beginning, the *Journal's* major theme was the junior college movement. During the first three decades of publication more than half of all article space was devoted to "proselytizing and educating" about the movement (Clowes & Towles, 1985).

Walter Eells of Stanford and Doak Campbell, of Peabody College, served as the *Journal's* first editor and associate editor. Twenty junior college leaders were named to the national advisory board, including Leonard Koos, George Zook, and Frederick Eby.

Eells later left Stanford for a position at the U.S. Office of Education in Washington, D.C. He took the *Journal* with him and set up an editorial headquarters at 744 Jackson Place. For the first time AAJC had an office of its own. From the Washington office Eells communicated by mail and telephone with Campbell and other junior college scholars. Eells continued to edit the *Journal* until 1945, when he resigned from the Association.

Through the years the *Journal* would change its name three times to reflect the diversified membership and evolving Association mission. After forty-two volumes under the title *Junior College Journal,* the publication became the *Community and Junior College Journal* in 1972, the *Community, Technical, and Junior College Journal* in 1985, and finally the *Community College Journal* in 1992.

AAJC FOUNDING FATHERS

Four men emerged as early leaders of AAJC: Leonard V. Koos, Doak S. Campbell, Walter C. Eells, and George F. Zook. Through their research and guidance, these individuals helped unite America's junior colleges into a cohesive national movement.

Born in Chicago, the son of an immigrant tailor, Leonard Koos began his education career at age nineteen teaching in one-room schools for $30 per month. The following year he entered Oberlin College, financing his education by tailoring for other students. During his graduate studies at the University of Chicago, Koos became intrigued with the late William Rainey Harper's concept of the six-year high school.

Starting in 1919 Koos served for ten years as professor of secondary education at the University of Minnesota, during which time he became America's foremost researcher on the junior college movement. In 1921 he began a detailed study of American junior colleges. This report, commonly called the Commonwealth Fund Investigation, identified four major purposes of the junior college, purposes that still apply to the modern comprehensive community college:

(a) providing the first two years of four-year baccalaureate degree programs.

(b) providing programs of occupational preparation which are completed in two years of college.
(c) offering programs of continuing education for adults.
(d) offering a two-year general college program for those who will not continue to senior college (Conger & Schultz, 1970, p. 29–30).

The Commonwealth Fund Investigation resulted in Koos's classic two-volume publication, *The Junior College* (1924), in its time the most comprehensive study of the national junior college movement. Over the next five decades Koos authored or coauthored seventeen books and more than 130 articles. With the publication of *The Junior High School* in 1927, Koos also proved to be a recognized expert on American secondary education.

Koos taught the first university courses on the subject of junior colleges, at the University of Chicago and the University of Minnesota, in 1921 (Eells, 1934). As the junior college movement grew, he continued to track its expansion, believing all along that vocational training should become an important role for junior colleges. To prove his point Koos isolated from the university curricula vocational and technical programs that could be easily shifted to the junior college domain. He coined the word *semiprofessional* for these training programs. Koos's studies and published works helped to shape the role of vocational education in American junior colleges.

Koos was the first researcher to use student testing as a way to gauge aptitudes for junior-college-level learning. Citing the results of the Alpha tests given by the U.S. Army during World War I, Koos argued that many students had the ability to pursue postsecondary education even though they might lack the ability to complete a four-year degree (Brint & Karabel, 1989, p. 39).

In 1929 Koos returned to the University of Chicago as a professor. Over the next seventeen years he taught a generation of future junior college leaders: Lamar Johnson, who founded the junior college leadership program at the University of California–Los Angeles; Maurice Seay of the Kellogg Foundation; James Reynolds, who became editor of the *Junior College Journal*; and S.V. Martorana, who headed the community college program at the State University of New York (Conger & Schultz, 1970, p. 29).

Through his writings and research Koos influenced many other junior college leaders. Doak Campbell based his 1930 monograph, *A Critical Study of the Stated Purposes of the Junior College*, on Koos's research. Other Koos disciples included Jesse Bogue, who headed AAJC from 1946 to 1958, and Leland Medsker, the "leading junior college scholar after World War II" (Brint & Karabel, 1989, p. 42). Koos also influenced Knox Broom, who directed the state planning in Mississippi, and James Wattenbarger, who played a major role in the planning of the Florida system. In fact, Koos served as a consultant in both of these states, as well as in a number of others later in his career.

Koos also helped to shape the early direction of AAJC. He spoke at meetings, wrote articles, and advised Association leaders. After retiring from the University of Chicago in 1945, he became the first research director for AAJC and editor of the *Junior College Journal*. These endeavors were jointly supported by the University of Chicago and the Association (Colvert & Littlefield, 1961).

In 1949 Koos turned the *Journal* over to James W. Reynolds at the University of Texas. During the next decade Koos helped with the development of junior colleges in twenty-two separate communities. He assisted in the state planning of junior college systems in Florida, Illinois, Maryland, Oregon, and Pennsylvania (Conger & Schultz, 1970, p. 27). In 1970, at eighty-nine years of age, Koos produced his final book, *The Community College Student*, a compendium of the major research on the primary populations served by American junior colleges.

Despite his other successes, Koos had one major professional frustration—the 6-4-4 plan. He was a strong supporter of this scheme for reorganizing American higher education, and although it received much scholarly attention, only a dozen or so institutions were ever established based on its principles. Still, Koos continued to advocate it throughout his career (Koos, 1970, p. 31).

Doak Campbell came from humble origins. He was born in a log cabin and was educated at a Baptist college in Arkansas. After college he served as Arkansas state secretary for Baptist Sunday schools (Brint & Karabel, 1989, p. 34). He later became president of a small Baptist women's college in Conway, Arkansas, converting the weak four-year school into a sound institution (Fawcett, 1973). At the 1922 Memphis convention Campbell was elected to replace Martha Reid as the second AAJC secretary.

By 1924 Campbell was serving as secretary-treasurer of the Association, and after the position was reconstituted as executive secretary, he took over most of the operations of the fledgling organization. He handled correspondence, minutes, and Association records while acting as associate editor of the *Junior College Journal*. Soon afterward Campbell became a professor at George Peabody College in Nashville, where he had recently completed a doctorate, and from there operated AAJC out of a large closet beside his office (Brick, 1964, pp. 37, 40–41).

In those early days Association presidents never served more than two years. While presidents came and went, Campbell remained as secretary and gained tremendous influence. Under his sixteen-year leadership AAJC became the booster of the nationwide junior college movement, which grew to over 520 institutions. It is reported that Campbell received no more than $100 a year for clerical assistance.

Campbell also conducted research on the history of the movement, compiling annual directories with statistical information on all known junior colleges (Eells, 1931, pp. 807–808). His dissertation, published in 1930 as *A Critical Study of the Stated Purposes of the Junior College*, is an excellent assessment of the early junior college movement.

Campbell resigned as executive secretary in 1938 when he became dean of the graduate school at Peabody. In 1941 he was named president of the Florida State College for Women (later Florida State University), and held that position until his retirement in 1957. During these years Campbell continued his interest in AAJC, chairing the Commission on Terminal Education from 1941 to 1945 (Brint & Karabel, 1989, pp. 33–37; Rutledge, 1951, p. 135) and assisting in the development of the new Florida system of community colleges.

Walter Eells was the first editor of the *Junior College Journal* and the first full-time executive of AAJC. A native of Union, Washington, Eells completed his master's degree at the University of Chicago. After teaching at the U.S. Naval Academy and Whitworth College, he earned a Ph.D. from Stanford University (Rutledge, 1951).

In 1927 Eells joined the Stanford faculty as an associate professor of education. Three years later he accepted the editorship of the *Junior College Journal*, which he managed even as he kept up a light teaching load, with clerical assistance provided by the Stanford University Press (Brick, 1964, p. 104).

The *Journal*, published monthly from October to May, was designed to meet the need for nationwide distribution of news and research relating to junior colleges. Eells declared that his journal would represent the "best in the junior college movement." In practice, however, the *Junior College Journal* was slanted heavily toward California. Eells defended this West Coast bias by explaining that California had the largest and most innovative junior college system in the nation. Many of his peers disagreed, complaining that the "Eells Journal" suffered from a bad case of "Californiaitis" (Brick, 1964, p. 105).

Eells eventually lived down the claims of his California bias, helping the *Journal* earn a nationwide reputation for scholarship and reporting. Eells's personal reputation increased with the publication of *The Junior College*, his 1931 compendium of the early junior college movement. On the negative side, *The Junior College*, critical of Koos's advocacy of the 6-4-4 system, caused a rift between the two leaders that continued through the rest of their careers (Reed, 1971).

Eells published, through the Carnegie Foundation for the Advancement of Teaching, *Surveys of American Higher Education* (1937d). When Campbell stepped down as executive secretary of AAJC, Eells was the logical successor. He took over leadership of the Association in 1938 and brought the headquarters to his office in Washington. He continued publishing the annual junior college directory, which had previously been published by Campbell, in the *Junior College Journal*. Eells was the Association's first full-time employee. He resigned in 1945.

After working briefly at the University Study Center in Florence, Italy, Eells served two years as chief of the education division

for the Veterans Administration (Rutledge, 1951, p. 138). In 1947 he traveled to Japan as a higher education adviser to General Douglas MacArthur, who at the time directed the Allied postwar occupation of that country.

George Frederick Zook organized the first national junior college conference in 1920. Although the conference was officially called by the commissioner of education, Philander Claxton, junior college leaders believed Zook to be the guiding force. Doak Campbell (1929) vouched for Zook's role:

> We are indebted to Dr. George F. Zook, who was then Specialist in Higher Education in the United States Bureau of Education, for calling the first group of junior college executives together for a conference.... Perhaps no man in America living at this time, has done more for the junior college than has Dr. Zook (pp. 14–15).

A native of Fort Smith, Kansas, Zook headed the U.S. Bureau of Education's division of higher education for five years (Colvert & Littlefield, 1961) before resigning in 1925 to become president of the University of Akron. Eight years later he was appointed by President Franklin Roosevelt as commissioner of education. He later served sixteen years as president of the American Council on Education (Brint & Karabel, 1989, p. 68).

In the 1940s Zook chaired the President's Commission on Higher Education, better known as the Truman Commission. The commission's report popularized the term *community college*, and its findings led to the massive expansion of comprehensive community colleges that took place in the 1950s and 1960s.

Whereas many junior college leaders saw university transfer as their only mission, Koos, Campbell, Eells, and Zook envisioned a much broader role. They reasoned that American high schools were producing thousands of graduates who had no need of a bachelor's degree.

These early theorists, believing that junior colleges should provide vocational, technical, and continuing education, pushed for comprehensive junior colleges that would meet the diverse needs of the American populace. Their research showed that such colleges

87

were not only feasible but essential. Without their efforts American junior colleges might have developed a much narrower focus, depriving millions of the opportunity to improve their lives and communities.

THE ACCREDITATION DILEMMA

By the end of the nineteenth century, definite standards had been developed for accrediting universities, high schools, and four-year colleges. The junior college, however, did not fit clearly into any existing definition. Although many junior colleges were housed in public high schools, their curricula clearly differed from those of the high schools.

On the other hand, junior colleges were not like four-year colleges and universities. Their budgets were generally smaller and their admission standards lower. More importantly, many junior colleges offered two-year degrees and vocational certificates rather than the traditional bachelor's degree.

The earliest junior colleges were accredited by nearby universities. In the 1890s William Rainey Harper created a network of high schools affiliated with the University of Chicago, and encouraged these schools to extend their programs to six years. The university acted as a kind of accrediting agency for these high school extensions.

In 1911 the University of Missouri developed a similar plan. The university's president began a campaign to convince small four-year colleges to drop their junior and senior years, offering, in turn, to accredit the colleges and accept their graduates into the junior class without examination. By 1929 eighteen Missouri colleges had been accredited (Eells, 1931, p. 65).

The University of Texas began accrediting junior colleges in 1914. Over the next two decades the universities of Illinois, Kentucky, Indiana, Michigan, and California followed suit, in most cases accrediting colleges only in their own state. This accreditation and coordination ensured an easy transfer of courses between a junior college and the state university.

In several states junior colleges were accredited by state education officials. In North Carolina, Utah, and Virginia the agency was the state education department; in Mississippi, the state accrediting commission. Church-related junior colleges often received accreditation from religious accrediting offices.

The standards of the several accrediting agencies varied greatly. In some states there was no accrediting agency at all, and for that reason junior college students found it difficult to transfer to other states without sacrificing credits earned. Clearly, regional or national standards were needed to assure the quality of these institutions and to make the transfer process easier for students.

The first attempt to set regional standards was made by the North Central Association of Colleges and Secondary Schools. Harper, J. Stanley Brown, James Wood, and other founders of the junior college movement had been active in this association. In 1903 Harper hosted an association meeting at the University of Chicago and used the occasion to advance the junior college concept.

Over the next fourteen years the North Central Association continued to study and discuss the junior college movement. Finally, in 1917, it adopted a set of standards and published the names of eight accredited junior colleges (Eells, 1931, pp. 162–166). By 1930 eighty-six junior colleges had been accredited. The association's standards defined a junior college:

> A standard junior college is an institution of higher education with a curriculum covering two years of college work which is based upon and continues or supplements the work of secondary instruction as given in any accredited four-year high school (p. 161).

The American Council on Education (ACE), the first national organization to propose junior college standards, in 1921 defined the junior college according to nine standards. After nearly three years of discussion and amendment, the standards were finally adopted. The ACE standards and those announced in 1922 by AAJC formed the basic national guidelines for junior college operations. The full text of the ACE standards reads:

Definition. The junior college is an institution of higher education which gives two years of work equivalent in prerequisites, scope, and thoroughness to the work done in the first two years of a college as defined elsewhere by the American Council on Education.

1. *Admission of students.* The requirement for admission should be the satisfactory completion of a four-year course of study in a secondary school approved by a recognized accrediting agency or the equivalent of such a course of study. The major portion of the secondary school course of study accepted for admission should be definitely correlated with the curriculum to which the student is admitted.

2. *Graduation requirements.* Requirements for graduation should be based on the satisfactory completion of 30 year hours or 60 semester hours of work corresponding in grade to that given in the freshman and sophomore years of standard colleges and universities. In addition to the above quantitative requirements, each institution should adopt qualitative standards suited to its individual conditions.

3. *Faculty.* Members of the teaching staff in regular charge of classes should have a baccalaureate degree and should have had not less than one year of graduate school; in all cases efficiency in teaching, as well as the amount of graduate work, should be taken into account.

4. *Teaching schedules* exceeding 16 hours per week per instructor, or classes (exclusive of lectures) of more than 30 students, should be interpreted as endangering educational efficiency.

5. *Curricula.* The curricula should provide for breadth of study and for concentration and should have justifiable relations to the resources of the institution. The number of departments and the size of the faculty should be increased with the development of varied curricula and the growth of the student body.

6. *Enrollment.* No junior college should be accredited unless it has a registration of not less than 50 students.

7. *Income.* The minimum annual operating income for the two years of junior college work should be $20,000, of which not less than $10,000 should be derived from stable sources other than students, such as public support or permanent endowments. Increase in faculty, student body, and scope of institution should be accompanied by increase of income from such stable sources. The financial status of each junior college should be judged in relation to its educational program.

8. *Buildings and equipment.* The material equipment and upkeep of a junior college, including its buildings, lands, laboratories, apparatus, and libraries, and their efficient operation in relation to its educational program, should also be considered when judging the institution.

9. *Inspection.* No junior college should be accredited until it has been inspected and reported upon by an agent or agents regularly appointed by the accrediting organization (Eells, 1931, pp. 162–164).

The ACE standards angered many junior college administrators. They viewed the sixteen-hour maximum teaching load restriction as gross interference in their internal affairs. Until that time many smaller private institutions were requiring teaching loads of eighteen hours or more. Junior college boards were also offended by the $20,000 minimum operating budget criterion. They felt that the minimum was unrealistic and would drive small colleges out of business (pp. 167–189).

The fifty-student minimum also concerned junior college leaders. Although the number of junior colleges had grown, the size of individual colleges was still quite small. A 1921 study found that 98 of 182 junior colleges surveyed had enrollments below fifty students. Many others were perilously close to the line. In fact, the national junior college enrollment averaged only sixty-one students. (Koos, 1924, p. 11).

As ACE debated its standards, AAJC was devising a second set of national standards. These standards, adopted at the Association's 1922 meeting, had a higher teaching load restriction than that of the ACE guidelines, with a maximum faculty load of eighteen hours. If a teacher taught both high school and junior college courses, the maximum was raised to twenty hours.

Although the AAJC standards echoed the $20,000 minimum for an annual operating budget as proposed by ACE, they broadened the definition of "stable" income by allowing church donations as well as endowment income. Many early AAJC members, as church-related institutions, derived a large portion of their budget from church contributions.

AAJC also added a number of standards not included in the ACE standards. For example, colleges were required to maintain a working library of at least 2,500 volumes. And wherever colleges and high schools operated jointly, the high school was required to be accredited. High school and college classes could not be mixed.

ACE and AAJC did not attempt to accredit junior colleges, but their standards had a strong impact on future accreditation guidelines. The standards were the primary tools for regional accrediting associations that attempted to set quantifiable minimum standards for the operation of junior colleges.

The Southern Association of Colleges and Schools, which began its interest in junior colleges in 1914 under the name Association of Colleges and Secondary Schools of the Southern States, adopted a set of standards for full accreditation of junior colleges nine years later. In 1925 Ward-Belmont, Inc., in Tennessee and Virginia Intermont became the first fully accredited institutions. The standards were revised in 1927, allowing Lon Morris College in Texas, Andrew College in Georgia, Hinds Junior College in Mississippi, and St. Mary's College in North Carolina to be admitted. By 1930 forty-six colleges had been accredited by the association (Eells, 1931, p. 165, 175).

The Northwest Association of Schools and Colleges adopted the ACE standards verbatim in 1922. In 1930 the association modified its standards to resemble more closely those of AAJC, including lowering the minimum annual budget and allowing faculty to carry a teaching load as high as twenty-two hours.

The Association of Colleges and Schools of the Middle States, which began considering junior college standards in 1919, adopted the ACE standards in 1927. For several years, however, the association refused to accredit junior colleges because of "problems" with the standards (Eells, 1931, p. 165).

The New England Association of Schools and Colleges adopted a stringent set of standards in 1929: standards for recognition and membership in the organization, *not* for the general accreditation of junior colleges. Their effect, however, was essentially the same (pp. 165–166).

Before 1930 there were clear national standards for junior colleges, as devised by the American Council on Education and the American Association of Junior Colleges. All five national accrediting agencies had adopted minimum standards for junior colleges and had admitted two-year schools to membership. In addition, junior colleges had their own national association and journal. The junior college had clearly become a recognized component of America's educational system.

CHAPTER 7

THE GREAT DEPRESSION (1929-1939)

Education is the strongest and cheapest social insurance that can be employed, and the nation that neglects it is inviting disaster.

— Doak Campbell

On October 29, 1929, America's economy fell from prosperity to poverty. The financial panic began on Wall Street but spread rapidly to every town and city in the nation. Stock prices plummeted, factories closed, and more than 5,000 banks failed. Foreign trade came to a virtual standstill. Overnight America was plunged into an economic abyss that affected virtually every family.

The Great Depression brought a decade of unemployment and despair. More than 32,000 businesses declared bankruptcy. By the end of 1931, 12 million Americans were out of work. For junior colleges, however, the Depression became a period of rapid expansion. The economic crisis brought government aid programs, a flood of new students, and hundreds of new campuses.

During the Depression a university education became an impossible dream for most American families. At the typical university, tuition, room, and board cost about $1,000 per year—more than the annual salary for most workers. Families that had saved for college saw their savings wiped out by bank failures. Student grant and loan programs were still decades away. As a consequence, university enrollments declined every year from 1929 to 1935 (Friedel, 1976, p. 212).

Public junior college enrollment, on the other hand, steadily increased (D.S. Campbell, 1931, 1932, 1933, 1934, 1935, 1936b, 1937, 1938). Junior colleges had already learned to serve working-class students by offering evening courses that met the needs of full-time workers and by allowing students to attend classes while living at home. Their vocational programs offered the unemployed masses an avenue back into the workforce. As the Depression worsened, thousands of unemployed adults turned to the tax-supported, low-tuition public junior college as a way out of their plight.

In the year before the market crash American junior colleges had graduated only 3,253 students. Three years later the graduating class numbered nearly 14,000 (Eells, 1931, p. 33). By the end of the decade nearly one-tenth of the students in American higher education were enrolled in junior colleges (Brint & Karabel, 1989, p. 42). American higher education had witnessed a cause and effect that would continue to the present: in every subsequent depression, recession, and economic downturn, enrollment in these two-year colleges would increase.

A NEW DEAL FOR JUNIOR COLLEGES

In 1928 presidential candidate Herbert Hoover had promised "two cars in every garage." Before the end of his administration, millions of Americans were standing in soup lines. The public blamed Hoover, and in 1932 he was soundly defeated by Democrat Franklin Delano Roosevelt. Hoover had tried to end the Depression by providing massive reconstruction loans to banks, railroads, and industry. His Democratic successor chose a different strategy: Roosevelt promised a "New Deal" for the American people. With the help of a Democratic Congress, he channeled billions of dollars into agricultural subsidies, public works projects, and government job programs.

Roosevelt's advisers, commonly called the Brain Trust, created a long list of new government agencies, including the Civilian Conservation Corps, Federal Emergency Relief Administration, Agricultural Adjustment Administration, Tennessee Valley Authority, National Youth Administration, Public Works Administration, Civil Works Administration, and Work Projects Administration. These "alphabet soup" agencies were designed to put unemployed Americans back to work. Several of these agencies had a direct impact on the growth of junior colleges.

Beginning in 1934 the Federal Emergency Relief Administration (FERA) allocated funds to communities to establish "emergency junior colleges." Emergency colleges soon appeared in Connecticut, Kansas, Massachusetts, Michigan, New Jersey, Ohio, and Texas (Greenleaf, 1936, pp. 25–28). Most emergency junior colleges were temporary high school extensions that used public school classrooms and equipment and operated in the evening only. Teachers were selected from the ranks of unemployed instructors and professors (Leuchtenburg, 1963, p. 123).

In most cases the emergency junior colleges were supervised by nearby state universities, which set admission standards, determined the curricula, and awarded credit. Generally, these new colleges offered a curriculum nearly identical to the freshman and/or sophomore year of the supervising university. They did not, however, provide the variety of vocational and terminal courses that was common at other public junior colleges. FERA provided funding based on the number of students enrolled. Although no tuition was charged, paying for books put a strain on many distressed families.

Michigan had the largest emergency college program, with 100 colleges enrolling more than 6,000 students. Divided into seven zones, each supervised by a different state college or university (the University of Michigan, Michigan State College, Wayne State University, and four teacher training colleges), these colleges brought higher education to the most remote portions of the state.

Michigan adopted new terms to categorize these colleges: freshman colleges, for the larger number of schools that offered only one year of coursework, and community colleges, for those that offered two years. This is the first known use of the term *community college*.

Ohio's version of the FERA college was called the Emergency Junior College Center. During the 1934–35 school year, such centers, established in thirty towns and cities, served more than 1,000 students.

Even more popular was the Emergency Junior Radio College, a program offered by Ohio State University in which faculty members broadcast their lectures over statewide radio to students at home who, following mail-in registration and the receipt of free lesson materials, then went to their local high school for discussion sessions. More than 1,700 students enrolled in these radio courses (Greenleaf, 1936, pp. 25–28).

In Connecticut the FERA institutions were known as Federal Colleges. The largest of these was in New Haven, home of Yale University. Students attended classes held at the local YMCA or YWCA and the Yale campus. Other Federal Colleges were established in Bristol, Farmington, Hartford, Meriden, and Winsted. For the 1934–35 year these colleges enrolled about 1,400 students.

New Jersey had six emergency colleges, located in high school buildings at Long Branch, Morristown, Newark, Paterson, Perth Amboy, and Roselle. At Morristown the local YMCA and YWCA provided physical education classes for the college students, and the high school cafeteria served evening meals.

The University of Kansas organized thirteen emergency colleges, supervised by the university extension division. The program offered sixty credit classes and a dozen noncredit classes, staffed by thirty-two instructors. The colleges were located in high school buildings in Atchison, Atwood, Colby, Horton, Houlton, Leavenworth, Marysville, Norton, Olathe, Phillipsburg, Plainville, St. Francis, and Stockton.

The Public Works Administration (PWA) supported 5,886 educational construction projects between 1933 and 1937, providing $89,683,445 in loans and $392,272 in grants. Many of these projects were at public junior colleges (Johnson, 1938, p. 234).

The Work Projects Administration (WPA) funded construction projects at thirty-nine public junior colleges in the South and West. The greatest award was a $368,400 grant toward a $1,313,620 classroom construction project at Pasadena Junior College in California. By 1939 the total amount of these awards had reached nearly $6 million (Eells, 1939a, pp. 302–304).

The National Youth Administration (NYA), founded in 1935 as a subsidiary of the WPA, created jobs to help needy students remain in school. Students worked as lab assistants, maintenance helpers, groundskeepers, and file clerks; helped create folk histories of their region; and even assisted in research projects. These NYA programs, under which some students were paid $7 a month, were the forerunner of today's college work-study programs. One of the agency's directors was Texas Democrat Lyndon Johnson, who as president three decades later would revolutionize public aid for higher education. African American students benefited from NYA funds through a subagency known as the Division of Negro Affairs (Popejoy, 1939). The division was headed by Mary McLeod Bethune, founder of Bethune-Cookman College in Florida.

The theory behind NYA was similar to that of the Civilian Conservation Corps (CCC). Both programs were designed to remove young people from the national job pool, thus reducing the unemployment rate. CCC focused on national parks, and NYA on colleges and universities. NYA was never highly funded. Although NYA spent only $2.6 million on financial assistance, it affected the lives of 100,000 students.

Doak Campbell, Walter Eells, and most other leaders of the American Association of Junior Colleges supported federal programs in the junior college. They maintained that public expenditures in junior colleges were the cheapest investment in a better America. A few junior college leaders, however, feared Washington's sudden interest. They believed that Roosevelt was imposing a new social order, similar to communism, and would use the junior college as his propaganda tool. In the *Junior College Journal* guest editors Katherine Denworth (1937) of Massachusetts and Edgar Knight (1937) of North Carolina described the New Deal programs as an attempt to indoctrinate America's unwary youth into New Deal socialism.

THE GROWTH OF PUBLIC COLLEGES

In the 1930s, as today, public junior colleges were the best value in American education. These institutions grew dramatically during the Depression, tripling enrollments to 140,545 by 1939 (Eells, 1939b). In that year nearly 71 percent of all junior college students were enrolled in the 258 public institutions. Private junior college enrollment also grew, though at a much slower rate, from 29,067 to 56,165 students (Colvert, 1956, p. 14).

More than eighty new public junior colleges were formed during the decade, fourteen in the state of California alone. Considering these colleges as extensions of secondary schooling, the state charged no tuition for district residents. The lure of free education, combined with California's population growth, drew thousands of students to the district colleges.

A comparison of two California junior colleges clearly illustrates the competitive edge of public institutions. Notre Dame, a private Catholic junior college, charged a tuition of $125 for the 1933 academic year. For $600 more the college could arrange room and board and books. On the other hand, nearby Long Beach Junior College, a public district college, charged no tuition. All incidental expenses such as books and laboratory fees were limited to $50. Most of its students lived at home and had no housing expenses.

Los Angeles Junior College became the largest two-year college in the nation. By 1934 its enrollment had risen to more than 5,000 students (Greenleaf, 1936, p. 157). The largest public junior colleges outside of California were Wright City Junior College in Chicago, with 1,600 students, and Kansas City Junior College in Missouri, with 1,100. Both of these colleges were city operated. In 1934 Wright City Junior College had an enrollment of 1,600, while Kansas City Junior College had about 1,100 students (pp. 60–65).

Despite its successes, the California junior college system was nearly eliminated in 1932 by the legislature, which considered a proposal to convert all junior colleges and normal schools into four-year colleges. At the height of this controversy the governor called for a study of California's education needs. This study, commonly known as the Commission of Seven Report and sponsored by the Carnegie Foundation for the Advancement of Teaching, became a milestone in the development of American junior colleges (Jensen, 1932).

Although no nationally recognized leaders active in the junior college field served on the commission, they clearly influenced its outcome. Walter Eells, editor of the *Junior College Journal*, attended many commission meetings. Leonard Koos, a friend of two commissioners and the Carnegie Foundation president, submitted information, including an important needs survey. Three leaders of the California junior college movement served on subcommittees, and George Zook, at that time president of the University of Akron, was a member (Commission of Seven, 1932).

The commission found that junior colleges were spending too much of their energy preparing students to transfer to Berkeley when the data showed that only a small percentage actually transferred. Instead of recommending the expansion of junior colleges into four-year colleges, commission members proposed a stronger emphasis on vocational education (Commission of Seven, 1932, p. 34), believing that 85 percent of junior college freshmen should enroll in vocational and technical courses (Walter, 1932). The Commission of Seven Report effectively ended the pressure to transform California's junior colleges into four-year institutions and over the next decade became a rallying point for proponents of terminal education (Eells, 1941a, p. 24).

California was not the only state to offer free tuition. Illinois, Kansas, Mississippi, Missouri, New Jersey, Oklahoma, and Pennsylvania all had some public junior colleges that waived tuition for residents. In most of the nation, however, public colleges charged at least a nominal tuition—usually less than $100 per academic year.

VOCATIONAL PROGRAMS: THE CHEAPEST SOCIAL INSURANCE

The demand for vocational and terminal programs grew rapidly during the Depression. The reason was all too obvious: Americans were desperate for jobs. Instead of enrolling in traditional liberal arts programs, which were expensive and offered no guarantee of employment, many Americans opted for programs that trained them for an existing job. And because junior colleges tailored programs to the needs of area employers, their graduates had a greater likelihood of employment. During the 1930s the legislatures of Colorado, Connecticut, Nebraska, and Pennsylvania passed junior college laws that required both vocational and academic classes. At the decade's end 70 percent of the nation's junior colleges offered at least one terminal program (Brint & Karabel, 1989, p. 54).

The vocations taught in junior colleges were considered inferior by many traditionalists, who complained that job training had no place in an institution that called itself a college. Despite these opinions, graduates of vocational programs often earned higher wages than university-trained professionals, such as ministers and teachers. With every passing year more junior college students were enrolling in vocational majors—a trend especially pronounced in public institutions. In California junior colleges, for example, the proportion of students who intended to transfer to a university decreased from 80 percent to less than 67 percent during the decade (Cohen & Brawer, 1987, p. 94).

To meet the demand, junior colleges increased their career offerings (Ingalls, 1937). By mid-decade junior college leaders were recommending an astounding array of vocational training, including accounting, architecture, art, automobile mechanics, aviation, banking, physician assisting, dental assisting, hairdressing, hotel keeping, laboratory assisting, lathe operation, cafe management, civil engineering, drafting, surveying, radio repair, finance, insurance sales, stock trading, physiotherapy, general business, home administration, office management, mechanical engineering design, machine operation, merchandising, music, nursing, police work, publications, recreational leadership, stenography, x-ray operation, and secretarial work ("The Junior College World," 1936, pp. 95–96; "Reports and Discussion," 1936, pp. 99–100).

Many of these career courses relied on equipment supplied indirectly by the Smith-Hughes Act, which provided matching funds for the purchase of high school vocational equipment. As nearly

85 percent of junior colleges still shared facilities with high schools during the Depression (Palinchak, 1973, p. 45), and the act provided no funds for junior colleges, the high school equipment was frequently used in junior college classes. The Smith-Hughes Act, designed to help high school "shop" classes, had the unintended effect of fostering career training in American junior colleges.

California junior colleges led the rest of the nation in developing career programs (Monroe, 1972, p. 84). Pasadena and Los Angeles were probably the most vocationalized junior colleges in the state. Pasadena Junior College, a pioneer in the use of counseling and testing, had two deans in charge of guidance and fourteen full-time and part-time counselors who steered students "scientifically" into career programs. Through the guidance program, students who were not likely to attain a bachelor's degree were diverted to a suitable terminal program (Eells, 1941b). Pasadena also created advisory councils of local business people to help tailor courses to the needs of their industry, and invited employers to campus to address students about opportunities in their fields. One of Pasadena's fastest-growing local industries was aircraft manufacturing. The college worked with manufacturers to create an aircraft technology program, which attracted a large number of students (Harbeson, 1939, p. 285). As a result of these innovations, Pasadena's vocational enrollment rose from 4 percent of the student body in 1926 to 67 percent in 1938 (Eells, 1941a).

Los Angeles Junior College established advisory committees of local employers and used employer surveys to develop new vocational programs. When a survey indicated the need for a new program, college staff studied the field and created a tentative curriculum, at which point employers were invited to campus to discuss the proposal. The employer feedback was used to develop the final program (Snyder, 1941).

Riverside Junior College developed the first junior college cooperative education program. The program granted vocational credit for supervised work at local businesses.

The use of testing programs for vocational students gained popularity. Before 1941 colleges in Colorado, Texas, and Vermont were employing extensive testing programs. Other California innovations, such as advisory boards, employer-needs surveys, and cooperative education, would also become a standard part of vocational programs nationwide.

Doak Campbell in 1934 supported vocational education as a remedy for the Great Depression and as protection against future disasters. He declared that education was the strongest and cheapest social insurance that could be employed, and the nation that neglected it was inviting disaster (Goodwin, 1971). Campbell foresaw a time after the current disaster when three quarters of all junior college graduates would be in vocational and terminal programs.

Walter Eells found a unique ground for supporting vocational education. He reasoned that America had limited need of university-trained professionals, and that with so many people graduating from college, the glut of doctors, lawyers, teachers, and ministers would force professional unemployment to soar. As a way to prevent this catastrophe, Eells proposed diverting high school graduates into semiprofessional junior college programs (Eells, 1931, pp. 46, 289; Medsker, Eells & Hollinshead, 1942).

The vocational movement also had its detractors. One of these was Robert Maynard Hutchins, president of the University of Chicago. Although Hutchins generally supported junior colleges, he denounced vocational specialization. Hutchins (1936) contended that higher education should concentrate on sharpening the intellect and fostering critical judgment, and he condemned the pragmatism of educators who dared to give the public what it wanted.

JUNIOR COLLEGE LIBRARIES

The first national study of junior college libraries painted a gloomy picture. The Carnegie Advisory Group on Junior College Libraries, funded by the Carnegie Foundation, found that some of the libraries were "little short of disgraceful," and that in some colleges the librarian was "untrained, nonexistent, or inexcusably ignorant of the possibilities of her position" (Eells, 1937c, p. 2).

Based on data collected by the advisory group in visits to the libraries of 184 junior colleges in all parts of the country, the foundation awarded $300,000 in grants to ninety-two of these institutions for the improvement of their libraries. The largest of these awards went to the Long Beach and Pasadena junior college districts in California, both of which had experienced tremendous growth during the Depression and were greatly underfunded (Lester, 1937, pp. 3–9).

The advisory group put together a "List of Books for Junior College Libraries" and drafted a set of standards, both of which the *Junior College Journal* used to create a "Junior College Library Analysis Chart" (Eells, 1937b, pp. 121, 123). This instrument allowed college librarians to compare their book collections with those of the strongest and weakest colleges in the nation and became a popular tool for seeking increased funding for books and staff.

Although the advisory group comprised primarily university professors and librarians, several AAJC leaders, including Walter Eells, Leonard Koos, and James Wood, served on the panel. At the end of the study, Eells (1937c) denounced the sorry state of many junior college libraries, concluding that "it is time for the administrators to take cognizance of such facts and see that they are remedied forthwith if the entire junior college movement, in some sections, is not to be brought into disrepute" (p. 2).

THE STUDENTS ORGANIZE

As enrollments grew larger, junior college students began to form campus organizations. By the early 1930s numerous groups, such as debating societies, honor societies, and honorary fraternities, flourished on junior college campuses. Several even developed into national organizations, as did the scholastic honor society Phi Theta Kappa.

Phi Theta Kappa was founded in 1910 at Stephens College, Missouri, under the name Kappa Phi Omicron. As Stephens was a women's college, the group started as a women's honorary association. It eventually changed its name to Phi Theta Kappa to indicate a similarity with the prestigious Phi Beta Kappa honor fraternity. In 1924 the group amended its constitution to admit male members, and two years later added the first chapter outside Missouri (Wilson, 1962). By 1936 there were seventy-two chapters nationwide (Eells, 1937a, p. 200).

Bolstered by AACC official recognition in 1929, promoted through its own national magazine, *The Golden Key* (established 1939), Phi Theta Kappa developed into the nation's largest and most prestigious junior college scholastic honor society. It remains today an integral part of junior college campus life.

For most students, however, who were not at the academic top 10 percent of their class, Phi Theta Kappa was too selective a society to join. They needed organizations of their own, for which membership would not be denied. As the demand for student organizations grew, other organizations were founded to fill the void. These included specialized honorary fraternities related to specific academic interests. By 1934 at least seven such fraternities were operating on a national basis: Alpha Mu Gamma (foreign languages), Alpha Pi Epsilon (secretarial), Beta Phi Gamma (journalism), Delta Psi Omega (drama), Phi Rho Pi (forensic), Phi Sigma Alpha (social science), and Rho Delta Epsilon (political science).

Even though most junior college students lived at home, social fraternities and sororities began to spring up on junior college campuses. The most popular of these, Sigma Iota Chi sorority, had twenty-three active and ten alumni chapters. Other popular fraternities included Eta Upsilon Gamma, Kappa Delta Phi, Phi Sigma Nu, Sigma Iota Chi, Theta Tau Epsilon, and Zeta Mu Epsilon. These Greek organizations formed the National Junior College Panhellenic Organization (Eells, 1937a, pp. 199–201).

Student government developed slowly in junior colleges. In the early years it was usually limited to class officers who arranged dances, picnics, and hayrides. Not always taken seriously by faculty or by their fellow students, these student leaders had little or no input into curriculum matters or college policy. At many colleges the editor of the student newspaper was more influential than all the student officers combined.

106

THE COMMUNITY'S COLLEGE

Unlike most universities, junior colleges, especially public junior colleges, had their roots in the local community. Whether high school extensions or district institutions, they answered to a local board and depended on local taxpayers for funding.

Local control forced the junior college to adapt to community needs. If the local factory needed welders, the junior college quickly produced a welding course. If local art lovers demanded cultural events, the junior college developed an arts series. If the public demanded flower arranging, the college hired a local florist. Courses from cosmetology to bricklaying sprang up to meet community needs. Even before the term gained popularity, these institutions had truly become community colleges.

The word *community* shows up frequently in early junior college literature. Alexis Lange predicted that junior colleges would form "a union of community experience and college activities" (Diener, 1986, p. 71). The Junior College Committee of Wyoming actually recommended that state aid to junior colleges be limited because "the largest support for a junior college should come from the community" (Hicks, 1930, p. 51). California's Commission of Seven, in its 1932 report, referred to junior colleges as "community institutions" (p. 34).

There is no clear record of who coined the term *community college*. William Boyce (1949) of Fullerton Junior College claimed that he suggested the adoption of the term to a group of California junior college administrators around 1935 (p. 445). At about the same time the FERA emergency junior colleges in Michigan were being called community colleges.

The first published use of the term *community college* was probably in a 1936 article by Byron S. Hollinshead, who proposed an agenda for making junior colleges more responsive to their communities:

That the junior college should be a community college, meeting community needs; that it should serve to promote a greater social and civic intelligence in the community; that it should provide opportunities for increased adult education;

107

that it should provide educational, recreational, and vocational opportunities for young people...that the work of the community college should be closely integrated with the work of the high school and the work of other community institutions (p. 111).

Clearly, Hollinshead was preaching to the choir. Many of America's junior colleges had already adopted his community college agenda.

AFRICAN AMERICAN COLLEGES

Racial prejudice and segregation kept some Americans from benefiting from a local junior college. The landmark *Plessy v. Ferguson* decision of 1896 had guaranteed equal rights under the law for all races. Unfortunately, it allowed "separate but equal" facilities, permitting the exclusion of African Americans from White-only schools and colleges.

Although de jure racial segregation was strongest in the South, African Americans were greatly underrepresented in higher education in all areas of the country. By 1935 they represented about 10 percent of the American population but less than 2 percent of junior college enrollment (Greenleaf, 1936, pp. 45-47). Many African American students were channeled into Negro colleges. In 1930 Eells found thirty-three such junior colleges in the nation, most of them in southern states, with Texas leading the nation with seven (Eells, 1931, p. 37). Lane (1933) listed nineteen, all located in one or another of the southern states. These were usually small private institutions, supported by African American religious denominations, averaging only 117 students—about half that of White junior colleges. Because most of these segregated schools received no public support, their tuition was usually above average and their quality questionable, since few, if any, were ever accredited.

Few of these segregated junior colleges were public institutions. The largest, Houston Colored Junior College in Texas, had a 1935 enrollment of 330 students and had fourteen faculty members. The other public institutions included Dunbar Junior College in Little Rock, Arkansas; Georgia Normal and Agricultural College in Albany; and Louisiana Normal and Industrial Institute in Grambling (Greenleaf, 1936, p. 72). Jackson (1940) expressed the concern of many who viewed these institutions as having great, but unrealized, potential for the education of minority youth when he cautioned that the junior college must become more interested in students and preparing them for a livelihood than preparing them for higher education.

The majority of America's private Black colleges had been established shortly after the Civil War, between 1878 and 1891. Though called colleges, even universities, most were little more than high schools, teaching basic skills to former slaves and their descendants. By the 1930s some institutions had become viable four-year colleges, while others had chosen to offer a two-year curriculum. Taylor (1972/1973), analyzing the funding patterns of Black private junior colleges in 1971, found fifteen largely church-supported colleges from Virginia to Texas enrolling from twenty-five to 672 students, with a total enrollment at that time of 3,873 students. Despite support by the Baptist, African Methodist Episcopal, and African Methodist Episcopal Zion churches, Black junior colleges still had grave financial difficulties (pp. 20-21).

In 1971 the Southern Association of Colleges and Schools' Commission on Colleges issued a report listing only four Black junior colleges as accredited: Mobile State Junior College and Theodore Alfred Lawson State Junior College in Alabama, Morristown College in Tennessee, and St. Philips College in Texas (Sweet, 1971). Other colleges were in existence at the time but were not accredited by the association. In fact, none of the fifteen identified by Taylor were listed by Sweet as accredited.

AAJC REORGANIZES

As the demand for junior colleges increased, the American Association of Junior Colleges prospered. In 1936 the total number of junior colleges was around 520 (Campbell, 1936a). Interest in

AAJC was also increasing: in 1930 about half of all junior colleges belonged to the Association; by 1940 about two-thirds did. California had thirty-six AAJC members in 1940—the largest number from any one state (Brick, 1964).

Between 1930 and 1940 the Association's largest increase in the number of institutional members occurred in the Northeast. In 1929 this region reported only a handful of two-year colleges. With the increase in FERA-funded high school extensions in Connecticut, Massachusetts, and Pennsylvania during the Depression, however, many of these emergency junior colleges were looking for guidance, and membership in AAJC seemed a logical choice. The Association's Massachusetts delegation grew from four to sixteen, while the Pennsylvania contingent jumped from six to twenty between 1930 and 1940 (Brick, 1964).

Most emergency junior colleges were abandoned after the Depression. When FERA funding ended, the AAJC delegations from Massachusetts and Pennsylvania dwindled. It would be many years before either state took a serious interest in forming a public junior college system (Brick, 1964, pp. 62–63). Massachusetts did not pass its first public junior college act until 1947, and Pennsylvania failed to do so until 1963 (Blocker, Plummer & Richardson, 1965, pp. 28–29).

Although the Depression was a boon for most junior colleges, a few were not as fortunate. In fact, six of the founding members of AAJC had failed by 1936 (Campbell, 1936a). Most of these were small private colleges. As a result, AAJC membership from Indiana, Louisiana, and Texas decreased slightly. All of the other states maintained or increased their membership during the decade (Brick, 1964, pp. 62–63).

AAJC received its first outside grants during this period. In 1937 Doak Campbell approached the General Education Board (GEB), a division of the Rockefeller Foundation, for funding to study terminal education. The board authorized a four-year grant of more than $100,000, which Campbell, as chair, used to direct the work of the Commission on Terminal Education (Brick, 1964).

The GEB grant resulted in three monographs published in 1941. These publications presented the results of surveys sent to terminal programs and of questionnaires answered by 1,900 leaders. The monographs, authored by Walter Eells, made a strong case for the expansion of terminal education (Eells, 1941a, 1941b, Engleman & Eells, 1941). The remaining GEB funds were used to finance twenty-four regional conferences and to conduct vocational experiments at eight junior colleges (Brick, 1964, pp. 124–127).

Doak Campbell stepped down as executive secretary in 1938, having served the Association for sixteen years. He noted (1939), in retrospect, that the most important decision of his tenure had come and gone when the Association chose to forgo the temptation to become a standardizing and accreditation agency and became, instead, a stimulating and developmental influence on the growth of the junior college movement. He pointed out that the selection of students for junior colleges was based upon economic rather than academic standards (p. 443).

Walter Eells was the logical choice as Campbell's successor, but despite his dedication to the movement, Eells had reservations. Campbell had served with no salary, managing the organization out of a closet. Eells had no intention of becoming a full-time volunteer. He wanted to head the organization, but only if the position included a salary:

> At this time when a reorganization of the Association is contemplated it is recommended that, if possible, the secretaryship of the Association and the editorship of the *Journal* be combined and that as soon as possible they be placed upon a basis to require the full-time services of one individual ("Minutes," 1938, p. 483).

The idea carried the weight of an ultimatum. Eells's full-time job with the Office of Education left little time for extra activities. If he was not approved as full-time executive secretary, Eells would soon resign as editor of the *Junior College Journal*. Losing both Eells and Campbell would have been a serious blow to the Association's leadership.

After considering Eells's reorganization plan, a committee chaired by former AAJC president Arthur Andrews recommended that the positions of executive secretary and editor be combined and that Eells be paid a professional salary to fill this post. In addition, the committee recommended that the Association maintain a national headquarters in Washington, D.C. To meet these expenses the Association would have to double its annual dues, from $10 to $20 ("Minutes," 1938, p. 475).

AAJC members approved the reorganization plan, as well as a new constitution and statement of purpose, at the 1939 convention. Gone was the original purpose of creating standards. Article 2 of the new constitution declared that the organization would be a promotional agency for the junior college movement:

> The purpose of this organization shall be to stimulate the professional development of its members, to promote the growth of junior colleges under appropriate conditions, to emphasize the significant place of the junior college in American education, and to interpret the junior college to the country ("American Association of Junior Colleges Constitution," 1939, p. 556).

It took nearly two years to raise the money for a full-time executive secretary. In the meantime Eells worked for a part-time salary, continuing to edit the *Junior College Journal* and perform the duties of executive secretary. In 1941 the Association's budget reached $21,000, and Eells was finally given a full salary.

With larger budgets and an office in the nation's capital, the Association became politically active. In the late 1930s AAJC made its first, though unsuccessful, attempt to lobby the Congress, for federal funding for junior college vocational programs. Congress, it seemed, preferred to spend such vocational funds on high schools and technical schools (Brint & Karabel, 1989, p. 65).

Almost all of the movement's early leaders had one thing in common—they were men. During AAJC's first seventeen years, no women had been elected to the presidency. At the 1927 convention Marion Coates was elected vice president, but unlike most vice presidents, she did not rise to the presidency. Finally, in 1938, Katherine Denworth, president of Bradford College, was elected AAJC president. Although she had served as vice president the year before, the nominating committee felt obliged to explain its choice, noting that the nomination was

...not to do honor to you as a woman, but because of your outstanding ability as an administrator and because of your interest and leadership in the junior college movement (Rutledge, 1951, p. 99).

The choice turned out to be a good one. Except for the FERA institutions, junior colleges had not found favor in the northeastern states. Denworth decided to attack the problem head-on by holding the 1938 convention in Philadelphia (Rutledge, 1951, p. 100). What with favorable coverage by newspapers, local radio stations, and even national radio networks, her campaign succeeded in stimulating the growth of junior colleges in the Northeast. Despite Denworth's success, the Association did not elect another woman president until 1951.

Walter Eells, as executive secretary, guided the Association through the difficult years of World War II. His tenure was a time of continuous growth for the junior college movement and AAJC.

CHAPTER 8

THE SECOND WORLD WAR (1939–1945)

The Junior College movement, including its philosophy, its facilities, and its momentum, had to be geared to the nation's needs as we found ourselves in a state of war.

— James Miller

In September 1939 the German army rolled across the border into Poland. Warsaw fell in a matter of hours under the terrible onslaught of the blitzkrieg. The most destructive war in human history had begun. Over the next six years, it would disrupt the lives of hundreds of millions of people in every corner of the globe. Its aftershocks will be felt for the rest of the century.

While Europe prepared for calamity, America felt secure in its splendid isolation. The Depression was finally ending, and Americans were going back to work. President Roosevelt was seeking his third term in the White House with a promise to keep America out of the war. America hoped to remain the fortress of democracy, producing airplanes, ships, and guns for the nations of Europe. Millions of Americans would be put back to work, but not a drop of American blood would be shed.

Junior college leaders shared this isolationist ideal. The European war was a boon to some of their vocational programs, such as aircraft mechanics and pilot training. They believed firmly, however, that American troops could and should stay out of the conflict. As Hitler's tanks rolled through Poland, the American Association of Junior Colleges was sending out a survey to 600 American junior college leaders, primarily college presidents, to gauge their opinions of the war. The 337 respondents were overwhelmingly against entering the war, even if American ships were sunk or the Western Hemisphere was invaded. Only in the event the American mainland or its territories were attacked did they deem America's entry into the war necessary.

On the other hand, these educators strongly supported national military mobilization and the "cash and carry" policy of selling armaments to England and France. Like most Americans they accepted Roosevelt's premise that America could affect the outcome of the war without being drawn into it (Eells, 1939c, p. 126):

Summary of Replies Received From
337 Junior College Administrators

	Percent Yes	Percent No
1. Under present conditions, should the United States enter the European war as an active fighting agent?	3	97
2. If Germany is defeated in the war, do you think the spread of the totalitarian form of government will be prevented?	42	58
3. Under the present conditions, should the United States sell munitions on a cash basis to any belligerent nation which can carry them away in their own ships?	64	36

4. Do you favor increased armaments and
   extension of armed forces in the United
   States at the present time?   61   39

5. Would you be willing to advise students
   to enlist and fight if:

   a. The United States proper were attacked? 96   4

   b. The United States territorial possessions
      were attacked?   74   26

   c. Any country in the western hemisphere
      were attacked?   42   58

   d. United States maritime rights were
      violated: i.e., if American ships were
      sunk with American passengers aboard? 29   71

   e. It became apparent that France and
      England were in serious danger of defeat? 23   77

Several college presidents passed the survey on to their students. The results of two of these surveys—at Custer County Junior College, Montana, and Itasca Junior College, Minnesota—were reported in the *Junior College Journal*. The student responses were remarkably similar to those of the college leaders. Of the 247 respondents, only 3 percent believed that America should go to war under the existing circumstances (Eells, 1939d, p. 214).

AAJC mirrored this isolationist sentiment. In October 1939 Executive Secretary Walter Eells suggested ten ways junior colleges could assist during the state of limited emergency, including the study of neutrality and preservation of academic freedom. Only two of these areas touched on preparation for military conflict ("Junior College World," 1939).

PREPARING FOR THE EMERGENCY

Although junior college leaders in general were against going to war, they became quite excited about responding to the growth of defense industries. The national mobilization created a demand for new and expanded vocational programs. A member of the AAJC executive committee called this emergency "a wonderful opportunity and a great responsibility" (Colvert, 1940, p. 3).

By 1939 forty-six junior colleges were participating in the newly approved Civilian Pilot Training Program, a defense-related effort sponsored by the Civil Aeronautics Authority to create trained pilots in case the limited emergency became a shooting war. These pilot training programs, located in colleges throughout the nation, had their largest concentration in California and Texas ("Junior College World," 1939).

In addition, junior colleges rushed to meet a potential wartime need for technicians, draftsmen, mechanics, welders, radio operators, health workers, and other vocational-program-trained professionals, training for whom universities largely eschewed. Although junior college leaders advocated isolationism and peace, they were clearly preparing for war.

JUNIOR COLLEGES GO TO WAR

While junior college leaders were debating neutrality, America was suddenly plunged into war. On a Sunday morning in 1941 the Japanese surprised the U.S. Pacific fleet at Pearl Harbor and, in the words of General Isoroku Yamamoto, awoke a "sleeping dragon." Overnight the entire nation geared up for war. An important component of that effort was the nation's junior colleges.

Normal college activities took a back seat as colleges prepared for the national war effort. By mid-1942 American junior colleges had added 135 new wartime courses to their curricula, including navigation, aviation training, airplane instrumentation, airplane repair, airplane drawing, blueprint reading, cartography and map reading, aerial photography, surveying, mechanical drawing, sheet metal drafting, radio repair, large diesel mechanics, riveting, synthetic rubber technology, ambulance driving, nurses' aides, and military correspondence. In some colleges shop programs functioned on an around-the-clock basis (Andrews, 1942; Anello, 1942, pp.

469–471). College faculties and administrators also got involved in working out the educational needs of Japanese American internees (Richardson, 1942).

Some college buildings were taken over by the military. At Phoenix Junior College, for example, the gymnasium was converted into a dormitory to house 150 military trainees (Wyman, 1944, p. 77). At Los Angeles Junior College the Army commandeered 35 percent of the classroom space for specialized military training ("Wartime Activities," 1943b, p. 176). The Florida Normal and Industrial Institute became an Army training center for African American radio operators ("Wartime Activities," 1942c).

Many colleges took their programs on the road in the cause of national defense. Los Angeles Junior College opened a flight training program at Lone Pine, California; Hardin Junior College offered evening courses at Sheppard Field, Texas; Stockton Junior College in California trained pilots at Carson City, Nevada. With the arrival of gas rationing, many students could not get to the college campus. Consequently, junior colleges set up extensions throughout their districts (Ballard, 1942, pp. 316–318), a practice that would serve them in good stead in later years and one that many would never give up.

With their students facing the military draft, junior colleges offered accelerated degree programs. Some, like San Bernardino Junior College, shortened the associate degree to three semesters. Trinidad Junior College in Colorado offered a four-quarter plan. Many colleges offered summer sessions for the first time, granting a degree after two standard semesters and a twelve-week summer session (Andrews, 1942).

As Americans struggled with wartime shortages, colleges offered patriotic noncredit courses. Citizens were trained to cultivate victory gardens, raise backyard poultry, and perform dozens of other do-it-yourself functions ("Wartime Activities," 1942a, pp. 469–471). Off-campus classes, noncredit courses, and summer sessions took root during the war. The defense effort also broadened the scope and acceptance of vocational programs as tailor-made and on-site training programs to meet the needs of industry became commonplace. These innovations remained after the emergency had passed.

AN ENROLLMENT ROLLER COASTER

The military draft cut deeply into junior college enrollments. Although the Selective Service Act of 1940 exempted college and university students from the draft, the official interpretation included only students in university transfer programs. Vocational and terminal students could still be drafted. Some local draft boards took a stricter interpretation and did not exempt junior college students. It took many months of lobbying to get these interpretations changed. In the meantime, thousands of junior college students were drafted or volunteered. Many others transferred to universities (Eells, 1942a, pp. 383–384; Eells & Winslow, 1941).

The number of junior colleges, both public and private, declined throughout America's involvement in the war. At the time of Pearl Harbor, there were about 627 junior colleges in America (Eells, 1942b, p. 279). Three years later only 586 such colleges remained (Eells, 1945, p. 219).

The private junior colleges that closed during World War II were primarily smaller schools. Even before the war, these colleges had been marginal. When their male students joined the military or took jobs in the defense industry, these schools slipped into insolvency. The remaining female students were not sufficient to see these colleges through four long years of war ("Wartime Activities," 1942b, p. 533).

The public colleges that vanished were primarily the high-school-extension emergency junior colleges that had been created during the Depression to keep young people out of unemployment lines. Following the attack on Pearl Harbor young adults were suddenly in demand as soldiers and defense workers. Consequently, the federal government cut its funding for these institutions, and most of them closed.

Iowa institutions experienced the worst decline, with fourteen of twenty-seven junior colleges closing during the first year of the war. Most of the casualties were small public colleges that had been formed haphazardly during the 1920s.

California, on the other hand, with its booming defense industry, actually gained ten colleges during the war. By 1945 the state had fifty-seven junior colleges, most of which were district junior colleges and charged no tuition (Long & Sanders, 1946).

National enrollment data for the war years are varied and often contradictory. It appears, however, that after the enrollment of most junior colleges peaked during the 1939–40 academic year, it declined steadily for three years. During 1943 enrollment declined by 77 percent in all junior colleges (Eells, 1940, 1943a, p. 137).

As the war drew to a close, enrollments suddenly skyrocketed. Largely owing to the influx of returning veterans taking advantage of the GI Bill, junior college enrollment for the 1944–45 academic year reached a record 251,290 students (Long & Sanders, 1946). Colleges were forced to adapt to the needs and schedules of adult students, many with jobs and families. These changes had a profound effect on the future mission of American junior colleges.

TROUBLED TIMES FOR AAJC

Walter Eells's six-year term as executive secretary, coincident with the war years, was a time of contention and change. The contention rose to the surface in 1942, when AAJC president John Harbeson proposed moving the national office to Chicago (Brick, 1964, pp. 42–45). Eells, who firmly believed that the Association should remain in the nation's capital, resigned in protest when the executive committee approved Harbeson's plan. Fearing that the Association might split, the executive committee backed down. The headquarters remained in Washington, and Eells rescinded his resignation.

Eells had other problems with Association leaders. Those representing public colleges complained that he was slanting the *Junior College Journal* toward private colleges. A rift also developed between Eells and Leonard Koos, whom Eells had criticized for his belief in the 6-4-4 system. This attack began a feud that undermined Eells's standing in the Association (Reed, 1971, p. 51).

The plummeting wartime enrollment at junior colleges also had an effect on the national Association. With the Association in a financial crisis in 1943, and debts beginning to mount, some members called for closing the Washington office (Reed, 1971). That year Jesse Bogue was elected AAJC president with a mandate to reform the Association's finances. Bogue called for an immediate audit of the Association's finances, moved to incorporate the Association and establish a formal budget, increased the dues, and solicited special contributions from the more affluent colleges. By the spring of 1944 "all accounts were paid, all indebtedness of the Association was liquidated and a substantial cash balance was established" (Reed, 1971, p. 47). These accomplishments established Bogue as a rising star of the junior college movement.

In the face of the Association's ailing financial situation, Walter Eells had issued a series of demands designed to upgrade his position. His insistence on tenure, pay raises, vacations, and a retirement allowance cost him the support of many close allies and strengthened his opponents. In the spring of 1945 Eells again tendered his resignation. This time it was accepted (Brick, 1964, pp. 42–45).

THE WAR WINDS DOWN

As early as 1943 the first wave of former soldiers, sailors, airmen, and marines was discharged from military hospitals. Advised to spend their convalescent time studying or preparing for a career, many of these wounded veterans chose to convalesce at a junior college. They were only the vanguard of the great wave of veterans who would fill college classrooms after the war.

While American forces fought the island-hopping campaign in the Pacific, the National Resources Planning Board (NRPB) prepared for their homecoming. As early as 1943 the NRPB predicted the impact of this mass repatriation:

When hostilities cease, many million men and women who have been members of the armed services or workers in war industries will need to find employment in civilian activities, many of which have little or no relationship to the work they have been doing.... Undoubtedly, several million of them will need either pre-employment training or retraining...financed almost if not entirely by federal funds ("Equal Access," 1943, pp. 55–57).

Eells agreed with the NRPB assessment but added his own prediction, forecasting that 35 percent of these returning veterans would be seeking "semiprofessional education, the distinctive field of the junior college" (Eells, 1943b, pp. 51–52).

The war changed or ended the lives of thousands of junior college students and staff. Several college presidents, including Charles Haines of Pueblo Junior College, John Mead of Amarillo College, and Dwight Baker of Modesto Junior College, volunteered for active duty. At San Francisco Junior College thirty-one faculty members were granted a leave of absence for military service. Perhaps the best known junior college serviceman was Army Air Corps ace Captain Ted Lawson. This graduate of Los Angeles Junior College authored *Thirty Seconds Over Tokyo*, one of the most inspirational accounts of the war ("Wartime Activities," 1943a, p. 243).

CHAPTER 9

THE GI BILL AND EXPANSION (1944-1948)

The junior colleges of America are well equipped to furnish the answer to the educational problems of our young veterans.

— General Omar Bradley

The conclusion of World War II could have created another national crisis, what with the millions of former service personnel and hoards of laid-off defense workers expected to exacerbate likely massive unemployment. Instead of postwar growth, America would be faced with another economic disaster.

The Roosevelt administration dealt with the crisis in the same way that it had battled the Depression: it created a government program to remove workers from the job pool. Like the National Youth Administration of the 1930s, this program aimed to channel young people out of the work force and into higher education. The official name of this legislation was the Serviceman's Readjustment Act; to millions of veterans, it was better known as the GI Bill of Rights, or simply the GI Bill.

Under the GI Bill any honorably discharged veteran who had served ninety days or was injured in the line of duty was entitled to a free college education. The government would pay for tuition, fees, and books at any approved educational institution. In addition, the veteran received a subsistence allowance of $65 a month, or $90 for veterans with dependents.

The GI Bill sailed through Congress on a wave of patriotic fervor. It was signed into law on January 22, 1944. Unknowingly, Congress had created one of the most successful social programs in America's history.

The GI Bill opened college doors to a generation of highly motivated young people. Never again would higher education be the exclusive province of the wealthy. For the first time the sons and daughters of farmers and laborers could afford to attend Harvard, Yale, or Stanford, and thousands of returning veterans did just that. Others chose a state university or liberal arts college. At some universities enrollments tripled.

For those veterans not academically prepared for a university, for those preferring career training, for those not wanting to sell their homes and uproot their families to attend a distant university, the best option was the local junior college.

After three years of declining enrollments, junior colleges scrambled to meet this sudden new demand. By the fall of 1946 nearly 43 percent of all junior college students were veterans. Yet, despite many previous farsighted attempts to increase capacity, 60 percent of the junior colleges reported that their classrooms were filled to capacity. There was no more space for new students (Reed, 1971, p. 63).

Again the federal government stepped in, creating the Veterans' Educational Facilities Program. Under this program the Bureau of Community Facilities (BCF) was formed to distribute war surplus structures, equipment, and furniture, mainly to educational institutions that served veterans. Thousands of Quonset huts, built for the Pacific war, became classrooms for returning veterans (Field, 1947, p. 376).

In its first six months in operation the bureau distributed surplus property to 1,368 institutions. By that time the federal government had spent over $61 million on the effort, mostly on the expense of dismantling, transporting, and reassembling surplus buildings. Through its Advanced Planning Program, the bureau also provided millions of dollars to help with public works projects. Junior colleges used these funds to design classrooms, office buildings, libraries, student centers, and other facilities (pp. 376–379).

In several instances, federal agencies actually operated junior colleges, such as the four colleges in Utah taken over by federal vocational officials and the junior college for convalescents at Percy Jones Hospital in Michigan established by the Army—which may be the first instance of a military service operating a junior college ("Wartime Activities," 1944, p. 321).

The U.S. Office of Education also developed a renewed interest in junior colleges since its sponsorship of the first national junior college conference in 1920 (Diener, 1970). In the interim the U.S. Office of Education had "only limited and spasmodic contact with the two year college movement" (p. 23). With the appointment in 1945 of its first "junior college specialist," William Conley, a former dean at Wright Junior College in Chicago, the office had reestablished a relationship with the junior college movement.

Franklin Roosevelt did not live to witness the success of the GI Bill. While the Allies were converging on Germany, Roosevelt died suddenly at his home in Warm Springs, Georgia. His vice president, Harry Truman, was thrust into the White House. Truman, who never attended college, would preside over the GI Bill and a historic national effort to expand access to higher education.

The GI Bill had created a taste for higher education in new segments of the population. College-educated veterans were able to build a better life for their families, and they instilled in their children and grandchildren the importance of higher education. Jesse Bogue was correct when he predicted that "great numbers of students are here to stay" (1947, p. 188).

THE POSTWAR BOOM

In November 1944 the *Junior College Journal* announced, "Enrollments are going up!" The news followed favorable reports from about 64 percent of 300 colleges surveyed. After three years of decline, the junior college movement was back on track (Eells, 1944a, p. 137).

Junior college enrollment nearly doubled in three years, from 251,290 in 1944 to half a million in the 1947 academic year. Much of the growth was at public colleges, which increased in number by fifty-eight for a national total of 328. By the fall of 1947 three of every four junior college students were enrolled in a public institution (Bogue & Sanders, 1948; Long & Sanders, 1946).

Once again, California led the nation, with eighteen new public junior colleges in the first five years of the GI Bill. Texas, a distant second, added nine (Bogue & Sanders, 1949). California's expansion was encouraged by the report of a state-mandated committee chaired by George Strayer (1948) of Columbia University, that assessed the state's future educational needs. The Strayer Committee made some predictions that seemed impossible at the time, predicting that California's population would soar as high as 15,092,000 by the year 1965, and that 30 percent of college-age students would enroll in higher education. To prepare for this onslaught, the committee recommended that California increase state funding for higher education. Although the Strayer Committee's estimates turned out to be extremely low, its recommendations paved the way for new junior colleges and the expansion of existing ones (Albright, 1948, pp. 112–115).

ADJUSTING TO SPECIAL STUDENTS

Junior colleges had always prided themselves on adapting to the needs of students, but in the postwar years this ability was severely tested. Overnight the armed services dropped thousands of nontraditional students onto the junior college doorstep: not compliant eighteen-year-olds, but seasoned combat veterans, with an unprecedented set of needs and demands, including housing, additional financial aid, and part-time jobs. By taking in the veteran, the local junior college also had to deal with some of the veteran's readjustment problems.

Mission

Each college manufactured its own solution to these problems. The experience of one North Dakota junior college was, in some ways, typical. The college expanded its dormitories and turned a former shop building into another dorm, and when these facilities filled up, it brought in a surplus Navy barracks and cabin trailers. College officials pleaded with local citizens to take in boarders, and some did. And the veterans kept coming. One brought his own solution: a truckload of lumber to build a cabin (Bell, 1946, p. 372).

Veterans also had special academic needs. A large number had not finished high school or had forgotten basic skills during the war. Some insisted on vocational courses that the junior college had never offered. A few had no objectives at all, but simply wanted the government subsidy. Most veterans, anxious to get on with their lives, demanded accelerated programs or credit for military experience. Newly discharged soldiers wanted to start classes immediately, even in midsemester (Black, 1945).

These former soldiers could be demanding and impatient. They had risked their lives to defend their country. Some had spent years away from their families under harsh conditions. They expected and deserved special consideration. In serving the veterans, junior colleges learned to adapt to a host of special academic and financial needs, and in the process became more responsive to the needs of their communities. Over the next three decades these lessons would help them serve racial minorities, women, senior citizens, persons with disabilities, and other special-needs students.

THE TRUMAN COMMISSION

Many commissions and agencies have studied America's junior college movement, but none of their reports has had a wider impact than that of the President's Commission on Higher Education (PCHE), better known as the Truman Commission. The commission's six-volume report, *Higher Education for American Democracy*, has become one of the best-known documents in educational history. Published in 1947, the report pushed the two-year college into the forefront of American higher education (Bonos, 1948, p. 426) and

129

assisted in changing the movement's family name from junior to community college (Boyce, 1949, p. 445).

The commission was appointed by President Harry S. Truman on July 13, 1946, to reexamine America's system of higher education. Truman and his advisers believed that higher education had remained elitist too long. The GI Bill had opened college doors to the average American, and Truman intended to keep them open. Truman instructed the commission, whose purview ran the gamut from curricula to access and financing, to create a master plan for "expanding educational opportunities for all able young people."

The appointment of George Zook, former commissioner of education, as chair of the twenty-eight-member commission was a boon for the junior college movement. He had been a lifelong advocate of junior colleges, having organized the first national junior college conference and helped found AAJC. For a dozen years Zook had served as president of the American Council on Education. There was no more eloquent spokesperson for the junior college movement.

Two other commissioners were also ardent junior college supporters: Henry Dixon, president of Weber College, the largest junior college in Utah, and Frederick Kelly, of the U.S. Office of Education, who had served on the advisory board of the *Junior College Journal*. The influence of these three men ensured that junior colleges would be written into the commission's blueprint for higher education.

The commission recommended a massive expansion of educational activity. Based upon the results of the Army General Classification Test, given to nearly ten million servicemen during World War II, the commission estimated that 49 percent of the American public had "the mental ability to complete 14 years of schooling" (President's Commission on Higher Education, 1947, vol. 1, pp. 40–41). To meet the educational needs of the underserved, the commission proposed a national effort to create new two-year colleges.

The proposed colleges would offer education through "the fourteenth grade." Like the junior colleges that William Rainey Harper had proposed half a century before, these institutions, mostly public, would be extensions of secondary education, "closely articulated with the local high school." They would be locally controlled but partially funded by state and federal governments (pp. 67–70). These colleges would offer not simply the "first half of a four year degree," but a wide variety of terminal, semiprofessional, public service, and recreational programs to fulfill local needs and to serve citizens of every age, race, and social class.

The commission strongly recommended that these democratic colleges take special pains to serve victims of poverty and racism, believing that every American should be encouraged to explore his or her full potential:

> The American people should set as their ultimate goal an educational system in which at no level—high school, college, graduate school, or professional school—will a qualified individual in any part of the country encounter an insuperable economic barrier to the attainment of the kind of education suited to his aptitudes and interests (p. 36).

A NEW FAMILY NAME

The college envisioned by the Truman Commission would "fit into a comprehensive state-wide system of higher education" as a "community center of learning" (President's Commission on Higher Education, 1947, vol. 1, pp. 67–70):

> Hence the President's Commission suggests the name "community college" to be applied to the institution designed to serve chiefly local community educational needs. It may have various forms of organization and may have curricula of various lengths. Its dominant feature is its intimate relations to the life of the community it serves (vol. 3, p. 5).

The Truman Commission did not create the term *community college*, however; the term had been around since the mid-1930s. In 1944 a book published by the Educational Policies Commission of the National Education Association, *Education for All American Youth*, had made wide use of the term (Boyce, 1949, p. 445). There is no clear record, though, of how the term found its way into the commission's report.

Soon after the commission's report appeared, Illinois changed the name of several two-year colleges from junior to community. Other states were slower to follow. Many institutions kept the name junior college, but referred to themselves generically as community colleges. Gradually, however, the name caught on and took root. The commission's definition of this institution remains remarkably accurate, four decades later:

> The Community College seeks to become a center of learn-
> ing for the entire community, with or without the restrictions
> that surround formal course work in traditional institutions of
> higher education. It gears its programs and services to the
> needs and wishes of the people it serves (President's Commis-
> sion on Higher Education, 1947, vol. 1, pp. 69–70).

Contrary to popular belief, the Truman Commission did not create the modern community college. By 1947 more than half a million Americans were already enrolled in two-year colleges, many of which were comprehensive institutions similar to those proposed in the report. In supporting these institutions' comprehensive mission, the commission made the community college a keystone of national educational policy and set the stage for the massive college growth of the next two decades.

TOWARD STATEWIDE SYSTEMS

In the 1940s educators focused more sharply on statewide planning for the development of junior colleges. George Stoddard (1944) claimed there was a universal need for "tertiary education" in state public education systems. Seashore (1940) emphasized that states needed to plan for the development of junior colleges so that a projected 1,346 junior colleges could serve more than 1.5 million full-time and part-time students living at home, and he even outlined three plans for combining the vocational and academic programs of these institutions under a statewide organizational structure (pp. 112–113). Starrak and Hughes (1948) predicted that each state would need to develop provisions for this next step in free public education. Deutsch, Douglas, and Strayer (1948) conducted several state studies with junior colleges in mind as part of the total state planning for higher education. Their highly influential master plan study for California, published in 1948, encompassed a tripartite system of junior colleges, state colleges, and the University of California, designed to meet the common and diversified educational needs of the citizens of that state (McGrath, 1966). McConnell (1962) further emphasized the place of junior colleges in the coordination and purposeful planning of higher education.

The years 1945 to 1948 were important ones for junior college legislation. The legislatures of Arizona, Idaho, Michigan, Nebraska, Utah, and Washington increased their financial support for junior colleges. Meanwhile, the states of Connecticut, Maryland, Massachusetts, Oregon, and Wyoming were establishing new public junior colleges (Bogue & Sanders, 1948; Eells, 1944b, 1945; Long & Sanders, 1946, 1947).

The New York state legislature created several kinds of two-year colleges during this period. Immediately after the war New York opened three "emergency two-year colleges" to accommodate returning veterans and then, in 1946, created five new two-year technical schools called Institutes of Advanced Arts and Sciences, which were added to the six existing technical institutes. Two years later the state authorized local agencies to establish community colleges. The same 1948 law put all postsecondary institutions under a coordinating body, the State University of New York (SUNY), and provided the basis for a statewide system (Medsker, 1960, pp. 252–253).

The Florida legislature passed the most sweeping educational law of the era, the omnibus Minimum Foundation Program (MFP) law of 1947. Prior to this date most Florida counties were divided into multiple school districts. The new law placed all public education in each county under one countywide district board of public instruction, which was authorized to add, with the specific permission of the state board of education, two new levels of education— a kindergarten and a junior college. These new levels became, when so approved, a part of the county school systems, jointly financed

133

by state and local funds. The provisions for curriculum as well as the purposes of these colleges were similar to those described by the Truman Commission.

This MFP law also provided a basis for a statewide system in that the state board of education could approve new institutions only in counties with a population of 50,000 or in combinations of counties totaling no less than 50,000, thereby forming a multicounty junior college district. Areas with a smaller population were not eligible to request approval. Academic and other standards for these junior colleges were to be set by the same state board of education. The statewide system began to take shape in 1955 when the Community College Council was formed with James L. Wattenbarger as its director and secretary, and a long-range plan was formulated (Wattenbarger, 1957).

The new law provided a home for the new junior colleges in the local county school systems, with a dean appointed as chief executive officer of the college reporting to the county superintendent of public instruction. As was the case with the other levels of public education, the junior college was supported by local taxation as well as by state-appropriated funds under a financial support formula authorized by the MFP and student fees authorized by the state board of education (Price, 1948, p. 440).

Before the 1947 law, however, Palm Beach Junior College was the only public junior college in Florida. Pensacola Junior College was approved in 1948, and soon afterward two private junior colleges, St. Petersburg Junior College and Chipola Junior College, became public institutions. No other public junior colleges were formed in Florida until the 1957 report of the Community College Council was approved.

The Maryland General Assembly appropriated $60,000 for public two-year colleges in 1947. Two years later the amount was increased to $100 per full-time equivalent student. There was no specific reference to community or junior colleges in Maryland state law, which were instead funded under a provision providing funds for continuing education. During this period three junior colleges were founded: Montgomery and Hagerstown junior colleges, both locally controlled institutions, and Baltimore Junior College, which began as an extension of a veterans' high school. No additional two-year colleges were founded for nearly a decade.

The Wyoming legislature had considered and rejected a series of junior college bills since the 1930s. Each bill had been strongly opposed by supporters of the University of Wyoming who feared competition. Finally, in 1945, a bill to extend high school adult education, amended to allow for junior colleges, was passed (Lahti, 1962). In the fall Wyoming's first junior college opened in the town of Cody, near Yellowstone National Park, followed the next year by a college in Powell, a wealthy oil community in the north. In the fall of 1948 two more colleges opened, in Sheridan and Torrington. After this rapid growth the movement suddenly stopped. No more junior colleges were built for eleven years (p. 93).

Agencies in several other states considered statewide planning for the establishment of systems of junior colleges, and some even employed consultants to conduct studies to determine the specific needs of the state and to make recommendations. Saylor (1949) reported that only twenty-six states in 1948 had general legislation authorizing junior colleges, and while a few had some special legislation, eleven had no legislation at all. Most states did little or nothing about the consultant recommendations prior to the presentation of the comprehensive Florida plan in 1957. This plan became a model for many states because the total state need for this level of education was considered and projected.

After a 1948 tour of junior college campuses, Jesse Bogue noted that he was "impressed, and sometimes almost depressed, with the scattered, haphazard, unplanned locations of the junior colleges," which were no better planned than "the location of trees and bushes in a wild forest" (1948, pp. 44–46).

AAJC COMES OF AGE

In May 1945 Walter Eells ended his tenure as AAJC executive secretary. For the next fourteen months his editorial assistant, Winifred Long, kept the Association functioning, acting as both editor and executive secretary.

The 1946 convention brought a series of bold changes and reforms. The Association adopted a reorganization plan, "Blueprint for the Future of the AAJC" (Bogue, 1946, p. 24), and to carry out its goals raised member dues from $30 to $50 per college and completely revised the constitution (Reed, 1971, p. 56). The reorganizing task fell to a research coordinating committee comprising the chairs of five operating committees—on administration, curriculum and adult education, legislation, student personnel problems, and teacher preparation—and headed by the Association's vice president (Colvert & Littlefield, 1961). The primary proponent of these changes was former Association president Jesse Bogue.

The revised constitution changed the name of the executive committee to the Board of Directors. The nine-member Board would include the president, vice president, immediate past president, and one director from each of the six regional areas (Rutledge, 1951, p. 26). The constitution also brought a new list of purposes, reflecting the growing scope of the organization:

> The purpose of this organization shall be to stimulate the professional development of its members and to promote the growth of junior colleges. In particular and to implement the philosophy of the preamble the purposes are: to promote through cooperative research and dissemination of information improvements in the services of the colleges to their students, improvements of their instructors and instructional practices, the organization and administration of the member colleges and to study and report on the best ways and means for financing junior colleges (American Association of Junior Colleges, 1967, p. 16).

Nevertheless, the basic structure of AAJC remained the same. Delegates to the annual convention still selected the president, vice president, and Board members, who, in nearly every case, were junior college presidents.

During the summer of 1946 the Association Board met to select a new executive secretary. After two days of deliberations the Board elected an "outstanding leader" from the Midwest, but when this individual declined the offer, the Board went back into session, working past midnight to choose among three remaining candidates. Curtis Bishop, a Board member from Virginia, explained the results:

> At four o'clock on the morning of the second night, Dr. Bogue was called out of bed, invited to the room in which the board was meeting and was informed that he had been elected Executive Secretary. In typical Dr. Bogue genteel fashion, he agreed not only to accept the appointment but confirm it by taking the members of the Board who were still willing to sit up to accompany him to an early breakfast (Reed, 1971, p. 58).

Eells's departure had left AAJC deeply divided. Bogue began an immediate effort to reunite Association members, becoming over the next dozen years the movement's most visible leader. Members could not accuse him, as they had Eells, of favoritism, for Bogue became a nationwide president (Reynolds, 1958), visiting hundreds of colleges throughout the country.

Like many junior college leaders, Bogue came from humble origins. One of eleven children born to a pioneer family in northern Alabama, Bogue worked his way through DePauw University as a lumberjack, coal miner, cowboy, and even deep-sea fisherman. In his spare time he served as a minister in the Methodist Episcopal church. A natural public speaker, he had been a preacher since age sixteen ("Jesse Parker Bogue," 1961, p. 22).

After serving as a field chaplain in France during World War I, Bogue became school superintendent in Bringhurst, Indiana, and then, in 1930, headmaster of the Troy Conference Academy, a private boarding school in Vermont. Bogue expanded the academy's curriculum, creating Green Mountain Junior College, and served as its president for more than fifteen years. In 1943 he was elected president of AAJC (Reed, 1971). When he was appointed executive secretary in 1946, Bogue was completing a term in the Vermont state legislature.

Eells's resignation also left the *Junior College Journal* without an editor. During the 1946 convention a special meeting was held in Chicago's Drake Hotel, at which it was decided to farm out the

Association's journal to a major university (Reed, 1971, p. 55). Many of those at the meeting wanted to contract it out to the University of Chicago, specifically to Leonard Koos, who had recently retired as a professor.

Once again, the longstanding feud between Koos and Eells became an issue. Eells loyalists did not want Koos to take over the journal that their friend had founded. As a compromise, Koos was given the editorship, but his term was limited to three years. During that period he also served as the Association's first research director. His salary was split between the university and AAJC. In 1949 the University of Chicago contract ended and the publication was moved to the University of Texas, with James Reynolds, a former student of Koos's, as the new editor.

CHAPTER 10

THE COLD WAR (1949-1958)

It's bad enough for our young men to fight in hell holes around the world; it's worse that they should be compelled to do so without knowing why.

— Jesse Bogue

The United States had emerged from World War II as the strongest economic and military power on the planet. American products and technology were the envy of the world. In Western Europe, America's Marshall Plan was rebuilding war-ravaged nations. In Asia, American troops had occupied Japan and imposed a Western style democracy. Even the fledgling United Nations chose America for its headquarters. Historians and politicians proclaimed the beginning of the American century.

A single dark cloud hung over the American horizon—the Soviet Union. Under the leadership of Joseph Stalin, political purges were carried out in which millions lost their lives. At the war's end, as Soviet armies seized Eastern Europe and imposed communist dictatorships, Winston Churchill declared that an "iron curtain" had fallen over the peoples of Eastern Europe.

In March 1947 President Truman announced that the United States would "support free peoples who are resisting subjugation by armed minorities or by outside pressure." The Truman Doctrine committed America to containing the spread of communism. The following year Soviet troops blockaded Berlin, forcing an eleven-month airlift.

In 1949 Chinese communists completed their takeover of mainland China after forcing out the United States-backed government of Chiang Kai-shek. In that same year the United States and Western Europe formed the North Atlantic Treaty Organization. The iron curtain nations formed their own military alliance, the Warsaw Pact. The cold war had begun.

A WAR OF WORDS

Following the Berlin airlift, anticommunist rhetoric became a pervasive part of American life. Even the American Association of Junior Colleges picked up the sentiment. At its 1949 convention Homer Rainey delivered a scalding assessment of the new enemy. "What has communism to offer the underprivileged peoples of the world?" he asked. "Under communism, it is the system that is all-important. The individual must conform, at the peril of his life, to its grotesque and inhuman set of rules" (Rainey, 1949, p. 507).

Two years later the Association's resolutions committee prepared AAJC members for what would likely be a continual struggle against a relentless enemy:

The United States and other nations of the free world are faced with a long-term contest of strength which involves three main aspects: ideological, technological, and military (Jenkins, Mohr, & Dodd, 1951, p. 513).

The committee's prediction proved correct for most of the next four decades. Two armed camps competed for world influence, building massive armies and arsenals of nuclear weapons and championing opposing causes in dozens of regional conflicts. The two superpowers also competed in technology, space exploration, athletics, and propaganda. This cold war competition shaped America's society and educational system. It also had a profound effect on the development of community colleges.

THE KOREAN CONFLICT

In the summer of 1950 the cold war suddenly became hot. On June 25 the armies of communist North Korea crossed the 38th parallel into South Korea. The United Nations Security Council demanded a withdrawal, but North Korean forces moved forward to the outskirts of Seoul. On June 30 President Truman ordered American troops into the conflict, where they were joined by troops of fifteen other democratic nations. In the fall China entered the war on the North Korean side. Only five years after the end of World War II, America was enmeshed in another international conflict.

Once again community colleges joined in the war effort. The AAJC Board "authorized a letter to [the] United Nations with approval of its stand in the Korean affair...[and] authorized the Washington office to make a survey of junior colleges with a view to their possible participation in national preparedness and defense" (Bogue, 1950b, p. 113).

As in the last war, junior colleges trained factory workers and technicians for roles in national defense, except this time they were joined by community colleges in the ideological battle. General education courses emphasized the superiority of American values over those of the communist enemy (Roberts, 1953, p. 250). Courses in Americanism or anticommunism were popular offerings at many community colleges.

Some colleges participated in the controversial Citizenship Education Project (CEP), founded at the behest of General Dwight Eisenhower to combat communist propaganda by training students in the ideals of American democracy. Sponsored by the Carnegie Foundation for the Advancement of Teaching, this program was taught in public schools but later spread to community colleges and four-year institutions (Johnson & Harless, 1955).

141

Many of these citizenship courses took their tone from the Truman Doctrine. They pictured America as a defender of freedom, helping other nations resist the forces of communist tyranny. Their supporters believed that such Americanism courses helped college students understand the ideals of America. Critics, however, viewed them as unabashed propaganda, designed to justify American intervention in Korea.

FIGHTING THE ENROLLMENT WARS

During World War II enrollments had fallen for three straight years, causing many small colleges to close. Some college leaders feared even greater declines during the Korean conflict. Enrollments had already dropped by about 35,000 students in the fall of 1948 as the use of the GI Bill declined. With thousands of young Americans headed to Korea, further declines seemed imminent. Despite the gloomy predictions, the conflict did not seriously affect enrollments. In the fall before the war, total enrollments jumped by 21 percent, reaching 562,786 (American Association of Junior Colleges, 1946; 1947), and for the next three years remained relatively stable, dipping only slightly in the 1952 academic year. This resilience was due to three factors: increased adult enrollment, educational draft deferments, and a renewed GI Bill (Bogue, 1956a; 1956b).

With experts predicting sharp enrollment declines, admission staffs began recruiting a vast but largely untapped clientele: adult students. To reach this audience, colleges turned to advertising and public relations ("Junior College Directory," 1950, p. 134), using the radio and television media to push evening and special-interest classes. College courses offering a new hobby, better job, or simply self-improvement were sold to an eager public.

Colleges also sold themselves through films, some of which were aired on television. Del Mar College of Corpus Christi, Texas, produced a black-and-white film praising the quality of the college's equipment, buildings, and instructional programs. Another Texas institution, Paris Junior College, did much the same thing, only in color (Bogue, 1951a, p. 411).

142

AAJC joined in, producing booklets such as *I Will Never Regret Junior College* by Raymond A. Crippen and *Shall I Attend a Junior College?* by Edward Mason. These and other AAJC publications became primary tools in the effort to maintain junior college enrollments (Fields, 1950, p. 57).

Adult recruitment was most successful in California (Kempfer, 1950), where in 1950 community colleges enrolled 127,252 adults. Long Beach College alone had more than 24,000 adult students (Bogue, 1952a, p. 350). Soon the rest of the nation followed California's lead. By 1957 more than half of America's junior college enrollment was adult education students (Bogue, 1958a, pp. 356–58).

Unlike World War II, the Korean conflict did not gain wide public support. America had not been attacked and Congress had not declared war. Thousands of young Americans were fighting in a place that most had never heard of. While some young people volunteered, many more were called up in the reinstated military draft. Some young men temporarily escaped the draft by attending college.

As in World War II, college undergraduates were given draft deferments to complete their education. Once again many draft boards had a limited view of the term college, considering a college course to be one that led to a bachelor's degree. In many cases vocational or terminal students were denied a deferment. Some draft boards believed that community colleges were not colleges at all. As one Selective Service official stated: "A college is a four-year institution of higher learning which grants the bachelor's degree" (Bogue, 1952b, p. 527).

Eventually most community colleges won their battles with the draft boards. The issue was settled permanently in March 1953 by Local Memorandum Number 53 from the Selective Service director, which stated clearly that draft deferments were available to all male students pursuing a "full-time course of instruction in a satisfactory manner" (Reed, 1971, p. 108). During the Vietnam and Korean wars, draft deferments convinced many eighteen-year-olds to enroll in a two-year college.

In 1952 the Veterans' Readjustment Act extended the educational benefits of the GI Bill to Korean War veterans (Reed, 1971,

p. 105). The effect of this legislation was immediate. Although the war dragged on, by the fall of 1952 over 800,000 veterans had been rotated back to the United States. Nearly all of them were eligible for the new Korean GI Bill (Bogue, 1952c, p. 56).

Initially, some states interpreted the bill to cover only those courses leading to a standard (bachelor's) degree, and required all other programs to submit detailed reports for a case-by-case evaluation. Fearing that funding for most junior college vocational programs would be slowed or eliminated, AAJC pressed the Veterans Administration to change this discriminatory interpretation. In March 1953 the administration complied by eliminating from the bill the sentence containing the words "standard college degree" (Reed, 1971, p. 108).

The returning veterans helped to cushion the conflict's impact on community colleges. All told, through January 1965 more than 2.3 million veterans took advantage of the Korean GI Bill ("Veterans," 1964).

While the draft and the GI Bill were increasing community college enrollments, another federal program was undermining those gains. The Reserve Officers' Training Corps (ROTC), a campus-based program designed to train officers for the five branches of military service, paid a stipend to students who enrolled in the program and conferred junior-officer-grade status on those who completed their degrees. Unfortunately, ROTC programs were not available to community college students. Jesse Bogue complained that four-year colleges "used this advantage to lure junior college students to the senior college campuses" (Bogue, 1952b, pp. 526–527).

Another Postwar Boom

With the return of thousands of veterans following the end of the Korean conflict in 1953, many of them choosing to get a higher education, community colleges began another era of postwar growth. In actual numbers this growth was larger than that of the period after World War II. Over three years the enrollment at

America's two-year colleges increased by about 299,000 students (Bogue, 1956a, pp. 358–360; 1958a, pp. 356–358). Although enrollment climbed, the total number of two-year colleges actually shrank. Most of the failures were private institutions that could not compete with expanding public community colleges. By mid-1955 there were only 596 junior colleges in the nation, down from a high of 663 in 1946 (Bogue, 1956a, pp. 358–360).

In 1955 enrollments rose by another 10 percent, reaching 765,551. This time the number of two-year colleges also grew, by thirty-nine, more than two-thirds of which were public community colleges. The next year enrollments were up again, to 869,720 students (Bogue, 1958a, pp. 356–358).

Nearly all of this expansion occurred in public colleges. In the first year after the war, as public colleges added 57,000 students, private college enrollment declined. By the 1957 academic year more than 89 percent of all two-year college students were enrolled in public institutions. (Bogue, 1958a, pp. 352–360; Colvert & Baker, 1955, p. 43). Once again California had the greatest growth, with 294,508 junior college students, nearly half the national total, at the war's end. To handle the increasing enrollments five new California colleges opened between 1950 and 1956. (Colvert, 1956, p. 15).

The California community college system was aided by an amendment to the state constitution known as Proposition 2. Approved by state voters in November 1953, this measure and its accompanying legislation increased state funding for adult education, vocational training, and general education at public community colleges. The legislature also revised a state law to allow community college districts to issue bonds, worth 10 percent of the college's assessed value, for the increase of budgets and improvement of physical plants (Martorana, 1954).

Michigan gained five new community colleges during this period: Alpena Community College, Kellogg Community College in Battle Creek, Macomb Community College in Warren, and Northwestern Michigan College in Traverse City.

Several other states also experienced rapid growth. By 1955 Illinois had the third highest enrollment, behind California and Texas, with 32,455 students. New York had built thirty-two two-year institutions, including junior colleges and technical centers, enrolling 23,415 students. Washington state's ten public junior colleges had grown to 18,762 students. Despite these gains, broad areas of the country were still unserved, including much of New England, Ohio, Tennessee, and the less populous western states (Colvert, 1956, p. 15).

By far, however, the most important development in education at this time was the implementation of a total state plan in Florida. Although Mississippi had developed a state plan some years previous, very little attention had been given to state planning in most states until after World War II. In fact, the concept that the state-level leadership had any responsibility for providing educational opportunity beyond the twelfth grade to all citizens was neither generally accepted nor understood. Yet, in 1955 the Florida legislature, encouraged by the leadership of Governor LeRoy Collins, established the Community College Council and instructed the council to formulate a long-range plan for the establishment and coordination of community colleges. The legislature defined the community college as "an educational institution offering (1) a program of general education consisting of classical and scientific courses parallel to that of the first two years of work at a senior four year institution, (2) terminal courses of technical and vocational nature, and (3) courses beyond the basic education courses for adults" (Wattenbarger, 1957, p. iii).

The council, made up of seven laypersons from various areas of the state plus the executive director of the Board of Control (the operating board for the universities), the state superintendent of public instruction, and the president of Chipola Junior College, designated James L. Wattenbarger as director and secretary to the council. Under Wattenbarger's leadership the council developed and presented to the 1957 legislature a master plan for community colleges. The legislature approved it, establishing six new institutions and implementing a priority-based plan for a total state system of twenty-eight community colleges within commuting distance of 99 percent of the state's population. The community colleges thereby became an integral part of the higher education system of the state of Florida, and the majority of students graduating from high school began to plan to attend their own local community colleges prior to attending four-year colleges or universities. In addition to serving those students, the colleges became a major location for the continued education of the total population as had been envisioned by many community college mission statements over the years.

The Florida plan was one of the first total statewide planning activities in the nation and provided a model for the development of higher education systems in a number of other states, even several that had had junior colleges for a number of years. The most critical features of the plan were the consideration of people in the entire state and the orderly growth of new institutions coordinated by a state agency. In addition, the plan called for a smooth articulation process for all students and equity for the junior colleges as an integral part of the higher education system of the state.

THE GLOBAL MOVEMENT

During the 1950s the community college movement spread to the United States territories and foreign countries. In 1952 the federal government established a territorial community college in Guam. The following year the territory of Alaska formed two district community colleges, and a third in 1956. The U.S. government also funded a junior college in the Panama Canal Zone (Bogue, 1949, p. 519; Martorana, 1954).

Community colleges also began to show up in other countries. Canada had two province-sponsored junior colleges: Nova Scotia Agricultural College and Prince of Wales College on Prince Edward Island (Bogue, 1949, p. 519). The fastest growth, however, was in Japan, thanks to the efforts of one man—Walter Eells, former executive secretary of the AAJC.

In 1947 General Douglas MacArthur, as supreme commander of Allied forces in Japan, had approved a bulky educational system for that country that included 599 specialized three-year junior colleges (Eells, 1951, p. 3). Eells, as higher education adviser, believed that these schools should be reorganized as comprehensive com-

147

munity colleges called *tanki-daigaku*—literally "short-term colleges" (Watanabe, 1964). Eells and others persuaded MacArthur and the Japanese minister of culture to accept the plan, whereupon the three-year colleges were reorganized into 181 comprehensive community colleges: 153 private colleges, twenty-four public colleges, and four national colleges. The new junior college system began classes in April 1950. Eells proudly proclaimed, "Nowhere in the world has such a large number of junior colleges been organized in such a short space of time" (Eells, 1951, p. 3).

THE EISENHOWER COMMITTEE

In the spring of 1956 President Eisenhower appointed a task force to study the problems of higher education in America. This new body was officially known as the President's Committee on Education Beyond the High School (1957), more commonly called the Eisenhower Committee. Like many political conservatives, Eisenhower was opposed to expansion of the federal government and believed that higher education should be financed and controlled at the state and local levels. In a 1957 message to Congress the president explained the purpose and limits of the committee:

Higher education is and must remain the responsibility of the states, localities and private groups and institutions. But to lay before us all the problems of education beyond the high school, and to encourage active and systematic attack on them, I shall appoint a distinguished group of educators and citizens to develop...proposals in this educational field... (Stahr, 1957, p. 491).

The Eisenhower Committee was vastly different in composition and attitude from the Truman Commission. In particular, it did not include influential supporters of the community college movement. The Truman Commission had been chaired by a lifelong junior college advocate, George Zook. The Eisenhower Committee, on the other hand, was chaired by Devereux Josephs, chair of the New York Life Insurance Company.

Few of the committee's members and staff, who were primarily conservative businessmen and university leaders, had any real expertise or interest in community colleges, and their recommendations were often contradictory and disturbing to community college leaders. For example, the committee accepted a prediction that by 1970 at least 50 percent of freshmen would enter a community college, and they foresaw a spectacular growth in student numbers. Instead of calling for new two-year colleges to meet the demand, as one might expect, the committee recommended caution:

> There are already too many colleges too small to be economical. Community planning must be closely related to state and regional planning in order to avoid the possibility of developing still more small, uneconomic units.... Without sound planning, what might have become a community asset may become a community disappointment (Diener, 1986, p. 157).

The committee's description of "small, uneconomic units" ran contrary to the facts. During the 1955–56 academic year, the average public two-year college had an enrollment of 1,882, and most colleges had seen a decade of steadily rising enrollments. They were hardly destined for failure. In reality they were poised for another era of growth.

The committee report angered many supporters of two-year colleges. Even staff members of the U.S. Office of Education spoke out against the report, attacking the accuracy of the committee's findings:

> The report reflects a basic lack of genuine sympathy, if not enthusiasm, for the two-year college, couching most of its recommendations in provisos, cautions, and qualifying statements that leave the reader more impressed with the "pitfalls" that may befall action than with ways that present serious problems can be alleviated. Some of the recommendations of the Committee also appear to be highly challengeable and weak in light of known evidence about the operation and practice in American higher education (Diener, 1986, p. 162).

In an earlier era the Eisenhower committee report might have had a chilling effect on the community college movement. In the late

1950s, however, its impact was relatively small. The demand for more two-year colleges was too great to be stopped by a federal report. The looming avalanche of baby boomers ensured that more and larger community colleges would be built throughout the nation.

SPUTNIK AND THE NDEA

The Korean conflict had ended, but the cold war grew more intense. America was no longer the sole possessor of nuclear weapons. The Soviet Union had them too. As politicians raised the specter of a sudden doomsday attack by the red menace, in towns across America civil defense agencies prepared for a nuclear alert. Against this backdrop of nuclear anxiety, the Soviets launched *Sputnik*, the first manmade satellite. On an October night in 1957 millions of Americans watched a tiny blinking light move across the autumn sky. For the most powerful nation on earth, it was a humbling and threatening experience. This sudden development caught America by surprise, and, like the Pearl Harbor attack of sixteen years before, galvanized public opinion. Citizens and politicians demanded action.

The national effort that followed *Sputnik* took two major forms: the building of a space program and a new commitment to science and technical education. National studies had indicated that American students were deficient in science, technical fields, and foreign languages. Congress passed a series of bills to correct these deficiencies. The best known, the National Defense Education Act (NDEA), authorized $887 million in grants and loans to college students in the targeted areas. Unfortunately, most of these funds were aimed at four-year institutions. Few community or junior college students benefited from this massive federal program.

The NDEA also provided funds for training technicians in occupations requiring scientific or technical knowledge. Despite appeals from AAJC, Congress placed all of this funding in secondary schools. As it had in the Smith-Hughes Act of two decades before, Congress refused to consider community colleges as a viable provider of vocational education (Brint & Karabel, 1989, p. 95).

FUNDRAISING FOR JUNIOR COLLEGES

Private fundraising is nearly as old as the junior college movement: the first annual giving program by a two-year college was inaugurated in 1906 at Midway Junior College in Kentucky. In the early years of the century most fundraising was by private and church-related junior colleges. By the 1950s, however, public junior colleges had also become active fundraisers (Timmins, 1962).

In 1959 the Council for Financial Aid to Education surveyed the fundraising activities of 172 public, church-related, and independent junior colleges. Not counting religious, government, and board support, for the 1958–59 year these schools had raised nearly $5.2 million, an average of more than $30,000 per institution. Surprisingly, less than 15 percent of contributions came from former students. The largest source of contributions was from individuals and friends, who contributed nearly 39 percent of the total. About 22 percent came from businesses, and the remainder came from nonchurch groups and other sources. These findings showed that junior colleges were attracting support far beyond their own alumni. More than 60 percent of their support was coming from businesses and from citizens who had not attended the college (Timmins, 1962).

THE RISE OF NURSE TRAINING

In postwar America people were living longer than ever before. Improved diets, inoculations, and wonder drugs had lengthened the average lifespan. These developments, along with a growing population, increased the demand for health care, for nurses in particular, whose numbers were critically low by the 1950s (Barker, 1969, p. 92).

The Cadet Nurse Corps Training Program during World War II had shown that good nurses could be trained in less than four years. Based on this experience many educational leaders advocated a shorter and revised nursing education program. The logical institution to offer this shortened program was the community college (W.K. Kellogg Foundation, 1980, p. 73).

151

The idea of an associate degree in nursing (ADN) was developed by Mildred Montag of the Teachers College at Columbia University, who in the early 1950s spent three years developing a basic curriculum. When the American Nurses Association recommended that nursing preparation take place in colleges and universities rather than in hospitals, advocacy for the ADN became a national movement.

In 1958 the W.K. Kellogg Foundation began funding curriculum and program development for an ADN project in California, Florida, New York, and Texas (p. 74). A later Kellogg grant helped set standards for faculty preparation, curriculum, consultation services, and demonstration sites. The importance of the program in Florida, for example, was emphasized by the fact that hospitals were closing their nurse training programs in the 1950s. Without the community college ADN programs, there would have been no source of nurses other than university baccalaureate programs. The same was true of other states (Anderson, 1966, p. viii).

In 1962 the National League for Nursing (NLN) began accrediting associate degree programs (Barker, 1969, p. 94). By the end of 1967 nearly 300 junior colleges offered nursing programs, about half of which were accredited or had received reasonable assurance of accreditation by the NLN. Nearly all of the accredited programs were coeducational and varied in length from eighteen to twenty-two months. The largest concentration was at public two-year colleges in the high-growth states of California, Florida, and New York (p. 92).

THE FIRST TV COLLEGE

Sputnik was not the only technological innovation that changed American life. By the mid-1950s millions of American families were raising the rabbit-ear antennas on their first black-and-white television sets. Community colleges quickly took advantage of this new medium.

In September 1956 Chicago City Junior College offered what were probably the first college classes by broadcast television

(Erickson, 1960). With a $475,000 grant from the Fund for the Advancement of Education, the college began a three-year experiment in remote education, offering through local public television such courses as English composition, national government, biology, and social science (Erickson, 1963).

The innovation attracted wide attention. Educators from around the world came to study the Chicago program, and it was written up in *Time* and *Life* magazines. As a result, the program became permanent, and the curriculum was greatly expanded. During its first seven years more than 100,000 students registered for fifty-five different classes. Incredibly, sixty-five students completed their entire associate degree by television (p. 22).

CHANGES AT AAJC

Disregarding the cautious report of the Eisenhower Committee, AAJC pushed for more and larger public community and junior colleges. Jesse Bogue became an evangelist for the junior college movement, preparing the way with predictions of ever larger numbers of new students. Traveling more than a million miles, visiting hundreds of community and junior colleges, writing more than 200 articles for the *Junior College Journal*, teaching dozens of seminars and workshops—Bogue became the most visible figure in the community college movement. He even found time to edit a volume called *American Junior Colleges*, a compendium of information on 600 institutions (Rutledge, 1951, p. 174).

Bogue also served as the AAJC liaison to the federal government. He arranged government meetings for community and junior college leaders, but most often did the lobbying himself (Reed, 1971, p. 97). He fought successfully against interpretations of the Korean GI Bill that shut out vocational students (p. 105) and won the battle to gain draft exemptions for junior college students (p. 107). He campaigned less successfully, however, for community college ROTC and direct federal support for two-year colleges. Whenever a federal agency needed the junior college viewpoint, it called on Jesse Bogue.

Bogue was a man with a mission. He had trouble saying no to any project that could conceivably benefit two-year colleges. Operating a growing national organization as a one-man show, with no professional staff support, by the mid-1950s the energetic executive was becoming increasingly exhausted.

In 1956 the Association undertook a $20,000 fundraising effort to create a public information program. The campaign was designed to promote community and junior colleges as an effective, low-cost alternative to four-year institutions. The targets would be foundations, businesses, and government (Brint & Karabel, 1989, p. 63).

By the Board's summer meeting the entire amount had been pledged. All that remained was to choose a director. The choice was the Association's vice president, Edmund J. Gleazer, Jr., who was vacationing in Norway at the time. Bogue offered him the job by cable and met him on his return in New York. Gleazer, then president of Graceland College in Iowa, asked his trustees for a one-year leave of absence. He would never return.

Gleazer had risen rapidly through the ranks of the Association, partially due to his friendship with Bogue. During his doctoral studies at Harvard, Gleazer had enrolled in one of Bogue's summer courses, and after returning to his duties at Graceland invited Bogue to the campus. Bogue reported his trip to Graceland in glowing terms:

> Under the vigorous leadership of 32-year-old Edmund Gleazer, Jr., Graceland College at Lamoni, Iowa, had recently added two new buildings to the campus of 350 acres.... The College is free of debt and has been since its founding in 1897.... Mr. Gleazer will attend Harvard this summer to continue his studies for the doctorate. (Reed, 1971, p. 118)

Gleazer was elected to the Board of Directors in 1954 and chaired the administration committee. Two years later he was elected vice president.

When Gleazer reported for duty in December 1956, he was given a desk next to Bogue's in the Association's two-room office. A few months later he was elected president of the Association. For a few brief months the two men, AAJC president and chief executive, shared the same cramped office.

In March 1957 Bogue announced that he was ready to retire. The Board offered the position to several old-line leaders of the Association, but in each case, the offer was turned down. Finally the Board decided to use the criteria developed to select the public information program director. Someone happened to note that Gleazer fit those criteria.

In July 1957 the Board unanimously tapped Gleazer as Bogue's replacement. Gleazer would continue as director of the public information program through the end of the year and take over the reins April 1, 1958 (Reed, 1971, p. 119). At Gleazer's suggestion, the title of the position was changed from executive secretary to executive director. William G. Shannon, named as Gleazer's assistant, would handle the commissions on administration and legislation.

Bogue remained as a consultant until his contract ended in August 1958, and a month later joined the education faculty of the University of Michigan. During the fall semester he became "noticeably fatigued" (p. 129). Soon afterward he was diagnosed with leukemia. Nevertheless, Bogue traveled throughout Michigan, creating ties between the university and two-year colleges. He died on February 5, 1960, at the age of seventy, having given a lifetime of service to higher education.

During Bogue's term of office national community and junior college enrollment had increased from 294,475 to 869,720 students. Association membership jumped to more than 500 institutions, and the Association's budget doubled to over $52,000 (Bogue, 1958b, p. 481).

In 1949 the Association contracted with the University of Texas to publish the *Junior College Journal*. James Reynolds, a former student of Leonard Koos, was appointed editor and C.C. Colvert research director. Reynolds and Colvert, both professors at the university, were paid by the institution. AAJC paid half the salary of a secretary and a large portion of the publication's expenses.

After 1955 most of the *Journal's* production costs were taken over by the Association. Colvert was promoted to coordinator of research, serving under the AAJC vice president. Reynolds, however, continued to edit the *Journal* on a volunteer basis. The *Journal's* headquarters remained at the University of Texas until 1962, when it was shifted to Washington. Still not a moneymaker for the Association, the *Journal* in 1960 cost $16,211 to produce but brought in only about $13,500 (Gleazer, 1961a, p. 500).

WOOING THE FOUNDATIONS

Despite their significant growth, two-year colleges had largely been ignored by major foundations. The last major foundation grants had come from the Rockefeller Foundation in the 1930s. Powerful foundations such as Ford, Carnegie, and Kellogg, which had a long history of supporting university and K–12 projects, ignored community and junior colleges.

As the baby boomers approached college age, this attitude began to change. Experts were predicting that high school graduates would double in number during the 1960s and that this wave of students would bring massive growth in two-year colleges. Clearly, existing colleges and universities would not be able to meet the demand. By the late 1950s these predictions were beginning to catch the interest of major educational foundations.

AAJC founded its public information program largely to attract foundation support. As an Association newsletter noted:

> There are now more than 7,000 foundations in the United States. It is believed that face-to-face contacts should be made with the top personnel of many of these foundations.... Publications designed especially for readers in the foundations... should be published and distributed (Reed, 1971, p. 114).

When the program's director, Edmund Gleazer, arrived in Washington in December 1956, he made it his mandate to go around the country and seek out sources of foundation funding. Although slowed at first by the retirement of Jesse Bogue and Gleazer's promotion to executive director, within a year the effort began to pay off (Gleazer, n.d.).

The first grant, for $3,500 from the Fund for the Advancement of Education at the Ford Foundation, supported a conference on community and junior college issues. Held in New York in February 1956, the two-day conference brought together eighteen educational and business leaders to discuss the future needs of two-year colleges. The meeting resulted in a $140,000 grant proposal to the Ford Foundation for training community and junior college administrators and teachers. The foundation turned the proposal down, but the experience derived from seeking the grant led to later, more successful efforts. On the heels of smaller grants, from the US Steel Foundation in 1958 for $10,000 and from the Sears Roebuck Foundation for a booklet on two-year colleges, came the first major grant—from the W.K. Kellogg Foundation. Gleazer (1991) describes the fortunate chain of events leading up to the grant:

> On January 27, 1957, just a month after arriving in Washington, I met with Robert Kinsinger who was consultant in Junior College Education for the National League for Nursing.... Soon after that, I participated in a meeting of the national advisory committee to the ADN program. Bob Kinsinger introduced me to Mildred Tuttle, Director of Nursing Programs at the W.K. Kellogg Foundation. Mildred told me that the Foundation was coming toward the close of support of its Cooperative Program for Educational Administrators, which focused on improvement of public school leadership, and the Foundation was looking for new areas of interest. Possibly one of these could be the junior college. She suggested that if I were in the vicinity of Battle Creek that it might be a good idea to drop in and talk with the officers of the Foundation.... On Wednesday, October 15, my oldest son's birthday, I flew out to Battle Creek.... The next morning at nine o'clock Bob Kinsinger and I were ushered into the office of Emory Morris, President of the Foundation, by Maurice Seay, Director of Educational Programs.

A foundation report described the meeting:

> The meeting began alone with the Foundation's president, Dr. Emory Morris. "Ed" Gleazer told his story so well and so convincingly that he was stopped again and again as other Foun-

dation officials asked to join them. By noon, six Kellogg executives lined the room (W.K. Kellogg Foundation, 1980, p. 32).

Gleazer (1991) remembers the meeting in great detail:

It was a friendly group, but their questions had bite to them. Is the junior college kind of a temporary aberration—an expedient developed to deal with mounting enrollments in post secondary education? Will they all want to grow up to be "regular" colleges—4-year institutions—as soon as this is feasible? Historically they have been related to the secondary schools. Will that be the direction in which they will go? How is a community college different from a junior college? Where does leadership come from? What should be the elements in a program of leadership? How different from programs for 4-year college administration? What are the problems and issues that will confront the growing numbers of junior colleges?

Maurice Seay, a former student of Leonard Koos's who had monitored the junior college movement for years, had become the foundation's primary advocate for junior college funding. At a February 1958 meeting in Washington, Seay proposed funding for university centers to train junior college administrators. The foundation was already funding similar centers for public school administrators under its Cooperative Program for Educational Administration.

The first Kellogg grant, approved in August 1959, provided $1.6 million for Seay's administrative training centers, now called Junior College Leadership Programs (JCLP). Eventually, JCLP centers were established at twelve universities nationwide. The grant also provided $240,000 in direct funding to AAJC. These funds were used to staff and cover expenses for the Association's commissions and to improve the publications program. Thomas Merson of Bakersfield College was brought in to work with the curriculum and student personnel commissions. Elizabeth Reed was named director of publications.

Three years later the Kellogg Foundation provided another $340,000 grant to the Association. Over two decades Kellogg would contribute $29 million to the community college movement. Although less than half these funds were funneled through AAJC, the support of the Kellogg Foundation had a profound effect on the Association. Gleazer (1991) described the initial impression on the AAJC Board:

> By accepting the Foundation grant we were committing ourselves to the maintenance of a new and higher level of operations. It would be expected that as Foundation funds were scheduled to decline over subsequent years that the Association would develop other resources, these would likely include greater income from the membership. There was serious and probing discussion of the implications of accepting such a grant. Now it appeared that this was not a gift. The grant had some strings attached and it was very large in terms of the experience of the Association and the size of its current budget. Was the Association's membership ready for such a big step? Do developments in our field nationally justify our taking a substantial risk? The thoughtful and enthusiastic decision made by that Board meant that AAJC had chosen to enter the "big time." And on that day it passed the point of no return.

During this period the Association also received smaller grants from the General Electric Foundation and the Lilly Endowment.

A FRIEND AT THE OFFICE OF EDUCATION

In 1955 Sebastian V. Martorana, a former AAJC researcher, became the specialist for community and junior colleges in the U.S. Office of Education. With his encouragement the Office of Education began to actively promote federal legislation in support of two-year colleges. Office staff wrote reports on bills, prepared papers for legislative hearings, and answered inquiries from members of Congress. Their efforts paved the way for increased federal support in the early 1960s.

Martorana also acted as a liaison between the U.S. Office of Education and state governments. Diener (1970) explained Martorana's role in the creation and growth of state junior college systems:

159

To states without junior colleges the office provided information on the two-year college concept, on alternative patterns
of organization and financing, and on the establishing of criteria and procedures. For a state with two-year colleges but
no coordinator of their activities, the office offered counsel to
individual institutions. More importantly, it assisted several
state governments in planning the sound development and
coordination of junior colleges. (p. 26)

Martorana planned and organized an annual conference for the
directors of statewide junior college systems. From the first conference, held in Washington, D.C., in May 1957, the office would
continue to sponsor these meetings into the mid-1960s. In 1957
Martorana was promoted to chief of the U.S. Office of Education
state and regional organization branch, where he remained a cham-
pion of junior colleges. He and other staff members defended junior
colleges against the critical statements of the Eisenhower Committee (Diener, 1970).

LOOKING TO THE FUTURE

In 1957 the first products of America's postwar baby boom
reached their teens. Four years later some of them would be entering their first year of college. This wave of students promised to
bring the greatest enrollment increase in junior college history. A
study by the American Association of Collegiate Registrars and
Admissions Officers predicted an unprecedented expansion of student populations. California alone, according to the report, would
see a 230 percent increase in the college-age population by 1970,
and Arizona, Maryland, Nevada, Oregon, and Washington a 150
percent increase. These were not wild predictions, but conservative
estimates, based on postwar birth rates (Bogue, 1954). Planning
such as that demonstrated by Florida caused the realization of these
projections.

By the late 1950s the junior college movement had experienced
seven decades of nearly continuous growth. Clearly, however, the

greatest expansion was yet to come. In February 1957 Jesse Bogue predicted: "The next ten to fifteen years will find our college enrollments doubled" (Bogue, 1957, p. 358). Events of the next decade proved Bogue's prediction an understatement.

STATUS REPORT (1959)

The so-called "tidal wave" of students is now at the very doors of our colleges and universities.

—Jesse Bogue

A t the end of the 1950s America was on the brink of enormous social change. Eight years of Eisenhower conservatism were drawing to a close. Presidential candidate John Kennedy was promising a "New Frontier." In the South civil rights leaders demanded a new world of equal opportunity. These calls for change would have a powerful impact on higher education. Like the GI Bill of the 1940s, these new democratic movements would open college doors to large segments of the public that had been untouched by higher education.

At the same time, the baby boom generation was about to graduate from high school. In the early 1960s this mass of students would descend on colleges and universities. Larger college-age populations and expanded access would combine to create a new era of record growth for higher education. Many of these new students would enroll in two-year colleges, creating the greatest period of growth in community college history.

On the eve of these great changes the Carnegie Corporation of New York sponsored a study of America's two-year college system. The research team was headed by former AAJC president Leland Medsker, vice chair of the Center for the Study of Higher Education at the University of California–Berkeley. For his study Medsker chose the systems of fifteen states, which at the time enrolled more than three quarters of America's two-year college students (Bogue, 1958c; "Junior College Directory," 1959, 1960). His selection included a wide variety of organizational structures, enrollment sizes, and funding mechanisms.

Medsker's study found America's two-year colleges to be diverse in mission, structure, and funding. Several states had built their two-year college system around the California model of local control and partial state funding. In other states two-year colleges were primarily extensions of the state university. In most states, however, two-year colleges had grown up with relatively little systemwide planning.

Likewise the curricula of two-year colleges followed no single pattern. The community college, slowly taking root in many states, offered a comprehensive curriculum. On the other hand, some two-year colleges still offered exclusively university transfer courses; others were simply postsecondary technical centers with no transfer curricula.

Published in 1960 as *The Junior College: Progress and Prospect*, Medsker's findings provided the most complete analysis of state two-year college systems since Walter Eells's *The Junior College* of three decades before. Medsker's publication, in this light, serves well as a status report on America's two-year colleges, on the verge of the New Frontier.

CALIFORNIA

California had the largest two-year college enrollment in America—a claim it had held title to for more than forty years. The state's sixty-three junior colleges were controlled by fifty-six funding districts, most of which were free-standing. Twelve junior colleges, however, were still controlled by unified (K–14) school systems and sixteen by high school districts.

Because California's community colleges were considered a part of the secondary education system, the state department of education oversaw their curricula, academic standards, and finances. Recently a bureau of junior college education had been created to handle these responsibilities. In most ways, however, the colleges were autonomous, answering primarily to the governing boards of their districts.

The largest funding source for California community colleges was local real estate taxes. The district board could assess as much as thirty-five cents for every $100 of property value. The state contribution, based on a complicated funding unit called the average daily attendance (ADA), in 1959 amounted to $125 per ADA. For districts with extremely low property values, the state could increase this appropriation.

State funds were also available for transportation and other special items, but the legislature appropriated no funds for land or buildings. All construction was paid for by the individual districts. In all, state funds accounted for about one-third of college operating expenses (Medsker, 1960, p. 208–209).

The California colleges had a liberal admissions policy. According to the state education code, they were open to any "high school graduate and any other person over 18 years of age who...is capable of profiting from the instruction offered" (p. 210). At most colleges this instruction included a comprehensive mix of transfer, terminal, and adult education programs.

By the fall of 1958 California junior colleges enrolled more than 300,000 students, over two-thirds of whom were part-time or adult education students. About 91,000 students were actually enrolled in full-time degree or certificate programs, thus accounting for nearly 73 percent of all freshmen and sophomores in the state (Tyler, 1969).

FLORIDA

Florida was a relative newcomer to the two-year college movement. The state's Minimum Foundation Law, which had legalized public junior colleges in 1947, though hailed by junior college leaders, had few immediate results. By the mid-1950s there were still only five junior colleges in the state.

The real changes began in the legislative session of 1955 when with strong backing from Governor LeRoy Collins the legislature provided building funds for the existing junior colleges and also established the Community College Council. After a needs assessment process, the council, under the direction of James Wattenbarger, identified twenty-eight areas or districts of the state that needed the junior college opportunity. The council proposed and the legislature approved a planned procedure for building, funding, and governing this statewide network (Wattenbarger, 1957).

The legislation to implement Florida's community college plan was passed by the 1957 legislature. The law created a division of community junior colleges in the state department of public instruction to coordinate and oversee this new statewide system, and Wattenbarger was selected as the first director, a position he held for the next ten years.

Florida's junior colleges could serve one or multiple counties. They were governed by the school board of the county in which the campus was located. In addition, each college had an advisory board, appointed by the state board of education. Unlike California's colleges, however, Florida's junior colleges did not offer free tuition. Full-time students were charged a "matriculation fee" of $37.50 per semester. Students from outside the district could be charged an additional tuition fee.

Most of the colleges' costs were absorbed by the state, through its minimum foundation program, under which funds were provided on the basis of a complicated full-time equivalency formula. By law the counties contributed less than 50 percent of the colleges' budget. In practice, however, some counties provided as little as 10 percent of college costs. The state also provided funds to build college buildings, but the counties were required to provide the site (Medsker, 1960, p. 216). By 1959 the junior college plan was proceeding on schedule. Medsker found that ten districts were already operating and four more had been authorized. In the counties served by these, 75 percent of the first-time-in-college students chose community and junior colleges. Half of the total plan was in operation.

At the beginning of the 1960s, community colleges were rapidly becoming an established part of higher education planning in many states. The rapid growth of this new level of education became phenomenal during the 1960s, with the equivalent of a new community college being established each week. This growth was based on the solid records of educational service that had been demonstrated in these local institutions and in the long-range statewide planning that Florida and several other states had demonstrated during the 1950s (Wattenbarger, 1969a).

GEORGIA

In Georgia most public junior colleges were state-controlled and came under the auspices of the university system. In 1959 there were six of these institutions: three former agriculture schools, located in small rural communities; two schools, located in Savannah and Augusta, that had been locally operated before they were acquired by the state; and a former university branch school.

These public junior colleges answered to the University of Georgia board of regents and its chancellor. The chancellor's staff controlled the colleges' operating budgets and approved requests for new facilities. In other matters the colleges maintained a large amount of autonomy. Each college had its own president, and curricular decisions were usually made internally (Medsker, 1960, pp. 217–218).

Several other two-year schools existed in Georgia. The University of Georgia operated seven branches throughout the state, enrolling 1,277 students. These two-year centers had their own administration and faculty. The Georgia Institute of Technology operated a two-year extension that trained technicians and engineers for certification. Georgia also had nine private junior colleges, two of which were military academies that operated without state funds (p. 219).

In 1958 the legislature authorized any "county, counties, independent school system or other political subdivisions" to establish a junior college (p. 221). The state would provide at least $300 per student to operate these institutions. By 1959 no colleges had been formed under this law.

ILLINOIS

The Illinois junior college system was dominated by metropolitan Chicago. Chicago City Junior College operated six campuses and was planning a seventh. The district's 1957–58 enrollment was 13,659—nearly 80 percent of the state total. The state's eleven other districts operated one college each, with an average of 250 students.

The Chicago colleges were funded and governed by the local school district. These institutions, most of which operated out of buildings of local high schools, offered a university transfer curriculum, including evening classes. Their terminal programs, however, were limited to business, medical technology, and drafting. All other vocational courses were handled by vocational schools and technical high schools. The junior colleges offered few adult education courses, leaving that role to the local high schools (Medsker, 1960, p. 224).

The colleges outside Chicago were also governed by public school districts. Seven of these were operated by high school districts, and the remainder by unitary districts. Primarily university transfer institutions, these schools offered only a few terminal and adult courses (p. 222).

Any Illinois school district that maintained a four-year high school could petition to start a junior college. The request went to the state superintendent, who made a survey of the needs and financial resources of the district. If the survey results were positive, the issue was placed on the district ballot.

In 1959 the legislature approved separate community college districts. A district could be formed in any "territory" with $75 million in property assessments that was not already served by a junior college. Over the next six years three new college districts were founded under this law (Erickson, 1969).

Like most states, Illinois based its junior college funding on enrollment data. The state provided $7.60 per credit hour for any student who enrolled in a course and completed at least half of that course before dropping out. School districts were allowed to levy as much as thirty-five cents per $100 in real estate evaluation for college operating budgets and capital improvements (Medsker, 1960).

Until 1959 Illinois's junior colleges were free for in-district students. In that year the legislature approved a measure to allow tuition charges, but limited these charges to one-third of the prorated cost of operating the college.

In addition, the University of Chicago maintained a two-year branch in Chicago. Southern Illinois University operated a branch in Alton and planned another for East St. Louis. Many two-year college supporters viewed these university branches as a threat to the growth of district junior colleges, reasoning that few communities would approve taxes for a junior college if they could get a state-supported university branch.

INDIANA

Vincennes University Junior College was the only junior college in Indiana in 1959. There were no district junior colleges. The state's thirteen public two-year colleges, all extensions of Indiana University and Purdue University, enrolled more than 14,700 students in credit courses. These off-campus centers received no local financial support and little state support; most of their funding, including building costs, came from student tuition. Consequently, the tuition at these centers was high, even by university standards. At the Indiana University centers students were charged $12 per credit hour, about 60 percent more than on the university's main campus (Medsker, 1960, pp. 228–229).

The Indiana University centers offered the first two years of liberal arts and business degrees. They also provided adult education and special-interest courses on a noncredit basis. Occasionally, the centers would offer upper-division or even graduate courses, but never terminal or vocational certificate courses. They were tightly controlled by the university, with their curricula and operations supervised by the division of university extension. Instructors were

169

approved by corresponding departments at the university's main campus in Bloomington, and every attempt was made to ensure that classes remained identical to those taught at Bloomington. The centers did not have their own chief executive officers, but were managed by directors.

The two-year centers operated by Purdue University offered transfer programs in engineering and science. They also offered terminal technical programs, approved by the Engineers Council for Professional Development (pp. 230–231).

Indiana had no plans for district colleges. Indiana University, however, planned to build new centers in areas not served by any other college (p. 228).

IOWA

While junior colleges expanded nationwide, the Iowa system shrank. During the 1920s towns throughout the state had established junior colleges, often without the students or finances to support them. At its height Iowa had thirty-four public junior colleges, but by 1959 only sixteen remained, and most of those were struggling. Five of these survivors had been forced to close at least once since they were founded. Total public junior college enrollment as of September 15, 1957, was only 2,402 full-time students (Medsker, 1960, p. 232).

Most Iowa junior colleges were situated in small towns. Des Moines, the state's largest city, had no plans for a junior college. All of the Iowa colleges shared facilities with their local high schools, and only three had any buildings of their own. About 84 percent of their instructors also taught in the high school. Because of their small size, these schools had limited course offerings and virtually no vocational programs. Most credit courses were a part of the standard university transfer curriculum. However, many of the colleges offered noncredit programs in the evening.

The funding for these colleges came largely from tuition and local taxes. Tuition ran as high as $90 per semester. After 1949 the state provided funding of twenty-five cents per day for each student, and then, in 1957, increased its support to one dollar per day. These funds applied only to students carrying a twelve-semester-hour class load. There was no state funding for part-time students, buildings, or other capital investment. For these reasons the future of most Iowa junior colleges continued to be uncertain (pp. 232–233).

MASSACHUSETTS

Higher education in Massachusetts was still dominated by private institutions. Its exclusive private colleges and universities attracted students from throughout the nation. The state also had a large number of private junior colleges with dormitories, many of which were former women's finishing schools or liberal arts colleges that had eliminated their upper divisions.

Public junior colleges were legalized by the Junior College Bill of 1948, but this law was little more than an authorization bill and provided no funding. Colleges were supported instead by student tuition and funds from the local school system. In 1957 the state legislature finally appropriated funds for its public junior colleges, with a cap of $100 per student.

In 1958 Massachusetts took the first steps toward creating a real community college system. The governor announced a three-year plan that would provide $24 million to create comprehensive community colleges. Soon afterward the legislature created a fifteen-member board, known as the Massachusetts Board of Regional Community Colleges, and gave this body $1 million in funds to conduct initial planning (Medsker, 1960, pp. 234, 239).

In the fall of 1959 Massachusetts had only four public junior colleges. A decade later the system had grown to thirteen colleges, with more in the planning stage (Taylor, 1969, p. 81).

MINNESOTA

Minnesota had nine small public junior colleges, the largest of which enrolled only 390 students. All but two colleges were housed

171

in local high schools, and each shared some of its faculty. The system had been virtually stagnant for two decades, with no new junior colleges formed since before World War II. There were no junior colleges in the Twin Cities or their suburbs, and none were planned (Medsker, 1960, p. 240).

One problem was opposition from the University of Minnesota, which, in 1959, dominated higher education in the state. As the only state university, it enrolled more than half of all postsecondary students. Although the university president officially favored junior colleges, many alumni and regents felt otherwise: they did not want a large junior college system competing for state funding. Some university leaders wanted to turn the five university-owned agricultural schools into two-year extensions, but junior college supporters feared that such a system might preclude the development of local junior colleges (p. 242).

All of Minnesota's junior colleges were controlled by local school boards. To create a college the school board was required to conduct a needs survey and hold a districtwide election. If the issue received approval by a two-thirds majority, the plan could proceed. The college campus had to be located at least thirty-six miles from any existing junior college or teachers college (p. 241). In this mainly rural state, where few school districts were large enough to support a junior college, the law did not permit multidistrict colleges. Consequently, community colleges remained financially unfeasible for most areas of the state (p. 243).

Initially, Minnesota's junior colleges were supported entirely from tuition and school district revenues. The state provided no funds until 1957, when the legislature appropriated $200 annually for each student, based on average daily attendance. Two years later that amount was raised to $250. Despite this new state support, no new districts had applied for junior colleges by 1959 (p. 241).

Most of Minnesota's two-year colleges were not comprehensive. They primarily offered a university-parallel curriculum, with the notable exception of the public junior college in Rochester, site of the Mayo Clinic, which offered extensive semiprofessional and technical training in health-related fields.

Left, William Rainey Harper

Below, J. Stanley Brown, the innovative principal of Joliet High School who began the school's postgraduate department in 1901. The department later became Joliet Junior College.

Above, George F. Zook, the higher education specialist at the U.S. Bureau of Education who organized the first national meeting of junior college leaders, at which the American Association of Junior Colleges was founded.

Right, Martha McKenzie Reid, first secretary of AAJC, 1920-1923. The position of secretary would evolve into president and CEO of the Association.

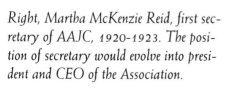

Left, David McKenzie, second president of AAJC, after James M. Wood. The chair of the Board of Directors was known as president in the early days of the Association.

Right, Doak S. Campbell

Below, nine living presidents of AAJC at the Association's 11th annual meeting on November 19, 1930, with Doak S. Campbell, secretary of the organization, at far right. Left to right, they are George F. Winfield, James M. Wood, Louis E. Plummer, H.G. Noffsinger, Lewis W. Smith, Edgar D. Lee, J. Thomas Davis, John W. Barton, and Jeremiah B. Lillard.

Left, Walter Eells, first editor of the Junior College Journal.

Left, Katherine Denworth, president, AAJC, 1938.

Above, Jesse Bogue

Left, Edmund J. Gleazer, Jr.

Right, Norvel Smith, who was elected to the AACJC Board of Directors in 1971. When the Association's nominating committee added three new seats to accommodate more minority representation but failed to nominate a single African American, the Black Caucus presented an entire slate of African American candidates. Smith became only the second African American AACJC Board member — Malcolm Hurst had been elected to the Board in 1970.

Left, Abel Sykes, first African American AACJC Board Chair.

Above, Dale Parnell

Above, Flora Mancuso Edwards, first Hispanic AACJC Board Chair.

Right, David R. Pierce

MISSISSIPPI

Mississippi had fifteen public two-year colleges, funded by fifty-eight counties. Most of these colleges were located in rural areas of the state and had grown out of agricultural high schools. In 1957 these colleges enrolled 8,932 students. State policy prohibited junior colleges in areas that were served by four-year state institutions (Medsker, 1960, p. 245).

Mississippi community colleges offered a comprehensive curriculum, including adult education and vocational programs. Each college attempted to offer one unique vocational program that would attract students from throughout the state. These students could live in college dormitories for $35 per month including meals (p. 247).

In addition to the two-year institutions, Mississippi had one four-year junior college. This college, operated by Meridian County, was based on the 6-4-4 system favored by many early junior college leaders (p. 245).

The statewide system was governed by a seven-member Junior College Commission. This board, composed of the heads of three junior colleges, the University of Mississippi, the State College for Women, and Mississippi State College, plus the superintendent of education, determined the location of new colleges and set standards for admission, curriculum, records, equipment, and facilities. A supervisor of junior colleges in the state department of education, who also served as secretary of the state junior college association, administered the system. Colleges were accredited by a state agency that worked closely with the commission.

Mississippi's junior colleges received about half their funds from the state. For the 1956–57 year the legislature appropriated nearly $4 million for junior colleges, all of which went toward operating expenses or vocational equipment. The state seldom funded buildings or capital improvements. Unlike most other states, Mississippi had no set formula for state support. Colleges were forced to campaign every year for funding. Most Mississippi junior colleges were supported by multicounty districts. State law allowed for bond issues to build or expand college facilities. The districts could levy taxes of three mills to support college operations and the same amount for capital improvements. In reality, none of the districts levied the full six mills (Medsker, 1960, p. 246; Todd, 1962).

NEW YORK

There were seventeen public two-year colleges in New York State: four comprehensive community colleges and the rest technical and agricultural institutes specializing in terminal courses. The coordinating agency for these colleges was the State University of New York (SUNY), which acted as an oversight agency for all higher education in the state (Medsker, 1960, p. 249).

Each of the two-year colleges was sponsored by a local agency— city, county, or school district. The sponsoring agency had broad powers over these institutions, appointing the president, choosing the curriculum, and approving the college budget. In most cases the agency appointed a majority of the college trustees. All of these decisions were subject to the approval of SUNY and the state board of regents. Construction and other capital costs were split evenly between the sponsoring agency and the state, with the sponsoring agency providing about one-third of the operating budget and the remainder coming from student tuition and state appropriations. The exception to this rule was the Fashion Institute of Technology in Manhattan, which was heavily subsidized by the garment industry and charged no tuition (Martorana, 1969; Medsker, 1960, p. 250).

New York also had a large number of private junior colleges, many of which were former women's finishing schools that had converted to junior colleges in the 1920s (Eells, 1931, p. 24). By the late 1950s there were more private two-year colleges in New York than in any other state (Medsker, 1960, p. 255). The influence of these established private colleges may have slowed the growth of comprehensive community colleges.

NORTH CAROLINA

North Carolina junior colleges had changed only slightly since the 1920s. Most of the two-year colleges were still private church-related institutions. In 1929 Eells had reported fifteen such institutions. Thirty years later the number had risen to seventeen. The number of locally supported junior colleges had remained the same—three—but they were now joined by a state-sponsored technical institute (Eells, 1931, pp. 24, 144; Medsker, 1960, p. 256).

In 1957 the legislature finally legalized public two-year colleges by passing the Community College Act, which created procedures for a county to establish a community college. To open a college, county commissioners needed approval of the state board of higher education, backed by a majority vote in a countywide election (Medsker, 1960, p. 259). The Community College Act also provided state funding, through which colleges could receive $3 for each quarter-hour taught, or about $135 annually for an average full-time student. This appropriation drew a strict line between community colleges and technical institutes. The former only received funds for academic courses; the latter could be funded for training in preparation for technical occupations. This formula prevented state funding for comprehensive community college programs. In 1957 the legislature appropriated $1.5 million in matching funds for capital improvements and allowed community colleges to issue bonds to raise their half. Despite the availability of state funds, no new colleges had been formed by 1959.

OHIO

There were no district junior colleges in Ohio. Instead, the state's five universities operated branches in twenty-two cities statewide, enrolling 8,000 students. Substantially different from community colleges, these branches, which operated only evening classes, offered a full four-year curriculum, plus graduate study, and were entirely supported by tuition. This system drove the cost of education beyond the reach of many students. In 1958–59 the full-time enrollment averaged fewer than sixty students per branch. Most of these students were in a two-year teacher training course.

Numerous studies and commissions had indicated the state's need for junior colleges. A 1958 report issued by the Ohio Commission on Education Beyond High School recommended three types of two-year institutions: technical institutes, two-year branches, and two-year colleges. The following year the legislature passed a bill allowing a county, city, or school district to create a two-year technical institute. The measure was later vetoed by the governor. At the end of the decade there was still no provision for public junior colleges in Ohio (Medsker, 1960).

OKLAHOMA

There were thirteen two-year colleges in Oklahoma: six locally controlled, which received no state funds, and seven operated and supported entirely by the state. The state two-year colleges offered both transfer and vocational programs. All but one of these colleges were located in small rural towns. Their 1957 enrollment varied widely, from 280 students to more than 1,200. Tuition, however, was standardized at $104 per year. The state institutions fell into three categories: agricultural colleges, agricultural and mechanical colleges, and junior colleges.

The two agricultural and mechanical colleges were originally mining schools that later added other vocational classes and a university-parallel program. The three agricultural colleges began as agricultural high schools and later added college courses. Like similar schools in Mississippi, these institutions later dropped their high school programs (Medsker, 1960, pp. 264–265).

Oklahoma had two state junior colleges: Oklahoma Military Academy, which offered both high school and junior college (strictly university transfer) programs, and Northern Oklahoma Junior College, a regional institution that offered both transfer and terminal courses. Governed by the Oklahoma Board of Regents, each of these colleges had its own president and administration. Junior college funding was appropriated in a lump sum by the legislature and allocated by the board of regents.

Oklahoma's six local junior colleges all began as high school extensions. In 1959 two were still operating in the local high schools; the rest had moved into facilities of their own. These colleges were financed through tuition charges and revenues from the local school boards. Despite repeated requests, local colleges had received no operating or building funds from the state. At the time of Medsker's study, state aid seemed unlikely (pp. 266–267).

OREGON

The state of Oregon had only two junior colleges. The older and larger of these was the Oregon Technical Institute, located near Klamath Falls. This institution offered postsecondary work in technical, industrial, and agricultural fields (Medsker, 1960, p. 271). It was entirely supported by state and federal funds, and was governed by the state board of higher education. In 1957 the ten-year-old institute enrolled nearly 1,000 students. The other junior college, located in Bend, had been founded in 1949 by the local school district. After 1957 the college received funds from several adjacent school districts and from the state legislature. Still offering only evening classes, the college enrolled about 250 students. A third state-supported two-year college had existed in Portland until 1955, when it was replaced by a four-year institution called Portland State College (p. 268).

Oregon's state colleges and universities offered general extension programs that served some of the functions of a junior college in towns throughout the state. In Eugene and Oregon City the school boards operated vocational schools that included postsecondary courses, charging tuition and offering one- and two-year terminal programs. Their extensive vocational offerings made them similar to the vocational division of a community college (p. 271).

A series of Oregon laws had been passed to encourage the development of junior colleges. A 1959 law allowed the creation of separate junior college districts and increased the level of state funding. Finally, in 1961 the legislature created a statewide community college system. State funding was doubled to $433 per full-time-equivalent student. The state also committed itself to 75 percent of junior college building costs, and the state department of education added an assistant superintendent to administer this system (Pence, 1969, pp. 44–53). Dale Parnell, who would later head the American Association of Community and Junior Colleges (AACJC) for ten years, was an educator and active political figure in Oregon in the 1960s and played an influential role in the creation of the Oregon system.

PENNSYLVANIA

Pennsylvania had a system of twenty-three private two-year colleges and public university extensions. In addition, the state had one unique public-private partnership, Hershey Junior College. This unusual institution, located in Hershey in western Pennsylvania, was financed by funds from the city's largest employer, the Hershey Chocolate Company. Although the college received no tax funds, it was administered by the local school board (Medsker, 1960, p. 273).

The twelve public two-year colleges were extension centers of Pennsylvania State University. All of them offered two-year vocational courses leading to an associate degree, and eight ran an evening technical institute, leading to certificates and technical diplomas. Only half of the centers offered full university-transfer programs, but at least six offered a curriculum comparable to that of a comprehensive community college (p. 274). The admissions standards for transfer programs were much higher than those for the typical community college, standards that also limited the centers' ability to serve local students (p. 278).

The university also offered extension courses in three other locations. University trustees, in fact, intended to expand the existing extension services into a statewide system of "diversified commonwealth campuses" (p. 278). The university centers were managed by a full-time director, who also handled relations with the local community. Even though the system was administered by the general extension division of the university, each center had a local advisory committee. University transfer courses were closely controlled by the academic departments on the main campus. With only about

20 percent of operating costs covered by the university, most of the centers' budgets came from student tuition. Consequently, student costs were far above junior college standards. The host communities were expected to provide a building and pay for any major repairs, which were usually handled through private fundraising drives (p. 274).

TEXAS

Texas had thirty-six public two-year colleges, two of which were sponsored by the Agricultural & Mechanical College of Texas, and the remainder of which were operated by college districts, including countywide districts, multicounty districts, and local school boards.

Texas had the nation's second highest public junior college enrollment, with nearly 35,000 students served by district colleges in 1956. Each of the district colleges offered a university transfer curriculum and a wide variety of vocational and technical programs. Both day and evening classes were available (Medsker, 1960, pp. 379, 382).

The district colleges were supervised by the Texas Council of Public Junior Colleges. The council, actually a division of the state education department and headed by an executive director, set standards and approved colleges for state funding. Its advisory board included the president of each approved public junior college (p. 381).

State funds for district colleges, appropriated on a sliding scale based on full-time-equivalent students, provided for courses that were offered only at state colleges or universities, and excluded many vocational courses. For the 1957 academic year the state's district colleges received over $4.7 million in state funds (pp. 380–381). Districts were allowed to levy taxes amounting to 1 percent of assessed real estate value. In reality, however, most charged less than half that amount. The overall costs of operating all colleges were shared nearly equally by state funding, local taxes, and tuition collections.

WASHINGTON

Washington's ten public junior colleges were a part of the secondary education system and hence controlled by individual local school boards. Multicounty college districts were not allowed by law. Junior colleges were banned from Seattle and other districts that had public four-year institutions (Medsker, 1960, p. 284).

Washington's junior colleges varied considerably in size, from 537 to 1,737 students in 1957. Most of the colleges had their own modern campuses and offered day and evening classes. Annual enrollment fees ranged from $90 to $100 per student.

The colleges received 64.5 percent of their operational funding from the state in 1957. About 20 percent came from local school districts, and the remainder from student fees. The state also contributed to building and capital improvements. On the state level, the colleges were supervised by the director of junior colleges.

Medsker did not choose Washington as one of the fifteen states for his original study. An analysis based on a trip to the state, however, was included in his final report.

WISCONSIN

Wisconsin had no comprehensive community colleges. Instead, it had three separate systems of two-year institutions providing specialized services: fifteen University of Wisconsin extension centers offering only university transfer and adult education courses, sixty city-funded vocational and adult schools offering vocational training, and twenty-three county-funded teachers colleges offering teacher training programs (Medsker, 1960, pp. 286–291).

The university extensions, known as freshman-sophomore centers, were located in major population centers but attracted relatively few students. The system had only about 2,100 students enrolled in credit classes and an additional 2,000 students in noncredit adult classes. The centers also offered lectures, workshops, and other community service activities.

Each center was managed by a director. Statewide coordination was handled by a director of freshman-sophomore centers in the office of university extension. Each of the university's twenty academic departments designated one faculty member to take charge of selecting, orienting, and supervising center faculty in his or her field.

The vocational and adult schools, on the other hand, were operated by local boards. State law specified that any town of more than 5,000 persons could operate such a school, but appropriated little money for the effort. Nearly 85 percent of school budgets came from local taxes and less than 4 percent from the state, with the rest provided by student tuition.

Eighteen of the vocational and adult schools operated only evening programs. The rest offered full-time day programs as well as part-time evening courses. Both one- and two-year programs were available. The largest of these, located in Milwaukee, offered associate degrees in business, graphic arts, telecasting, commercial cooking, and six industrial fields. For the spring semester of 1959 these schools enrolled more than 5,000 students.

Prior to 1959 vocational and adult schools operated on a city-wide basis. In that year the legislature passed a law permitting area districts, which allowed schools to increase their funding base to one or more contiguous counties. The measure was designed to encourage the creation of additional vocational schools and the expansion of existing schools. It did not, however, appropriate any additional state funding. There was no immediate rush to take advantage of this provision.

Teachers colleges, remnants of the normal schools that had once trained teachers throughout the nation, had existed in Wisconsin since the nineteenth century. Extremely small, they enrolled as few as thirty students. They were supported by their counties with some funds from the state.

Together, these three types of institutions offered all the services of comprehensive community colleges. Several bills had been introduced to create local junior colleges, but had failed to gain legislative approval. The legislature instead created a coordinating committee to link all postsecondary institutions. In 1959 this committee recommended against forming local junior colleges, deciding that "educational opportunities of the community college type" should be provided through the existing institutions (p. 294). Although turned down, the proposal became the framework for later successful grants.

SERVING THE TOTAL POPULATION (1960-1969)

There were more people and more people who

wanted to go to college.

— Edmund J. Gleazer, Jr.

T he 1960s was a time of growth and upheaval for American society. It began with the promise of John F. Kennedy's New Frontier and ended with the Vietnam War. In higher education the sixties ushered in a period of historic expansion. A new generation, born to returning World War II veterans, was coming of age. Not only were there more high school students, but a greater percentage of them planned to attend college. Nationwide, colleges scrambled to hire teachers and complete buildings to accommodate the rising tide of students.

Despite optimistic predictions, the decade started on a sour note. Community and junior college enrollment actually shrank during the 1959–60 academic year, to 640,527—its lowest level in six years. The decline was due to twenty-six institutions that added upper-division classes and were dropped from the list of two-year colleges (Gleazer, 1961c, pp. 354–355). The following year was only slightly better. For the moment, the predicted increase in students seemed far away (Gleazer, 1960b, 1960d, 1961b).

URBAN AMERICA GETS JUNIOR COLLEGES

The summer of 1962 marked the seventeenth anniversary of the Japanese surrender. That fall the advance guard of baby boomers climbed the college steps. That phenomenon alone would have caused a significant increase in junior college enrollment. But there were other trends afoot that not only would bring waves of students, but would change forever the nature of the junior college movement.

In the 1960s many of America's urban centers discovered the junior college. By 1961 Chicago already had nine junior colleges, Los Angeles had six, and New York City had five. Twenty-four junior colleges in these and a few other large cities were serving 118,555 students. But in 1960 most junior colleges were in small communities and rural areas, locations not served readily by a university, and many of America's major cities had not yet seen the need. In the 1960s colleges were established in Cleveland, Dallas, Fort Worth, Denver, Detroit, Miami, Phoenix, Philadelphia, Pittsburgh, St. Louis, Seattle, and a host of other urban centers. Chicago, Los Angeles, and New York greatly expanded their already existing systems (Warburton, 1969/1970; Watson & Luskin, 1969/1970). By 1980 sixty-eight colleges in seventeen urban centers were serving 640,770 students (Gernhart, 1981; Gleazer, 1963).

Impressive as these numbers were, they reflected only size. Community and junior colleges created to serve urban areas soon found they were serving the total range of urban populations: affluent and poor, academically talented and deficient, minorities and immigrants, and citizens of all ages. For many in the cities, the local two-year college offered training for jobs, an opportunity to learn English, and access to a college education. No institutions of higher education had ever tried to serve such diversity. There were no models. Community and junior college faculty were forced to be pioneers in the creation of new systems of student services and instructional programs. There was little time to prepare, for as fast as colleges were established, students filled them.

ONE COLLEGE PER WEEK

In 1962 enrollments jumped by 13.4 percent. This was only the beginning. The fall of 1963 set another record, with 927,000 students enrolled nationwide. In a single year New York enrollments increased by 35 percent, and Florida enrollments jumped 31 percent. Recognizing the need, twenty-four states added new junior colleges. By the fall of 1965 nationwide enrollments had reached nearly 1.3 million students. Since the previous year, California's community colleges had gained 57,000 students, New York had added nearly 25,000 students, and fifty new colleges had opened in eighteen states.

Funding from the Korean GI Bill ended in January 1965, but its demise was barely noticed in the barrage of new students. The first veterans of the Vietnam War were also beginning to arrive on college campuses. Other young Americans registered for college classes to avoid the military draft.

While colleges hurried to recruit faculty and build new campuses, the student boom continued unabated. By the fall of 1970 there were 1,091 junior colleges nationwide, an increase of 413 colleges in ten years. After accounting for colleges that were dropped, America had built nearly one community or junior college per week for a decade. Several of these new colleges had opening enrollments of more than 3,000 students (Holt, 1969/1970).

The experts had predicted that enrollments would double during the 1960s. Instead they nearly quadrupled! By the decade's end junior colleges were operating in all fifty states with slightly fewer than 2.5 million students (American Association of Junior Colleges, 1965, 1966; Gleazer, 1961d, 1962, 1963, 1964; Harper, 1967, 1968b, 1969, 1970; Harper et al., 1971).

After the boom had passed, Edmund Gleazer, executive director of the American Association of Junior Colleges, explained the reasons for this historic expansion:

185

There were more people and more people who wanted to go to college. The number of Americans between the ages of 14 and 24 increased by 52% during the 1960s, more than five times the rate of increase of the preceding three decades. And it was this increase in the young adult age group coupled with national social goals and individual aspirations that led to the greatest decade of expansion in the history of post-secondary education. The community college was a significant part of that expansion (1973/1974, p. 6).

THE OPEN DOOR

During the 1960s the concept of the open door college gained near religious importance among community college leaders (Huther, 1971). With hundreds of new campuses, the vast majority of Americans had a two-year college within commuting distance of their home. These colleges had lenient admission requirements and charged little or no tuition. As James Thornton (1972) noted:

> The basic admission policy of many community junior colleges is starkly simple: any high school graduate, or any person over 18 years of age who seems capable of profiting from instruction, is eligible for admission (p. 25).

A 1971 study of two-year college catalogs showed that many colleges did not even require a high school diploma. About 46 percent of the two-year colleges accepted students whether or not they were high school graduates (Thornton, 1972).

The open door even extended to current high school students. In the fall of 1959 Fresno City College began admitting selected test-subject high school seniors into college classes. Without the teachers being told which students were from the high school, these students enrolled in regular college classes and were "in every way treated the same as other college students" (Hansen, 1960, p. 193). During the program's first semester the high school students passed 98 percent of their college courses. Their grades were significantly above the college average. During the 1960s similar advanced placement programs became commonplace, opening the college door to exceptionally talented high school students.

The wide diversity of students coming through the open doors of community and junior colleges included high school dropouts and others with marginal academic achievements, adult students returning to college, and students with limited command of English. To serve these students, most colleges developed remedial programs. Usually, these programs included basic mathematics, grammar, and study skills. Students could enroll in these developmental courses to prepare for the regular college curriculum. With the arrival of new technologies, many colleges opened learning centers that allowed students to work at their own pace.

The greatest threat to the open door policy was rising tuition costs. By 1968 only 18 percent of public junior colleges, primarily in California, offered a tuition-free education. Most others charged over $200 per year. Combined with the cost of books and commuting, rising tuition could create hardships for lower income students (Thornton, 1972, p. 27).

THE JUNIOR COLLEGE TEACHER

The growing enrollments brought about a higher demand for community and junior college teachers. As the decade began there were more than 20,000 full-time junior college faculty nationwide, and this number was expected to double within ten years. Junior college leaders were faced with the need to find not only enough instructors to meet the demand but faculty members qualified to work with the diversity of students who attended.

The *Junior College Journal* ran numerous articles on recruiting new faculty, recommending such sources as retired military personnel and former Peace Corps volunteers ("Colleges Needing Teachers," 1968; Litton & Rogers, 1965). The *Journal's* classified section listed hundreds of teaching and administrative jobs at colleges nationwide. A typical advertisement was placed by Ulster County Community College in New York:

Faculty—September 1965. Accounting/data processing; business administration; English; biology; medical technology/ engineering science; electronic technology/engineering science; physics/physical science.... Master's degree and experience desirable ([Classified Advertising], 1965, p. 46).

The faculty shortage was particularly acute in the fast-growing states of California, Florida, Michigan, and Texas (Gleazer, 1960a). Colleges in these states took out full-page advertisements in the *Journal*, trying to lure instructors to their campus. In one striking advertisement faculty members relaxed under the shade of umbrellas on the sun-drenched campus of Miami-Dade Community College.

The California system was the hardest hit. During the 1950s California's population had grown by one-third. By 1960 the state's junior colleges had 6,597 instructors, and that number was expected to more than double by 1970. To meet these demands, college administrators frequently traveled to the East in search of new teaching talent (Gleazer, 1960a).

Most junior college instructors were former high school teachers. Nationwide, more than 31 percent of new junior college teachers had taught in a high school the year before. In California alone former high school teachers accounted for fully 45 percent of new faculty. Only about 20 percent of beginning faculty came directly from graduate schools.

In most cases junior college salaries were extremely competitive. A 1960 study found that many instructors at public junior colleges had higher average salaries than professors at four-year colleges and universities, with nine- to ten-month instructors making an average of $6,550 a year. Similar instructors at four-year institutions received only $6,430 (D'Amico, 1960, p. 89). The average president of a public junior college made $11,890 a year (Morrison, 1962).

Larger public junior colleges paid the highest salaries. The average eleven- to twelve-month instructor at a small private college, for example, made only $4,960 a year, whereas the same instructor at a public college with more than 2,500 students made $8,150 (D'Amico, 1960, p. 89). The low salaries paid at small private colleges were partially due to location. Most of these schools were located in rural areas of the South and Midwest, where living costs were generally low. The larger colleges, on the other hand, were located in metropolitan areas or in California, where costs and salaries were relatively high. As competition grew, the larger colleges increased their salaries to draw instructors from throughout the nation.

Colleges also offered relatively generous packages of fringe benefits. A 1968 study of public junior colleges found that 99 percent provided a retirement plan, with most plans provided by state employee pension funds. Faculty members were usually required to participate, but could withdraw their contributions if they left the system. More than 90 percent of the colleges offered health and major medical insurance, and 50 percent paid the full cost of health insurance. Nearly all of the colleges offered sick leave at full salary. About 94 percent of public junior colleges reimbursed their faculty for professional travel. Most colleges also offered life insurance. A few even provided unusual benefits such as faculty housing, moving expenses, and personal loans (Roberts, 1968).

As enrollments rose, colleges increased their use of part-time faculty (Guthrie-Morse, 1979). Part-time instructors, many of whom were local professionals and business people, were much more plentiful and easier to find than qualified full-time instructors. They also had several distinctive advantages over full-timers. According to Bender and Hammons (1972), part-time faculty were paid much less than full-time instructors, usually on the basis of semester hours or contact hours. The per-course instructional costs could be half those of a class staffed by a full-time employee. Part-time faculty received no fringe benefits, required no office space, and needed little secretarial help. They did not have long-term contracts, tenure, or other guarantees of employment, and so could be hired for a single course with no further commitment. Because they were usually local residents, they helped to build a relationship between the college and the community. Finally, part-time faculty taught weekend and evening classes that were difficult to staff with regular faculty members. By the end of the decade more than 38 percent of all community college faculty were adjunct, part-time employees (p. 21). Although most part-timers taught only one course per semester, they had become an indispensable part of the junior college faculty.

A DECADE OF INNOVATIONS

The 1960s was a decade of change, both in American society and in America's community and junior colleges. The civil rights, antiwar, and women's rights movements changed the national self-image and the educational aspirations of many American citizens. Technology continued to advance with ever-increasing speed. Breakthroughs in computers, automation, and telecommunications changed the American workplace. As the workplace changed, so did the educational needs of the American worker. A trend began that would continue unabated into the 1990s—high unemployment of unskilled workers and a shortage of workers with technological training. Businesses and industries discovered that continuous change was necessary if they wished to remain competitive and that their employees needed continuous retraining to cope with new technology.

Americans were discovering their local community colleges, and community colleges were discovering the diverse educational needs of their communities. The colleges were also learning to harness the new technologies to provide more educational opportunities. These developments sparked changes at every community and junior college campus in the nation. Some of these changes were passing fads; others became permanent fixtures. Those discussed below are a small sampling of innovations from colleges throughout the nation.

Pensacola Junior College in Florida became the first two-year college to use a nuclear reactor. The Atomic Energy Commission licensed Pensacola to use fissionable materials in a subcritical nuclear reactor in its electronics program (Gleazer, 1960c, p. 112).

Bronx Community College in New York installed video cameras in eight hospital rooms used for nurse training. Using this network instructors could monitor several students without actually being in the room.

The St. Louis Junior College District in Missouri used computers to plan three new college campuses. The technology was provided by the McDonnell Automation Center, a division of nearby McDonnell Aircraft Corporation. The computers determined the number of rooms by various sizes and uses that should be built on the new campuses (Cosand & Tirrell, 1964).

Orange Coast College in California operated a push-button lecture hall. The speaker's podium was equipped with a television and screen, wireless microphone, electronic pointer, slide, filmstrip, opaque and movie projectors, tape recorder, and turntable. Lectures were videotaped for viewing in the college library.

Daytona Beach Junior College in Florida offered a radio counseling service called *Profiles in Education*. The program paired a student with a professional in the student's career field to discuss the rewards and pitfalls of that field for the listeners of WNDB radio ("Daytona Beach," 1969).

Harford Community College in Maryland offered master's degree programs in education and business under the supervision of Towson State College, George Washington University, and the University of Maryland. Most of the instructors, however, came from the Harford faculty ("M.A. Degree," 1971).

Chicago City College published an American Indian history handbook and a Black studies directory. These publications were designed to help public school teachers present an accurate account of minority history (Shabat, 1969/1970, p. 13).

Cuyahoga Community College in Ohio was another pioneer in African American studies. The college formed an ad hoc curriculum committee to explore new offerings in this area and was developing a special certificate in Black studies (Decker, 1969/1970, p. 15).

Stephens College in Missouri developed a long-distance lecture system. The system, which used an amplification unit attached to a normal telephone line, allowed special guests, including authors, labor leaders, a governor, editors, and business executives, to address college classes. Students could speak to their guests through microphones.

Santa Fe Junior College in Florida offered a unique air pollution technology program. Students engaged in hands-on pollution mon-

191

itoring with the local health department (Fordyce & Bromley, 1969/1970, p. 49).

Seattle Community College acquired a 189-foot boat to use as a "floating classroom." The boat was used for courses in marine engines, navigation, marine refrigeration, and marine cooking (Erickson, 1969/1970, p. 52).

San Bernardino Valley College in California had its own television station. The station, assembled by college students, provided up to twelve hours of educational programming per week and included television courses like those pioneered at Chicago City Junior College in the 1950s (Johnson, 1964b, p. 14).

Delta College in Michigan began scoring tests with an IBM 360 model 40 computer to provide prompt individualized reports of student performance. This innovation quickly became a standard practice at all levels of American education (Carlyon & Wolf, 1969/1970, p. 22).

Peralta Junior College District in California offered basic encounter groups for its students. In these group therapy sessions for problem students, a counselor led twelve students at a time through "intensive interactions to dilute the psychological barriers which impede progress in classroom situations" (Dunn, 1969/1970, p. 43).

Foothill Junior College in California offered a unique audiotutorial biology course in which students performed laboratory experiments to tape-recorded instructions. Students saw the instructor only once per week for a discussion session (Flint & Ewing, 1969/1970, p. 24).

Florida Atlantic University opened in 1964 as the nation's first upper-division university with a curriculum beginning with the junior year. This innovation fulfilled William Rainey Harper's dream that junior colleges would allow universities to drop their lower divisions (Snyder, 1963).

TRAINING COLLEGE LEADERS

Soon after World War II universities began to sponsor seminars and workshops for junior college administrators and faculty. By the late 1940s nearly forty institutions were operating such programs. AAJC promoted these workshops and often assisted with the instruction (Reed, 1971, p. 77). One widely recognized six-week annual seminar, held at Harvard University in 1949, attracted thirty-three participants from fourteen states (p. 87).

As community and junior colleges changed and developed in unique and innovative ways to provide for the educational needs of their communities, leaders were wanted who had the skills and training necessary to advance these institutions. Yet, despite the success of summer seminars, few universities offered graduate programs specifically designed for junior college leaders. In 1959 the W.K. Kellogg Foundation announced a program that would fill this gap: it would provide $1.6 million to begin a junior college leadership program (JCLP) at ten major universities.

The first JCLP began with a chance visit to AAJC headquarters by B. Lamar Johnson of the University of California at Los Angeles. Johnson had come to discuss his recent tour of overseas junior colleges with Edmund Gleazer, who, in the course of the conversation, mentioned the new grant. A report by the foundation (W.K. Kellogg, 1980) noted:

Gleazer's news of the Foundation decision was just what Johnson had long desired. He took immediate steps to initiate the JCLP at his home institution.... The total package that Dr. Johnson and his staff prepared with the help of the advisory council became a prototype for the Junior College Leadership Program. It included workshops, seminars, summer conferences, pre-service and in-service training, internships and laboratory materials about the entire junior college community (pp. 34–35).

Johnson unveiled his new program at the Western Conference on Junior College Administration held at UCLA in July 1961. The conference "marked the beginning of the first organized systematic effort of this kind in the preparation of junior college administrators" (American Association of Junior Colleges, 1967, p. 6).

The University of California at Berkeley and Stanford and Columbia universities soon joined the program. Eventually, centers were added at Florida State, Michigan State, and Wayne State universities and the universities of Colorado, Florida, Michigan, Texas, and Washington (W.K. Kellogg, 1980).

The JCLPs were given continuity by the AAJC's commission on administration, a Kellogg-funded national advisory board for the programs, whose role was to provide public relations and publications, recommend research areas, hold meetings, and evaluate program results (Giles, 1961).

The JCLP centers were pioneers in community and junior college research and administrator training. Training thousands of future leaders, they thrived during the boom years of the movement, only to be gradually phased out beginning in 1972. In most cases the programs were taken over by their host universities (W.K. Kellogg, 1980, p. 35).

THE LEAGUE FOR INNOVATION IN THE COMMUNITY COLLEGE

Culminating the "Decade of Innovations" and growing out of a Kellogg-funded junior college leadership program was a new community college organization dedicated to innovation (Fox, 1989). Its primary sponsor was B. Lamar Johnson. In addition to the hundreds of doctoral students who studied under him in his leadership program at UCLA and went on to become leaders in community colleges across the nation, Johnson (1964a) will be remembered for two major contributions to the community college movement: his 1964 landmark book *Islands of Innovation* and his role in the creation of the League for Innovation in the Community College. Johnson's concern for innovation and his work leading to the formation of the league has been described as follows:

In *Islands of Innovation*, B. Lamar Johnson...described representative innovations and experiments in the utilization of faculty services in American community colleges.... Despite citation of these innovations, Johnson lamented that although most of the colleges included in the survey were selected because of their reputation for innovative practices, most of the practices were found in a scattering of colleges only.

Johnson...coined the term *islands of innovation* to refer to the clusters of community colleges or departments within colleges that engaged in instructional experimentation and innovation. He issued the call for an increase in focus on cooperative efforts among colleges, for conferences and publications to report and discuss innovation, and for "bold and imaginative thinking at all levels" in community colleges (Johnson, 1964[a], p. 14). Johnson planted the seeds for the inception of the League for Innovation in the Community College with these ideas. (Fox, 1989, pp. 45–46)

Johnson had written earlier, "Assembling at the nation level a group of heretics, 'young Turks,' to share daring and often unworkable ideas and dreams might well point to the needed directions and opportunities for junior college development" (Johnson, 1964b, p. 15). In July 1967 he did just that. He invited a group of community college leaders he considered innovative to a conference, "The Experimental Junior College," out of which grew a task force that resulted in the formation of the League for Innovation in the Community College in 1968.

The charter members of the League for Innovation were twelve colleges whose chief executive officers were nationally respected leaders in the community and junior college movement: Oscar Shabat, Chicago City Colleges, Illinois; Norman Watson, Coast Community College District, California; Bill Priest, Dallas County Community College District, Texas; Donald Carlyon, Delta College, Michigan; Calvin Flint, Foothill College, California; Edward Simonsen, Kern Community College District, California; Stanley Warburton, Los Angeles Community College District, California; Walter Coultas, Los Rios Community College District, California; John Dunn, Peralta Junior College District, California; Joseph Cosand, St. Louis Junior College District, Missouri; Joseph Fordyce, Santa Fe Junior College, Florida; and Ed Erickson, Seattle Community College District, Washington.

From the beginning the League for Innovation, an exclusive organization with a fixed number of members, was widely criticized as an elitist organization made up of colleges supposedly opposed to elitism. Terry O'Banion, current executive director, described the founding of the League for Innovation and its elitist image:

> In 1968, two national community college organizations were created that flew in the face of the egalitarian values of the community college movement. The League for Innovation in the Community College and Group Ten for the 70s were created as selective, exclusive organizations limiting their membership to a small group of community colleges. Their creation was viewed by some as brazen, by others as clearly elitist. In half jest, one community college president, informed about the exclusive nature of the League, vowed to create "The League for Tradition" as a counter movement....

To the extent that anecdotal history, passed through an informal twenty-five-year history is correct, the League was founded not so much on the basis of elitism as on the basis of a commitment to working together in a small group to accomplish common tasks. Founding members to the present day remind those who are currently involved "We wanted to keep it small enough so that we could sit around a common table and share ideas and get things done" (O'Banion, n.d., pp. 2, 4).

Today League for Innovation membership is still held to twenty colleges that show evidence of meeting the League's membership criteria. Even though dues are quite high, several times those of the American Association of Community Colleges, there has always been a waiting list of colleges wishing to join. Membership requirements have been strictly adhered to, and over the years several member colleges have either voluntarily resigned or had their membership removed.

The League for Innovation in the Community College has done exactly what Johnson called for. It has encouraged innovation and experimentation among its members, and the outcomes have been shared widely with community colleges throughout the nation. Its partnerships with businesses and industries, notably computer companies, have provided grants allowing member colleges to pioneer the use of computers in instruction and student personnel services. Its partnership with the University of Texas has acquired sizable funding from the W.K. Kellogg Foundation to establish leadership training programs involving personnel from hundreds of colleges, both member and nonmember. Through its support of this program, the Kellogg Foundation has continued the work it began in 1959 with the junior college leadership program. Thousands of community college faculty and administrators have attended the League's leadership conferences, and many more receive League publications ("Mexicans to Train at League Colleges," 1980).

PROVIDING FOR MINORITIES

The 1954 Supreme Court decision in *Brown v. Board of Education* increased the speed of desegration in public education. This decision became the law of the land coincident with a movement in many states to expand educational opportunity, particularly to African American and other minority populations. College attendance for African American students was heavily concentrated in the South in institutions serving almost exclusively this minority. In a lecture on the history of higher education for African Americans in the United States, Pifer (1973) made no mention of junior college contributions except to indicate that there were twenty minority two-year colleges in existence at the time.

In 1933 Lane identified nineteen junior colleges for African Americans: six in Texas, three in North Carolina, and ten others scattered among eight other southern states. He reported that these were both public and private institutions and that the oldest was a church-related junior college in Mississippi established in 1895, Mississippi Southern Christian Institute. Ford (1936) indicated that African Americans should "demand the public junior colleges for the masses in preference to the state universities for the classes," and predicted that the junior college would be the "cornerstone of the Negro's education haven" (p. 594). This anticipated growth in junior college education for African Americans did not occur, how-

197

ever. Walker reported twenty-one such junior colleges in existence in 1950, with only eight accredited at the time. By 1958, according to Walker, this number had dropped to six. A brief increase developed after 1958 when the Florida community college program began. Today there are no public junior colleges operating for African Americans and very few, if any, private ones.

Ford's promotion of junior colleges as an educational boon to African American students was not typical of later educators. Coombs (1973a, 1973b, 1973c, 1973d, 1974), in a series of articles in *Change* in the early 1970s, made no mention of such colleges. Nor did the National Association of State Universities and Land Grant Colleges in its 1974 factbook on historically Black public colleges. In his history of Negro education in the South since 1619, Bullock (1967) does not include either "junior college" or "community college" in the index. These omissions do not seem to be accidental, nor are they the result of poor scholarship. Most students of African American higher education have not considered the community or junior college a viable opportunity for minority students, although they recognize the segregated two-year college as an especially poor substitute (as accreditation reports seem to indicate). Those who still defend and support the existence of historically Black four-year colleges and universities do not recognize or value historically Black junior colleges with equal enthusiasm.

During the years when community colleges were being established at the rate of one a week, several of the southern states, in an attempt to expand educational opportunities for African American youth, established "predominately Black" junior colleges, often in connection with an existing high school—a procedure that had been followed quite often in junior college development in general. This expansion coincided with a growing educational concern for a statewide approach to a system of community colleges.

Florida is a case in point. During the 1950s and early 1960s, as new community college districts were being established, twelve Florida districts chose to establish two colleges each, one predominantly White and one predominantly Black. Florida's first Black public junior college, Booker T. Washington Junior College in Pensacola, had been created in 1949 as part of the same district that operated Pensacola Junior College. When Florida authorized its second Black public junior college, Gibbs Junior College, in 1957, there were only nineteen predominantly Black junior colleges in the United States, six of which were public. By 1962 ten more of the new Florida districts established predominantly Black junior colleges. Of these twelve colleges, Gibbs Junior College in St. Petersburg was the largest, with a peak enrollment of 991 (Smith, 1991). The AME church also operated a private Black junior college, Edward Waters College, in Florida during this period.

In 1960 the pattern of opening two colleges in each district was broken when Dade County Junior College (later to become Miami-Dade Community College) was established as a single county college. New districts began to follow Dade County's lead, and in previously formed districts between 1963 and 1967, the predominantly Black junior colleges were disestablished even more rapidly than they had been established. The colleges were reorganized as campuses of other larger district community colleges, and the process of integration eradicated their separate identities.

A study of African American higher education in 1966, supported by a grant from the U.S. Office of Education, pointed out the shortcomings of these colleges and encouraged integration:

> ...discussions with Negro specialists in this field invite the conclusion that the Negro junior college structure should be abandoned and a strenuous effort made to integrate Negroes fully into the regular two-year system which show signs of being a stimulating and enriching experiment in American education (Robbins, 1966, pp. 48–49).

The extension of educational opportunity had been a concern of the community college leadership since the early days of the junior college movement. Minority leaders, however, in most cases had not favored the community college as providing an educational opportunity for African American students even in integrated institutions. As Godwin (1970) pointed out, two-year colleges needed to adopt specific "action programs" to encourage recruitment of minority students. The establishment of Black junior colleges was not the answer, either. As Morris (1991) observed, "The toughest battles and most vocal challenges came from black ministers, teachers, doctors and civil-rights leaders who thought the black community colleges promoted segregation" (p. 1C).

Obviously, the establishment of these specific colleges did not provide enough encouragement for minorities that had not been, historically at least, active participants in higher education (Gilbert, 1979a). Other and more innovative solutions, such as described by Clarke and Ammons (1970), were needed in order for community colleges to better serve this special population.

SLOW GROWTH FOR PRIVATE COLLEGES

By 1960 private colleges accounted for only 13 percent of all junior college enrollments. Most of these 273 institutions were small schools with fewer than 400 students. Nearly two-thirds of private junior colleges were church affiliated, with sixty alone sponsored by the Roman Catholic church. There were also twenty-eight Baptist, twenty-four Methodist, and fifteen Lutheran institutions.

The boom of the 1960s nearly bypassed private junior colleges. By the fall of 1969, only 244 of these institutions were left. Their total enrollment had dropped for three straight years to end the decade at 134,779 students (Harper, 1970). Private junior colleges also lost out on most federal funding programs, and their role in AAJC was increasingly eclipsed by the larger public schools. Many private college leaders felt that they needed an organization that could speak for their unique interests. Responding to their plight, AAJC in 1968 conducted a study of the problems and concerns of the nation's private junior colleges, and issued a report, authored by Kenneth MacKay, recommending that "the private colleges establish a steering committee for a purpose of giving leadership and direction to the cause of the private junior college" (Gernhart, 1969, p. 42).

The following year a group of private junior college leaders founded the National Council of Independent Junior Colleges under the aegis of AAJC. The council, partially funded by AAJC and given an office in Association headquarters, was opened to

AAJC member colleges that were accredited or candidates for accreditation.

The council held its first regular meeting in October 1969 at Sullins College, Virginia. The meeting attracted representatives from sixty-seven colleges in twenty-seven states, who pledged $150,000 over a three-year period to support council operations. Most of these funds went to hiring a full-time executive director (Gleazer, 1970). Council members agreed that their most pressing job was to seek a greater voice in formulating future federal programs (Gernhart, 1969).

THE GLOBAL MOVEMENT

As early as 1937 AAJC expressed interest in international education. Eby (1937), in his speech to the seventeenth annual meeting of the Association, called for four emphases in the junior colleges: to provide for youth who are shut out from the ranks of labor; to prepare citizens to live in a society that is dependent upon social equality; to maintain educational opportunity until vocational competence is achieved; and to include international education as a part of the total curriculum (p. 423).

In February 1970 AAJC sponsored an international assembly in Honolulu that attracted educators from eighteen nations in Asia, the Pacific, the Middle East, and North America (Carroll, 1989; Yarrington, 1970). The message of this conference was clear. Junior colleges—the great American invention—had spread throughout the globe. The largest foreign junior college systems at the time were in Canada and Japan, with a combined enrollment of nearly 170,000 students.

The Japanese junior college system began in April 1950, when Walter Eells reorganized Japan's 599 three-year colleges into 181 comprehensive community colleges (Eells, 1951, p. 3). By 1960 there were 289 of these institutions with an enrollment of 81,528 students. Some of the colleges, primarily terminal institutions, offered the usual two-year curriculum, while others offered three-year programs (Gleazer, 1961e, p. 117). Most students majored in academic fields, such as fine arts, literature, philosophy, and history, but few transferred to a university (Walker, 1970).

Japan's junior colleges operated under article 109 of the School Education Law, which unfortunately branded them as temporary higher institutions and thus undermined their credibility. This temporary status was not changed until July 1964 ("Japanese Diet," 1964). Another problem for Japanese junior colleges was their designation as *tanki-daigaku*, or "short-term colleges." This designation lowered their perceived status among educators and the public. Some elitists referred to them as "half colleges" (Watanabe, 1964).

In Japan private junior colleges, primarily women's schools— over 72 percent of their daytime students were female—were much more popular than government-supported institutions. In 1960 the country's 214 private colleges enrolled nearly 80 percent of junior college students. Private colleges could be ten to twenty times as expensive as public institutions, with tuition running as high as 200,000 yen, then about $560 (Walker, 1970).

Japan's national government operated twenty-eight junior colleges. These male-only institutions had a combined enrollment of only 3,100 students in 1963. Local governments operated twenty-five junior colleges, which enrolled 5,380 students of both sexes. Students at public junior colleges paid tuition as low as 8,100 yen, then about $23.

Canada developed a diverse system of two- and three-year colleges. By the fall of 1969 there were 106 of these institutions, most of which were less than ten years old. About 80 percent of the colleges were funded by provincial governments. Data from 96 of these showed a total enrollment of 85,933 students, of which nearly 70 percent were male (Campbell, 1969, p. 44).

In 1966 the Canadian Commission for the Community College was formed. Many of the commission's early operations were funded by the W.K. Kellogg Foundation. Two years later the commission sponsored a national meeting of community colleges in Ottawa, at which delegates created the Canadian Community College Association (Shannon, 1971a).

Because they were oriented toward community service, the various types of Canadian two-year colleges were classified under a generic name—community college—even though actual institution names did not always include the term "community college." Unlike American community colleges, however, none of these institutions granted a degree. The nature of their curricula varied greatly, for nearly half of these colleges were actually technical institutes, and most of the others offered a combination of transfer and vocational programs.

Ontario operated a system of technical institutes called Colleges of Applied Arts and Technology, or CAATs. The system was created by a 1965 provincial law. Four years later there were twenty such institutions, each controlled by a local board of governors that acted as a crown corporation and held responsibility for the college's operation and development. Statewide coordination was provided by a fifteen-member council of regents (Campbell, 1969, p. 46).

Each CAAT was divided into three divisions: applied arts, business, and technology. The colleges offered no university-parallel programs, and few of their students ever transferred, but they did offer extensive evening courses, designed for part-time and employed students.

Quebec developed a system of postsecondary schools called *collèges d'enseignement général et professionnel*, or CEGEPs. These colleges, created by the General and Vocational College Act of 1967, were not all new institutions, but were built around the province's old classical colleges. Twenty-three French language CEGEPs were in operation by 1969, and an English language college was preparing to open. Entirely supported by the provincial government, they charged no tuition.

The CEGEP curriculum included university transfer courses as well as two- and three-year vocational programs. When the colleges were formed, it was anticipated that more than 70 percent of the students would elect to take occupational training. In reality, the opposite took place. By 1969 more than three quarters of CEGEP students had enrolled in university-parallel courses.

British Columbia legalized community colleges in its Public Schools Act of 1958. These two-year colleges could be sponsored by a single school district or a consortium of districts. To be established, each new college required a majority vote of the participating districts. By the fall of 1968 four colleges were established and two more were scheduled to open the following year. These six colleges were sponsored by forty school districts, but most of their operating budget and capital funding came from the provincial government (p. 44).

By enacting the Colleges Act in 1969, Alberta created a provincewide system of junior colleges governed by the Alberta Colleges Commission. Before this time most junior colleges had been affiliated with local school boards. This measure put them under an independent board of governors, and it replaced local tax support with provincial funds. In the fall of 1969 Alberta had five public junior colleges, all designed to offer both vocational and university transfer programs. There were also three private church-related colleges in the province.

Canada's other provinces did not have a unified system of community colleges. There were, however, individual junior colleges and technical institutes in Newfoundland, Nova Scotia, Prince Edward Island, and Saskatchewan (p. 48).

Chile established a system of five university colleges in remote areas of the country between 1960 and 1965. The colleges, built with loans from the Inter-American Bank, were operated by the University of Chile. Their curricula, similar to those of comprehensive community colleges, included intermediate-level career education, general education, and academic studies. Instructors were trained at the University of California–Berkeley, under the supervision of Leland Medsker, with funding provided by the Ford Foundation (Jacobsen, 1968, p. 10).

From the beginning, the university colleges ran into trouble with the national university system. Their graduates could transfer to the university but were not given any unit credit for the work they completed at the college (p. 10). By 1964 only three colleges with 1,201 students remained. The following year the university colleges were changed into five-year university branches, thus ending Chile's first experiment in public junior colleges.

The University of California also fostered the junior college movement in Colombia. In 1967 the Colombia Association of Universities and Berkeley issued a national higher education plan recommending the establishment of colleges called *institutos univer-sitarios*. Their curriculum would include general education and pre-professional education programs in the behavioral and social sciences, the natural sciences and mathematics, and the humanities and arts, plus vocational, adult, and remedial programs (Jacobsen, 1968, p. 12).

Following this report the Colombiano de Especialización Tecnica en el Exterior arranged to convert three existing institutions in Bogotá, Medellín, and the state of Santander del Sur into *institutos universitarios*. Sixty faculty and five administrators from these institutions went to Berkeley for training. Their studies included an internship at a California community college. Matthews (1982) concluded that colleges similar to Colombia's *institutos universitarios* had also assisted in democratizing Venezuelan higher education.

Jordan had a network of six junior colleges, all government-operated institutions controlled by the Ministry of Education. Four of these colleges were dedicated to teacher training, two for men and two for women. Another college specialized in agriculture. The sixth college, dedicated to business administration, was captured by Israel during the 1967 war (Gilliam, 1969).

Ceylon (now Sri Lanka) established six junior university colleges in January 1969. As even admission operations for these govern-ment-funded and -controlled colleges were centralized, students had to apply to the National Council on Higher Education, indi-cating their preferences, and were assigned to a specific college. The primary founder of this system, I.M.R.A. Iriyagolla, was inspired by junior colleges in the United States and Japan (Iriyagolla, 1969, pp. 26–27). Fred Kintzer (1970), a professor at the University of California–Los Angeles, contributed greatly to this development, as he later did with a similar program in Kenya (Kintzer, 1989).

The first junior college in the Dominican Republic opened in February 1966. The new college, located in Santo Domingo, was founded by a business group, the Acción Pro-Educación y Cultura. Much of its initial funding came from the Ford Foundation and American foreign aid. Technical advisers from Bryant College in Rhode Island organized the college curriculum. During its first six months of operation, the college's enrollment jumped from 141 to nearly 400 students. (Green & Cavallo, 1969, p. 31).

Over the years many of these community and junior college programs begun in other countries failed or were abandoned by their sponsoring countries. Seeds were sown, however, that continue to germinate now and again as many nations around the world recognize the need for expanded educational opportunities (Martinez, 1982).

NEVADA MAKES FORTY-NINE

Nevada was one of the last states to establish a community college system (Wattenbarger, 1969b). The founding of the Nevada system was due primarily to the determined citizens of Elko. For years many of Elko's 10,000 residents had talked about establishing a junior college, but two things stood in their way: financing and state approval. In 1967 the town raised $50,000 and hired a college president. When the legislature soon after legalized junior colleges but appropriated no money, the town was left with approval for a college that did not exist (Lein, 1970).

Billionaire Howard Hughes brought the idea back to life by contributing $250,000. The publicity surrounding the Hughes gift caused the Nevada legislature to relent, and in 1969 the legislature agreed to fund the college at $1,000 per full-time-equivalent student. Elko Community College was dedicated in July 1969 and began classes in a former elementary school. This humble opening had historic importance. Seventy-seven years after it began, the junior college movement had a foothold in forty-nine of the fifty states.

THE ASSOCIATION PROSPERS

AAJC became the national center for research and studies relating to community and junior colleges, and the host of annual meetings featuring the most respected and recognized leaders in the movement: William C. Bagley, Walter C. Eells, Robert M. Hutchins, Charles H. Judd, Grayson N. Kefauver, Leonard V. Koos, Earl J. McGrath, Homer P. Rainey, George F. Zook, and many others. These scholars made speeches, reported research, and urged the colleges to implement the philosophy that represented the movement.

AAJC took its greatest strides during the 1960s. By the decade's end it was one of the best funded educational associations in the nation, with a membership of more than 1,000 institutions. With this growth came increasing prestige and funding from foundations and the government. This new prestige was evident in the expansion of the AAJC budget and staff. As late as 1956 the Association had only one professional employee, the executive secretary, who operated the Association out of a two-room office in the American Council on Education headquarters. In 1960 its membership income was still only $51,000 per year (Gleazer, 1961a).

By 1970 dramatic changes had taken place. The Association had moved into its own Washington headquarters at One Dupont Circle, the full-time headquarters staff had risen to twenty-eight professionals, and membership dues were bringing in more than $273,000 a year. When combined with income from publications, foundation grants, and special projects, this amount grew to $1.8 million.

A revised constitution was approved at the 1965 convention. The revision added three members to the Board of Directors. It also removed the requirement that Board members come from a specific geographic area (American Association of Junior Colleges, 1967, p. 12). The commission structure, however, remained largely unchanged. The five operating committees that Jesse Bogue created in the 1940s were now called commissions. With the exception of the adult education committee, which had been replaced with an instruction commission, their names and functions remained essentially the same (Colvert & Littlefield, 1961).

With the constitutional changes came a new statement of purpose. It seems awkward and is phrased in legalistic terms; according to an AAJC (1967) report, the statement was carefully worded to meet the requirements of the Internal Revenue Code:

Pursuant to these purposes, the Association shall promote the sound growth of community and junior colleges and shall help create in them an atmosphere conducive to learning. Thus we will direct our activities toward the development of good teaching, suitable curriculums, effective administration, appropriate student services, and communication with local, state and national communities. We believe that through our mutual efforts we can advance these goals (p. 17).

Despite these changes, a large portion of the two-year college community still had no voice in the Association. Nearly all AAJC directors and officers were college presidents and White males. Faculty members, ethnic minorities, and women were seldom represented on the Board. In fact, there had been only two female presidents in Association history and none since 1952. These inequities would lead to protests and a major reorganization during the next decade.

In January 1962 James W. Reynolds reluctantly stepped down as editor of the *Junior College Journal*. Reynolds had edited the publication for fourteen years as a part-time volunteer, producing the magazine in his basement (Reynolds, 1962, p. 183). When the publication was moved to AAJC headquarters in Washington, he was replaced by a full-time editor and paid staff, funded primarily by grants from the W.K. Kellogg Foundation (1980, p. 32).

The new editor, Roger Yarrington, changed the plain scholarly appearance to a glossy magazine format, with photographs, graphics, and an eye-catching layout ("Journal Circulation," 1968). The Association hoped that the new format would expand its circulation (Gleazer, 1963). It was not disappointed. By the end of the decade the *Junior College Journal* had increased its circulation from 7,500 to to more than 42,000 copies (American Association of Junior Colleges, 1969).

In addition to the *Journal*, the Association produced two newsletters: *PR Exchange* and *Research Review*. The latter was published in cooperation with the ERIC Clearinghouse for Junior Colleges (Gleazer, 1972a). The Association produced several other newsletters and publications under foundation grants.

A RUSH OF FEDERAL AID

Traditionally, junior colleges had been shortchanged in federal funding. Congress preferred to spend vocational funds on local high schools and technical centers. Higher education programs, such as those funded by the National Defense Education Act, went primarily to universities. Because junior colleges could not mount the lobbying effort of secondary schools or universities, their needs often fell between the cracks of federal funding.

In the 1960s junior colleges finally began to gain federal attention, owing in part to increased enrollments and relentless lobbying by the AAJC. At its 1961 convention in Washington, for example, the Association successfully prevailed upon the secretary of health, education, and welfare to deliver the keynote address. The 572 delegates, at the behest of the Association, visited their legislators and federal agencies, drumming up support for junior college legislation (Gleazer, 1961a).

The first major success came in December 1963 when President Lyndon Johnson signed two landmark education spending bills: the Higher Education Facilities Act and the Vocational Education Act. At Johnson's side were AAJC director Edmund Gleazer and AAJC president Donald Deyo. Both of these laws included large appropriations for community and junior colleges ("Two Legislative Landmarks," 1964, p. 4).

After this initial victory AAJC created a governmental and urban affairs office. The office acted as the Association's liaison with Congress and federal agencies. It produced a newsletter, *AAJC Special*, to alert its members to pending action on Capitol Hill (American Association of Junior Colleges, 1969). It also conducted workshops for college administrators and arranged meetings with federal agencies. Over the next three decades program directors John Mallan, Selden Menefee, and Frank Mensel became familiar figures on the Hill.

Congress soon became aware that there was a community or junior college in almost every congressional district. The success of AAJC in mobilizing local support was largely responsible for the boom in government spending for junior colleges. At the end of the decade the U.S. Office of Education listed fifty-eight programs that

209

impacted junior colleges. Several of these bills were specifically written (or rewritten) to include junior colleges.

The Higher Education Facilities Act of 1963 provided $1.2 billion for postsecondary construction projects, of which $690 million was authorized as matching grants for undergraduate institutions. Public junior colleges and technical institutes were guaranteed 22 percent of these funds—more than $151 million. Private junior colleges could apply for a portion of the remaining undergraduate funds. In addition, junior colleges were eligible for a portion of $360 million in low-interest loans ("Two Legislative Landmarks," 1964, p. 5).

The Vocational Education Act of 1963 provided $450 million in new funds for construction and operation of vocational education schools. These schools could be departments or divisions of junior colleges. The act was amended in 1968 to fund equipment grants, exemplary programs, consumer and homemaking education, and curriculum development.

Federal loan and grant programs directly benefited two-year college students, as well. The National Defense Student Loan and Guaranteed Student Loan programs provided financing for academic students, and the National Vocational Student Loan Insurance Act provided financing for vocational students. The College Work-Study Program funded student jobs on college campuses. Economic Opportunity Grants provided direct funding to students in financial need (Mensel, 1969, p. 16).

Title III of the Higher Education Act was amended in 1969 to guarantee funding for two-year institutions. Under this change 23 percent of funds provided under the title were designated for two-year colleges. Much of this funding went to support the Programs with Developing Institutions project, administered by AAJC, which used the funds to provide program evaluation, planning, workshops, and teacher training for more than 300 junior colleges nationwide (Chapman, 1970; Gleazer, 1972a; Menefee, 1971).

The Manpower Development and Training Act of 1964 was amended to make junior colleges eligible for funding to train and retrain unemployed persons.

The National Defense Education Act of 1958, Title V-A, was amended to provide grants to support guidance counseling in junior colleges and technical institutes. Most other provisions of the act still excluded junior colleges unless they were operated as part of a local school system (Mensel, 1969, p. 19).

The Educational Research Information Center (ERIC), funded by the U.S. Office of Education, opened a junior college clearinghouse in 1967. Based at the University of California–Los Angeles, the clearinghouse acquired and indexed some 2,000 documents relating to two-year colleges during its first two years of operation (Cohen, 1970).

In the midst of this bonanza of federal funding the movement lost its representation at the Office of Education. In 1965 the office's junior college and associate degree specialists both resigned. Their positions remained vacant throughout the remainder of the Johnson administration (Diener, 1970).

President Richard Nixon took office in January 1969 and appointed Robert Finch as secretary of health, education, welfare. From the first, Finch "made it abundantly clear, in repeated statements," that he supported two-year colleges (p. 18). Finch recruited an AAJC staff member as his junior college specialist, and also appointed a special task force to recommend junior college policies. These developments led the *Junior College Journal* to declare: "The Washington climate is different than six months ago—or even six weeks" (p. 14).

FOUNDATION FUNDS TAKE OFF

The massive growth of the 1960s attracted millions of dollars in contributions from private foundations. Most of these funds were channeled through AAJC (Gleazer, 1972b). The W.K. Kellogg Foundation announced its first grant to AAJC in 1959, for $240,000, which allowed the Association to hire new staff and improve the *Junior College Journal*. Three years later the foundation added another $377,000 in AAJC funding, and then in 1965 awarded a five-year grant to encourage occupational education programs. This $1.5 million award allowed the Association to increase its staff and publish a monthly *Occupational Education Bulletin*, and also paid for five regional conferences involving nearly 1,000 faculty and administrators.

211

In 1967 Kellogg sponsored the AAJC Community Services Project (American Association of Junior Colleges, 1967). Through consultative services and publications—a newsletter and a booklet, *Community Services in the Community College* (Myran, 1969)—this project encouraged junior colleges to improve their community service and continuing education programs. It resulted in the formation of the National Council on Community Services and Continuing Education, an affiliated council of AAJC.

The Ford Foundation provided partial funding for the AAJC Minority Group Programs Office. It also funded a demographic study to determine the attitudes of minority young people toward two-year colleges.

The US Steel Foundation funded a 1966 attitude study of junior college teachers. The research resulted in recommendations regarding faculty recruitment and training. To implement those recommendations, the Carnegie Corporation the following year funded the Faculty Development Project, which sponsored workshops and developed models for faculty training programs.

In addition to these major programs, the Association received smaller grants from AT&T, the Automobile Safety Foundation, the Cities Service Foundation, the Danforth Foundation, Educational Facilities Laboratories, the Esso Education Foundation, General Motors, Gulf Oil Corporation, the IBM Foundation, the Insurance Institute for Highway Safety, the Lilly Foundation, the National Science Foundation, the Pren-Hall Foundation, the Sears Roebuck Foundation, the Shell Companies Foundation, and the Sloan Foundation. By the end of the decade, through the personal campaigning of Gleazer and his staff, the AAJC special projects budget had climbed to more than $1 million a year, nearly all of which came from foundations and the federal government.

Despite these successes, some junior college administrators criticized the Association's handling of foundation funds, arguing that Gleazer had used the funds to create a huge bureaucracy in Washington. According to Gleazer, these administrators wanted more funds channeled directly to individual colleges. Channeling Association grant and project funds to member colleges would become a priority under Dale Parnell in the 1980s.

In reality, significant foundation funding did reach individual colleges. In March 1964 the Kellogg Foundation announced $1 million in grants for innovative semiprofessional and technical curricula (Seay, 1964). Kellogg also continued its longstanding practice of funding associate degree nursing programs and programs for auxiliary health-care and dental workers ("Kellogg Grant to Palm Beach," 1965; "Kellogg Grants $75,900," 1964; W.K. Kellogg Foundation, 1980).

CHAPTER 13

MASTER PLANS AND STATEWIDE SYSTEMS (1960-1969)

Without sound planning, what might have become

a community asset may become a community

disappointment.

— The Eisenhower Committee

To deal with massive numbers of new college students of the baby boom generation, California, in 1960, adopted a master plan for higher education. The plan, formulated by a commission headed by Clark Kerr, then president of the University of California, remains the basis for California higher education today—and it is still controversial.

The California plan created a three-tiered system of higher education. To implement this plan California placed new restrictions on admissions to state colleges and universities. High school graduates with a B average were no longer automatically admitted to the University of California system. Instead, freshman admissions were limited to the top 12.5 percent of high school graduates. The upper 41 percent of graduates could enter other state colleges and universities. The remainder would be diverted to the state's junior colleges.

The California plan is often criticized for consigning the academically poorest students to two-year colleges. In reality, junior colleges provided a nurturing environment for those students who were less well prepared. Many students who would have been eliminated from a state university succeeded at the local junior college.

Before the end of the decade, nearly half of the states had adopted statewide plans. Many of these were patterned, in major ways, after the California master plan and the Florida community college system.

In 1967 Kerr became chair of the Carnegie Commission on Higher Education, a high-profile group sponsored by the Carnegie Foundation for the Advancement of Teaching. Over the next six years the commission made an exhaustive study of the problems and potential of American higher education. Its findings favored a tiered system, similar to the California model. Specifically, the commission recommended that more students be channeled into two-year colleges, particularly into vocational programs. The commission's findings helped to mold America's emerging statewide community and junior college systems.

The California plan was not the first statewide plan for these institutions, however. Mississippi had in place the basic structure for a statewide system in the 1920s and 1930s, even though a definitive plan was not formalized until some years later. The state plan developed by James Wattenbarger (1953) for Florida, however, did provide a model that encompassed several basic principles that had become important in Mississippi, California, and Florida as well as other states involved in statewide planning for community colleges. His model envisioned institutions located within commuting distance of the total population of the state, local boards for operational control with state-level coordination, close association with local school systems and clear articulation policies with the state universities, comprehensive programs of study, low tuition, and broad state financial support. Following refinement to Wattenbarger's initial study, Florida adopted a comprehensive statewide plan in 1957. Over the next two decades a number of other states carried out similar statewide planning activities.

BUILDING STATEWIDE SYSTEMS

The new state of Hawaii passed its first Community College Act in 1964. The idea was championed by the state's second governor, John Burns. While Burns was preparing for his 1962 campaign, he gathered an advisory group to develop his platform, a group that included Teruo Ihara, who had written a doctoral dissertation on the need for a junior college system in Hawaii (Kappenberg, 1990, p. 5). With Ihara's encouragement, two-year colleges became a part of Burns's political agenda.

Burns's election captured the governorship and legislature for the Democratic party. The new leadership, determined to carry through the promise of a statewide community college system, in 1963 commissioned a feasibility study by the University of Hawaii. Richard Kosaki (1965), formerly a political science professor, was assigned to the project.

Kosaki (1964) became the architect of Hawaii's community colleges. He visited two-year colleges in California, Florida, New York, and Pennsylvania, picking up ideas. The structure he developed, based on New York's state university system, placed Hawaii's community colleges under the university, to be governed by the university's board of regents and guided by individual local advisory boards. This system fit with the Hawaiian tradition of centralizing political power in Honolulu (Harper, 1968a).

The new community colleges were housed in the buildings of state technical schools. The first of these colleges opened in 1967 on the island of Maui, and was followed in 1968 by four others, one on Kauai and the rest on the populous island of Oahu. Initially, the plan authorized no college for the island of Hawaii, which already had a two-year branch of the University of Hawaii (Kosaki, 1965, p. 6).

In 1970 the American Association of Junior Colleges welcomed the new Hawaii system by holding its fiftieth annual convention in Honolulu. Although campuses have since been added and student

enrollments have multiplied, the centralized Hawaii system sur-
vives largely unchanged into the 1990s, according to Richard
Kosaki.

The Pennsylvania legislature had defeated junior college laws
nearly every year since 1937 (Eldersveld, 1969). When the state
finally passed a community college law in 1963, some educators
hailed the law as a miracle. The new law identified "community colleges as part of higher education with their own identity and locally
governed by a board of trustees" (Bender & Shoemaker, 1971, p.
13). The Pennsylvania board of education adopted a master plan
calling for twenty-eight community college districts to serve the
entire population of the state. By the end of the decade, fourteen
community colleges had been founded, with a 1970 enrollment of
45,000 students.

The Arizona legislature created a state board of directors for
junior colleges and authorized it to establish a two-year college system. The board could place a college in any area that had the
potential to provide at last 320 students. It chose college sites,
established standards, and purchased property.

Under the Arizona plan the state paid half of the capital costs of
a new college, up to $500,000, and provided $525 for each of the
first 320 full-time-equivalent students and $350 for each additional
student (Gleazer, 1960c, p. 113). With the new legislation, enrollment grew quickly. By the decade's end Arizona's ten public colleges had an enrollment of 35,000 students. More than three quarters of these students attended the four colleges of the Maricopa
Junior College District, which served Phoenix and Maricopa
County (Hannelly, 1969, p. 36).

In May 1963 the Alabama legislature created the Alabama Trade
School and Junior College Authority and authorized it to expend
$15 million to build junior colleges and vocational schools
throughout the state. Funds would come from a one-cent increase
in the state beer tax. The major proponent of this legislation was
Alabama's governor, George Wallace (Katsinas, in press). A site
commission recommended the construction of ten new junior colleges and twelve trade schools. The number of colleges, all operated by the state board of education, actually grew to seventeen by

the end of the decade. Along with the six private junior colleges, two of which received state funding, the statewide two-year college total was twenty-three institutions. In 1969 these colleges enrolled more than 19,000 students (Graham, 1969, p. 135).

The Virginia General Assembly authorized a system of technical colleges in 1964. Three institutions were founded by 1966, when the assembly passed the Community College Act, which transformed the technical colleges into comprehensive community colleges under the governance of a state board and the guidance of local advisory boards (Wellman & Hamel, 1969). The Virginia system grew rapidly. By the fall of 1968 the state had eleven community colleges. Two area vocational schools had also added transfer programs. These thirteen institutions had a total enrollment of 16,000 students. A state master plan called for twenty-two community college regions, some with multiple campuses.

The Ohio legislature passed its first community college bill in 1961. Originally intended to establish technical institutes (Chapman, 1964), the bill was transformed into a community college law through a unique legislative ploy:

> The day [the technical institute law] was presented to the senate was one of the most unusual in Ohio's legislative history. As the bill was presented, Senator Frank King, the minority leader, jumped to his feet and moved to amend. He said "Strike the words technical institute and substitute community college." He did this at least a score of times.... Within an hour, Ohio had a community college law. (p. 9)

In September 1963 Cuyahoga Community College became the state's first public community college. The college, located in Cleveland, opened with about 3,000 students. Over two hundred more were turned away because of a shortage of faculty (p. 8). By the end of the decade three additional community college districts were in operation ("Sinclair," 1987).

Michigan adopted a new constitution in 1961 expressly requiring the state legislature to "provide by law for the establishment and financial support of public community and junior colleges." Each college was to be controlled by a locally elected board. Article 7 of the constitution also created a state board of community and junior colleges (Gannon, 1969, p. 108).

In 1964 the legislature passed Act 237, which defined the role of Michigan's community colleges. This law established college districts as "charter units of government" (p. 112), and as such, they were given the authority to issue bonds and levy property taxes, if approved by a local election. The following year state support for junior colleges was raised to $275 per full-time-equivalent student. By the end of the decade, Michigan had twenty-nine community college districts serving more than 95,000 students.

The Connecticut legislature had passed its first junior college law in 1959. The bill, introduced by the citizens of Norwalk, allowed local school boards to operate public junior colleges. Two years later a second law permitted groups of towns to operate a college. Neither law provided state funds for these colleges; however, three colleges were founded under these laws: Norwalk in 1961, Manchester in 1963, and Northwestern Connecticut in 1965 (Nader, 1969, p. 33).

In 1965 Connecticut Public Act 330 created a higher education system through a state board of trustees for regional community colleges. Within three years state-financed community colleges had been formed in Middletown, New Haven, Stratford, and Waterbury. During this period the state's three local colleges converted to state-controlled institutions (p. 34). In the 1968 academic year Connecticut's public community colleges had a full-time-equivalent enrollment of 7,570 students.

North Carolina also created a statewide two-year college system (Boozer, 1969). A 1957 law had provided funding for junior colleges but limited their curricula to academic subjects. All vocational programs were delegated to the state's twenty technical institutes. In 1963 the state assembly merged the three existing public junior colleges with the technical institutes. The result was a two-year college system made up of community colleges, technical institutes, and technical colleges. This system grew rapidly, from about 52,000 students in 1963 to more than 350,000 in 1971 ("North Carolina," 1988).

Missouri had only six public junior colleges in 1961, with an enrollment of about 3,500 students. In that year a group called the Missouri Citizens Committee for State Aid for Junior Colleges launched a campaign for a statewide junior college system, inducing 7,000 supporters, through letters, telegrams, and telephone calls, to influence state legislators. As a consequence, a junior college bill was passed on June 29, 1961, by an overwhelming majority. The Missouri legislation permitted the creation of junior college districts and provided $200 in state funding for each full-time student. Each college district was to be governed by an elected board of trustees with taxation and bonding powers; systemwide regulations and accreditation were delegated to the state department of education. Under the new system junior colleges expanded rapidly. By the end of the decade Missouri had twelve districts with an enrollment of more than 26,000 students. The largest was the three-campus St. Louis district (Bastian, 1969).

The Maryland General Assembly passed a community college governance bill, which created local boards of trustees for the state's thirteen two-year colleges and established a state board for community colleges to oversee the operation of these institutions. Between 1964 and 1968 the state's junior college enrollment jumped 143 percent to 26,594 students (Pesci & Novak, 1969, p. 29).

The New Jersey legislature passed the County College Law in 1963 to provide funding for a statewide system of two-year colleges. These colleges could be established by the county board of freeholders with permission from the state board of education. The state would provide 50 percent of construction costs and provide a maximum of $200 per full-time-equivalent student; remaining costs would be borne by the county and through student tuition. By the fall of 1969 there were twelve county colleges with a total of 15,800 students (MacKay, 1969).

The Illinois Board of Higher Education adopted a state master plan in 1965. The enabling legislation included House Bill 1710—the Public Junior College Act—which created a junior college board to oversee the statewide system. Under this act junior colleges, no longer secondary schools, were made a part of the higher education system. Colleges were given financial incentives to separate from local school systems and form separate junior college boards. By the end of the decade, the state had thirty-four public junior college districts serving 100,169 students (Erickson, 1969).

The Washington state legislature debated several junior college laws during its 1965 session. In the end it passed the problem to the state education department. The state superintendent was directed to prepare a statewide plan and present it to the 1967 legislative session (Giles, 1969, p. 102). The plan, as adopted, called for twenty-two junior college districts, each responsible to a five-member board of trustees. A state board of community colleges was created to supervise the system. The legislature also created a council for vocational-technical education to coordinate the vocational activities of community colleges and public schools.

The Minnesota legislature created a state junior college board in 1963 and charged it with establishing fifteen junior colleges. By the following fall the state's eleven existing district junior colleges had signed an agreement of takeover. After two of the colleges merged, the system numbered ten (Helland, 1969). The legislature also appropriated operational and capital funds directly to the state board, which had the authority to decide how the funds were to be distributed. Local colleges, headed by deans, had their own advisory boards. All purchases, payrolls, and payments, however, were made by the state office. In 1965 the state board recommended that the system be expanded to seventeen colleges, with five alone in the Minneapolis-St. Paul metropolitan area. By the end of the decade all seventeen colleges were operating and an eighteenth was nearing completion. Between 1964 and 1968 statewide enrollment nearly tripled, reaching 15,361 students.

The Iowa board of public instruction developed a statewide plan for postsecondary education in 1962, which the state legislature adopted three years later. The new law permitted county school boards to create community colleges or vocational schools. Community colleges were required to offer transfer, vocational, and adult education curricula. Any county that supported a community college, however, was not allowed to operate a separate vocational school (Newsham, 1969).

Because many Iowa counties were too sparsely populated to support a community college, the law permitted the school boards of two or more smaller counties to form area districts. Initially, each district received $2.25 per student day in state funding. Fifteen area districts, representing ninety-two of the state's ninety-nine counties, had been formed by 1967: eleven supporting community colleges and four supporting vocational schools. The new districts absorbed all the local junior colleges that existed before 1965. By the end of the decade enrollment had nearly doubled, reaching 21,000 full-time-equivalent students.

Kansas had passed its first junior college law in 1917. This law permitted local school districts to form high school extensions supported with real estate taxes. The law remained largely unchanged until 1965, when the legislature passed a community college act incorporating the state's seventeen junior colleges into a statewide system. Under this law junior colleges were removed from the high school district and given separate boards of control, faculties, facilities, and administration. The law also increased state funding and authorized two new junior colleges. The colleges were placed under an advisory council for junior colleges, which began work on a comprehensive statewide plan (Heinrich, 1969). Kansas's junior colleges prospered under this system. By 1968 two new colleges had been opened, twelve had moved into new campuses, and four others were completing new campuses. All of the Kansas junior colleges offered a mix of transfer, vocational, and community service programs.

The Kentucky community college system, authorized by the state legislature in 1962, was operated by the University of Kentucky, but had local advisory boards appointed by the governor. In 1964 the University of Kentucky's extension center in Covington became Northern Kentucky Community College. By the fall of 1969 Kentucky had sixteen community colleges, enrolling nearly 10,000 students.

The Colorado legislature passed the Community College and Occupational Act in 1967. This law formed the Colorado Board of Community Colleges and Occupational Education and charged it with establishing colleges, appointing college administrators, and approving budgets and curricula. Existing junior colleges could get increased state funding if they joined the system, but were required to give up their local tax base and much of their autonomy. Under this plan college districts were disbanded and their governing boards reduced to advisory boards called college councils. (Hodson & Crawfurd, 1969). Initially, three existing colleges—Lamar, Otero, and Trinidad—joined the Colorado system. The other four colleges decided to remain independent. By 1970 two new colleges had been added to the state system, including the multicampus Community College of Denver. During this period two new independent colleges were also formed. Some state leaders expressed concern that Colorado was creating two separate junior college systems.

The Montana legislature passed a new junior college law in 1965 allowing any contiguous area of the state to form a junior college district. The only requirements were that the area have 700 high school students and $30 million in assessed property value. Each college was to be governed by a seven-member elected board, with statewide supervision provided by the state board of education. Considered a part of the public school system, the colleges were funded on the same formula used for other schools (Blake, 1969). Before the 1965 law Montana had only two junior colleges, both of which moved into new campuses in 1967. In that year a third college was opened. No additional colleges were added by the end of the decade.

THE SOUTHERN REGIONAL EDUCATION BOARD

During the 1960s several regional consortia of states carried out research projects of interest to their constituencies. The Southern Regional Education Board (SREB), a membership organization of southeastern states, provided the legislatures and governors of its member states with research and other information relating in particular to planning for higher education. Each year the SREB would host a special conference for legislator leadership. During the 1960s every conference had some part of its program devoted to community and junior college issues.

Winfred Godwin, the executive officer of the SREB, coauthored with James Wattenbarger a status report on community colleges in the South (Wattenbarger & Godwin, 1962), and A.J. Brumbaugh, a staff member and consultant to the board, wrote several monographs on planning for higher education. Of particular value were two monographs dealing with planning and coordination: *Guidelines for the Establishment of Community Junior Colleges* (1963a) and *State-wide Planning and Coordination of Higher Education* (1963b). These publications provided the members of the southern legislatures with understanding and encouragement to develop sound legislation for higher education in general and community and junior colleges in particular. SREB staff also assisted the member states in conducting studies and need projections for higher education. The Western Interstate Commission on Higher Education (WICHE), with headquarters in Denver, also made available similar research support. WICHE's major efforts, however, came during the 1970s and 1980s.

U.S. OFFICE OF EDUCATION

In addition to the regional associations, the U.S. Office of Education provided assistance to states wishing to develop plans for community colleges. Under the leadership of Sebastian V. Martorana and Grant D. Morrison, several publications were developed to help states and localities in forming a community college survey committee. Other publications of particular value issued at this time include *Criteria for the Establishment of 2-year Colleges* (Morrison & Martorana, 1961) and *Procedures for the Establishment of Public 2-year Colleges* (Morrison & Witherspoon, 1966). The office also provided consultive assistance to state agencies. These activities emphasized the official and unofficial concerns that were being expressed about the two-year colleges and their place in higher education.

MODEL STATE LEGISLATION

After World War II there was a great deal of interest in the establishment of community and junior colleges in most states, and the demand for model state legislation, or at least guidelines for such a model, became very strong. The U.S. Office of Education, with the interest and active support of George Zook, provided some help to states wishing to extend educational opportunity to those citizens not well served through existing institutions. The work of Morrison and Martorana provided specific guidance to state leadership, and the guidelines and procedures they published (Morrison & Martorana, 1961; Morrison & Witherspoon, 1966) emphasized the need to alleviate the barriers of finance, access, and curriculum diversity in order to expand opportunities for postsecondary education. There continued to be, however, a strong demand for a model legal basis for community college development. The Council of State Governments had developed model legislation for other topics, and some educators felt that higher education should be similarly fashioned.

A difficulty lay in the fact that hardly any state had developed higher education in the same pattern as any other state. Even though there were some similarities in the general purposes of colleges and universities among the states, there were fifty different structures for higher education and a wide variety of institutions. Although the federal Land Grant College Act of 1862, the famous Morrill Act, had provided basic expectations for state colleges and universities, there were still many differences in organization, structure, and control of these institutions among the states. These dissimilarities were further complicated by fifty different implementations (by well-established state bureaucracies) of the various federal vocational acts that provided funds to the states. The use and the definition of such terms as secondary education, vocational education, colleges, universities, and even higher education were peculiar to each state. Obviously, model legislation would be extremely difficult for anyone to develop. It would be especially so for the Office of Education, which avoided any semblance of dictating to the states in matters relating to education.

Fortunately, AAJC had become active in promoting and assisting in the establishment of these new two-year institutions. The Association's commission on legislation led the way (Fariss, 1947). Under chair Kenneth Skaggs, a former community college president, the commission developed and published principles for legislative action that gained wide use (Commission on Legislation,

1960; Skaggs, 1962). The commission's model for state legislation drew from the research carried out by subsequent commission chair James Wattenbarger and other state and university researchers, as well as from the experience of AAJC's institutional leaders. It was greeted with enthusiasm around the nation and was used as a guide in the development of community and junior college laws by a number of states that adapted it to their own situations and legislative structures (Commission on Legislation, 1961; McLeod, 1983).

A number of state agencies sought commission participants and others experienced in developing community and junior colleges as consultants to assist in conducting surveys and recommending state plans for two-year colleges. These surveys and plans became the basis for state systems in Iowa, Kansas, Maryland, Massachusetts, Missouri, New Jersey, Oklahoma, and Virginia, to name a few. In some states, however, the plans were shelved, and the expansion of educational opportunity grew without much guidance.

The expansion of opportunity for postsecondary education was a major topic of concern in most states during the 1960s, and many legislators and governors were voicing their interest (Kintzer, 1980). Statewide planning for higher education became a familiar theme across America, and community and junior colleges played an integral part in it (Hurlburt, 1969).

THE AGE OF ACTIVISM (1970-1979)

Other forms of postsecondary education—such as a two-year community college...are far better suited to the interests of many young people.

— Richard Nixon

I n the late 1960s the "love generation" arrived on university campuses with beards, beads, sandals, peace symbols, and protests. The days of the clean-cut college student were gone. Community colleges, in fact, had begun to attract too many students of all ages to resemble typical four-year college campuses. Middle-aged retired service personnel shared classes with antiwar protestors. Women returning to college after raising a family shared classes with students the ages of their children. As the Vietnam War crept to a conclusion, the number of returning veteran students grew. This lost generation of veterans created special challenges for two-year colleges.

Other influences were also changing the community college. The civil rights movement raised troubling questions about how colleges served ethnic minorities and about the ethnic balance of their faculties. The women's rights and handicapped rights movements caused colleges to reassess their service to the whole community. These movements put community colleges in the uncomfortable role of social activist.

While colleges struggled with social change, demographic shifts slowed their growth. Nineteen-year-olds enrolled in more community college courses than any other age group, but by the mid-1970s there were simply fewer nineteen-year-olds to go around (Sheldon & Grafton, 1978, p. 38). As enrollments stagnated, community and junior colleges had to face other problems as well. Taxpayer revolts, such as California's notorious Proposition 13, and competing priorities slowed the growth of public funding. Increased tuition shut the open door for some potential students. After a century of growth, many colleges were facing a period of retrenchment.

THE BOOM WINDS DOWN

The enrollment boom did not end with the 1960s. The fall of 1970 was greeted by twenty-nine new two-year colleges, two of which opened with more than 3,500 students. All told, junior college enrollment increased by more than 11 percent, hitting an all-time record of nearly 2.5 million students. Buried in these optimistic figures, however, was the fact that enrollment at private junior colleges had declined for three straight years. In 1970 private enrollments dropped by another 6.2 percent (Harper et al., 1971).

Public enrollments more than made up for the private college slump. For the next five years, total enrollments rose until by the fall of 1975 nearly 4.1 million students were enrolled in American community and junior colleges. Enrollments had peaked. In the fall of 1976 two-year college enrollments grew only 0.4 percent (Drake, 1976). Even this slight growth was deceptive: all of it came from part-time students. Full-time enrollment, on the other hand, was beginning to decrease. This gradual decline in full-time students signaled a change in community college demographics that would continue into the 1990s. More students found it convenient to attend college only while holding down a full- or part-time job; more were full-time homemakers; and more wanted only a course or two rather than a total program. The fact that most community colleges offered a full range of classes in the evenings and on weekends made it easy. For many colleges, however, this meant a drop in both tuition revenues and state funding. The passing of the baby boom was one reason for the enrollment decrease. Another was higher tuition. By 1975 more than 45 percent of public community colleges charged annual tuition and fees of more than $300 (Lombardi, 1976).

A report by the data office of the (by then renamed) American Association of Community and Junior Colleges drew some dire conclusions about the years to come (Gilbert, 1979b):

> Many state people believe that a new era has started for the two-year college. For the next two or three years enrollments will hold rather steady. Then in 1982, a period of modest decline will begin. There are many reasons.
> 1. There will be fewer 18-year-olds to enter college.
> 2. It will take more older students with their small part-time loads to take the place of a full-time 18- to 21-year-old.
> 3. There will be fewer veterans.
> 4. State budgets will tend to hold enrollments down.
> 5. With increasing tuition in many places, the pay-by-the-credit plan will produce a market effect that will hold down the average credits taken (p. 58).

Enrollments climbed slightly in the fall of 1979, but by midyear many two-year colleges were suffering. In the Chicago system enrollments dropped by 4.4 percent, and in the California system a phenomonal 9 percent. Clearly, the era of double-digit growth was over. One pessimistic state official declared, "We're starting a new chapter [in community college history]. Enrollments may not go up again for 20 years" (Gilbert, 1979b, p. 58).

STUDENT PERSONNEL CONCERNS

From the earliest days, as noted by Leonard Koos, Walter Eells, and almost every other person who has written about community and junior colleges, there has been mention of the special need for student services, including counseling, testing, and myriad other activities. As community colleges began to serve an increasing number of nontraditional students—the academically unprepared, older students, working students, immigrants, and minorities—the need for and interest in student services increased.

Several studies basic to student services in community and junior colleges were carried out. Most had the financial support of a foundation and were conducted under the general supervision of university personnel. A major study in this area was a Carnegie Corporation-sponsored project supervised by AAJC. The Project for Appraisal and Development of Junior College Student Personnel Programs, completed in 1965, was directed by Max Raines of Michigan State University, who was advised by a national committee chaired by T.R. McConnell of the University of California at Berkeley (Raines, 1965). Jane E. Matson (1972), a member of the advisory committee, directed a follow-up study in 1971 for AAJC. These two studies provided a baseline for further evaluation of student service issues.

Along with the concern for the open door came the criticism, often justified, that the door was in fact a revolving door when unprepared students failed because they did not receive appropriate assistance. The emphasis upon orientation, testing, counseling, advisement, student activities, and a number of other areas of responsibility became a vital concern of those persons working in the community college field (Collins, 1967).

Educators to this day are defining and describing the student personnel services that a community college should provide (Thurston, Zook, Neher & Ingraham, 1972). Recent efforts by several individuals and organizations have emphasized the importance of these services. In 1987 the League for Innovation developed a policy statement addressing the role of student development professionals in assuring student success. Alfred, Peterson, and White (1992), in analyzing the student services at 136 community colleges, posited six characteristics of colleges that contribute to student success:

1) They "reach out" to students through academic and out-of-class activities.
2) They provide proactive services which meet student needs for quality, convenience, and cost while preventing negative outcomes from occurring.
3) They continually assess performance through research carried out on program and service quality.
4) They use assessment results to improve quality.
5) They have established a reputation for quality that is shared by staff, students, and external groups.
6) They have a facilitating culture—an approach to management and leadership that empowers staff to help students achieve goals (pp. 25–26).

ARTICULATION

If students are to transfer credit for the first two years of a baccalaureate degree from a community college to a four-year institution, the process must be smooth and guarantee that the students will be given every opportunity to succeed in the receiving institution. The majority of students enrolled in the third year of degree-granting colleges are transfer students. In the 1960s and 1970s, the articulation process was a matter of institutional and even systemwide policy concern throughout the community college movement (Sandeen & Goodale, 1976).

In California Spindt, Bird, and others began in the early 1940s to express concerns for assuring a smooth transfer between the junior colleges and the four-year baccalaureate programs. Puttman (1954) carried out a status study that became a dissertation at the University of North Dakota. Bird (1956) listed four recommended procedures that institutions should adopt for a clear mutual understanding of the transfer process, including policies governing transfer, machinery for coordination, and periodic evaluations of student performance (p. 93).

This concern for mutual understanding and clear policies that protected students became the basis for articulation studies during the decades since the 1950s. A monumental study under the direction of an interorganizational committee chaired by James Wattenbarger, with research carried out by Dorothy Knoell and Leland Medsker (1966), in the 1960s emphasized even further these procedures and developed suggested policies for statewide adoption. The cooperation between the three organizations that were represented on the Joint Committee on Junior and Senior Colleges—the Association of American Colleges, the American Association of Junior Colleges, and the American Association of Collegiate Registrars and Admissions Officers—illustrated the national attention that was increasingly given to articulation. The publication of this committee's studies, *Guidelines for Improving Articulation between Junior and Senior Colleges*, became influential in the state policies that were developed in Florida, Illinois, and a number of other states (Wattenbarger, 1965).

Subsequently, Kintzer (1973), Willingham (1972), and many other individuals and institutions, as well as state systems, often sponsored and encouraged by such organizations as the Educational Testing Service, American Council on Education, American College Testing, and, occasionally, interested foundations, conducted studies and held conferences focusing upon the articulation problem. A steady stream of publications was released dealing with various specific problems as well as general attitudes toward transfer.

Florida is an example of a state that has developed specific policies relating to transfer. These policy statements were based upon the work of Kintzer, Knoell, Medsker, and Wattenbarger and became state board of education regulations and later were even included in the Florida statutes. They specifically affected statewide requirements for general education, a common course numbering system, an achievement testing program, institution-to-institution liaison procedures, and an advisory committee that adjudicates appeals when needed. Studies of transfer students (e.g., Walker, 1969) as well as a series of annual studies on articulation were conducted by the Florida State Board of Community Colleges (Florida State Board of Community Colleges, 1988).

The most controversial part of these procedures has been the statewide testing programs, called the College Level Academic

234

Skills Test (CLAST) in Florida. Although several other states have instituted statewide testing (Engelhart, 1950), Florida is unique among the states in requiring successful performance on the CLAST as a basis for receiving the associate in arts degree and in order to continue college work. The pros and cons of this policy have been discussed by Blee (1985) and Nickens (1985), with strong arguments from each point of view. There is no question, however, that the use of CLAST in this manner does interfere with student progress, particularly with minority students, and to that extent is contrary to the community college philosophy.

Accreditation agencies have always emphasized as a measure of quality the importance of the records of transfer students (Palmer, 1990). The more recent emphasis upon student success and mission accomplishment has increased the concern for well-developed transfer procedures and policies. A publication of the League for Innovation (Doucette & Hughes, 1990), *Assessing Institutional Effectiveness in Community Colleges,* emphasizes these procedures in measuring institutional effectiveness.

FINALLY—THE COMPREHENSIVE COMMUNITY COLLEGE

From the beginning of the movement, community and junior colleges espoused a comprehensive three-part mission: preparing students for transfer to a four-year college, providing vocational training, and serving as a source of continuing education for the community. Although examples of all three emphases can be found in colleges throughout community and junior college history, they have not always received equal attention. Created as a needed access to higher education, early junior colleges concentrated on preparation for transfer. During and following World War II training for employment became important. As technology expanded, creating thousands of job categories requiring education beyond high school, preparation for immediate employment took precedence, even to today, when as many as 65 percent of the nation's community college students are enrolled in vocational, occupational, and technical programs. Despite eloquent statements by a

235

number of leaders from as far back as the early 1900s, however, community continuing education received far less attention throughout much of the history of the movement.

Emphasis on the community education function of the college seems to have grown almost in direct proportion to the use of the term *community* rather than *junior*. In fact, one of the clearest definitions of the college's role in the community comes from the report that urged the creation of community colleges, that of the President's Commission on Higher Education, the Truman Commission (1947). In that report the commission called for colleges that are centers "of learning for the entire community, with or without the restrictions that surround formal course work." Predating a basic tenet of community-based education by a quarter of a century, the report recommends that this new community college gear "its programs and services to the needs and wishes of the people it serves..." (vol. 1, pp. 69–70).

The community continuing education function of community and junior colleges emerged slowly over the years, becoming widely known as the community service function. By the end of the 1960s, a great many community colleges were involved in providing a variety of services to their communities, and many colleges had included the function in their organizational charts. Depending upon the size and organization of the college, the function was assigned as a full-time duty to an administrator or as one of many duties of the chief instructional officer. With the development of the community continuing education function, the final phase in the evolution of what would become known as the comprehensive community college was nearing completion.

In 1967, with the aid of a grant from the Alfred P. Sloan Foundation, AAJC contracted with Ervin L. Harlacher, a vice president at Oakland Community College in Michigan, to conduct a study of the community services function at a number of community colleges throughout the nation. Based on Harlacher's report, the importance of the community service function was recognized by the W.K. Kellogg Foundation with a grant to fund the AAJC Community Services Project. Harlacher's work (1969) was published as *The Community Dimension of the Community College*, the first major book

236

devoted entirely to the community service mission of community colleges. In it Harlacher concluded prophetically:

The community services function, while still emerging as a major aspect of the program of these colleges, is the element that may best fit them for a unique and highly significant role in future patterns of American education (p. 107).

In 1969, with support from the Kellogg Foundation, the Association published *Community Services in the Community College* by Gunder A. Myran. Reprinted in 1974 when community-based education was an even higher priority for the Association, the monograph stands today as one of the best analyses of the community service function. Written when he was dean of instruction at Rockland Community College in New York, it established Myran as one of the leading scholars in the field.

In 1974 Edmund J. Gleazer, Jr., by then president of the recently reorganized American Association of Community and Junior Colleges (AACJC), began a series of articles that launched AACJC's emphasis on community-based education, a term that soon replaced community services. In his first article, "After the Boom... What Now for the Community Colleges?" (1973/1974), Gleazer took his cue from the enrollment data being gathered by the Association. He pointed out that the boom period of growth for community colleges was rapidly coming to a close and that colleges must begin to look carefully at their markets. Gleazer suggested that the colleges begin to consider the total community as potential students, not just those who choose to come to the college.

In 1974 two national conferences were held that further established community-based education as a major concern of the Association and an increasing number of colleges. In April Valencia Community College in Florida hosted a national conference, titled "Beyond the Open Door—The Open College," which more than 250 college leaders and community service practitioners attended. Gleazer's keynote address was later printed in the *Community College Journal* (1974). Other speakers included Ervin L. Harlacher, the newly appointed chancellor of the Metropolitan Community Colleges in Kansas City, Missouri; Gunder Myran; Max Raines, of Michigan State University; Benjamin Wygal, president of Florida Junior College at Jacksonville; and James Gollattscheck, president of the host college.

Later that year, in November, AACJC sponsored a national assembly with support from the Kellogg Foundation. More than a hundred college leaders and lay citizens were invited to attend. The report of the assembly was published by the Association as *A Policy Primer for Community-Based Community Colleges*. In it William Shannon, AACJC senior vice president and moderator of the assembly, stated the purposes of the assembly:

> The main responsibility of the Assembly was to recommend ways that barriers to community-based education might be breached, not on a program-by-program basis but in terms of policy required for sustained and continuing effort (American Association of Community and Junior Colleges, 1975, p. 1).

In October 1975, with the support of the Charles Stewart Mott Foundation, AACJC established its Center for Community Education. Under the direction of Suzanne Fletcher, the center conducted an international survey of community education commitment at 1,275 public and private institutions in the United States and Canada (Fletcher, Rue & Young, 1977). The survey found that of the 67 percent responding, 95.7 percent accepted the definition that community education is made up of:

> courses and activities for credit or noncredit, formal classrooms or nontraditional programs, cultural, recreational offerings specifically designed to meet the needs of the surrounding community and utilizing school, college and other public facilities. Programming is determined with input from the community being served (p. 12).

The center held regional meetings and published a series of monographs, newsletters, and papers during its period of funding.

In 1976 Gollattscheck, Harlacher, and Wygal, three community college chief executive officers who had worked together on the Valencia conference and who were active promoters of community-based education at their colleges and on the national scene, and Eleanor Roberts, a staff member at the Metropolitan Community Colleges, presented an agenda for community-based education in a book titled *College Leadership for Community Renewal: Beyond Community-Based Education:*

> A college for community renewal...must be linked to the community in such a manner that it determines its direction and develops its goals through college-community interaction, uses the total community as a learning laboratory and resource, serves as a catalyst to create in the community a desire for renewal, provides a vehicle through which the community educates itself. Such a college will be committed not just to degrees and credentials, not just to job training, and not just to service *for* the community. It will, rather, be committed to the continual improvement of all aspects of community life and dedicated to the continual growth and development of its citizens and its social institutions (pp. 6–7).

In 1979 ten community colleges with a common interest in community-based education created COMBASE, a consortium with the express purpose of sharing expertise and experience. The organization continues today with more than fifty institutional members in twenty-two states.

In 1978 AACJC received a grant from the National Endowment for the Humanities to establish an office of community forums to help colleges involve their communities in addressing local issues. Under the leadership of Diane U. Eisenberg, project director, the Association conducted workshops, selected colleges for demonstration sites, and provided materials for community forums on the topic "Energy and the Way We Live." More than 450 colleges were involved in the project. Through the community forums series conducted by Valencia Community College in Florida, Ted Turner volunteered his new television station in Atlanta to conduct a nationwide forum, one of the first national teleconferences (Eisenberg, 1980). With support from the Shell Companies Foundation, the Ford Foundation, and the National Endowment for the Humanities, the Association conducted a national assembly that resulted in the monograph *Forums for Citizen Education* (American Association of Community and Junior Colleges, 1978).

Community-based education remained a priority for AACJC throughout Gleazer's tenure as president. In his final book as president of the Association, *The Community College: Values, Vision, and Vitality* (1980), he expressed what he felt should be the new mission of community colleges: "to encourage and facilitate lifelong learning with community as process and product" (p. 16). Dale Parnell, Gleazer's successor and a charter member of COMBASE, would take community-based education in new directions in the 1980s. Promotion of partnerships with business and industry would become a major thrust of the Association as member colleges and their communities wrestled with unemployment and a nationwide economic downturn.

The final validation of the community college mission that had been carried forward as community services and then community-based education occurred in 1988 when the Commission on the Future of Community Colleges released its report, *Building Communities: A Vision for a New Century*, stating:

> We propose, therefore, that the theme "Building Communities" become the new rallying point for community colleges in America. We define the term "community" not only as a region to be served, but also as a climate to be created. (1988, p. 7).

THE WOMEN'S MOVEMENT

Junior colleges had always prided themselves on serving the entire community. From the early days of the movement, these institutions were known as the "people's colleges" and "democracy's colleges." In the 1970s this egalitarian image was called into question by members of the women's movement (Reinfeld, 1975).

The feminist movement was ignited in the 1960s by Betty Friedan's book *The Feminine Mystique* (1963). Feminists demanded parity with men in politics, employment, and education, and they charged that employers, schools, and social institutions were not sensitive to their needs (Rossi, 1976). Higher education was a primary target for feminist criticism. Although women accounted for

THE AGE OF ACTIVISM (1970–1979)

about half of America's postsecondary students, faculties remained a male domain. The community college was no exception.

Critics claimed that the people's colleges were being operated by White males. In fact, only eight public community colleges were headed by women as of late 1975 (Rossi, 1976, p. 43), and by fall of the next year women made up only 35 percent of faculty and 20 percent of administrators (Drake, 1977). With their employment record under scrutiny, colleges began aggressively to hire and promote women. By the end of the decade about 40 percent of faculty and 31 percent of administrators were women (Brawer, 1977).

College programs were also called into question. Feminists claimed that counselors channeled women into traditionally female-dominated programs, such as home economics, secretarial-type programs, and nursing (Bulpitt, 1977, p. 4), and that colleges did not provide day care and programs for mature women. These complaints were given added weight by Title IX of the Federal Education Act amendments of 1972, which prohibited discrimination on the basis of sex in education programs and activities that receive federal funding (Rossi, 1976, p. 41).

Under mounting criticism from female students and faculty, two-year colleges developed programs and services to meet the needs of women. Many colleges created a campus women's center, a term loosely used to cover a wide range of facilities and activities. At some colleges the women's center housed meeting rooms, child care, guidance counseling, workshops, and job placement. At others it was simply a lounge or room set aside for "brown bag luncheon groups" (Bulpitt, 1977, p. 6).

Women's programs were extremely popular during the 1970s. Some of these programs offered a reentry curriculum aimed at former homemakers who wanted to return to the workforce. Other programs were designed for low-income women with poor educational backgrounds. A 1974 survey found that 50.8 percent of junior colleges operated a women's program (Nichols, 1975/1976, p. 7). Programs at two California schools illustrate the ambitious nature of these efforts.

The Vocational Internship Education for Women program, sponsored by the Foothill-DeAnza College District, was aimed at

241

skilled, educated women, most of whom already held bachelor's degrees. They were given technical internships at the National Aeronautics and Space Administration's Ames Research Center for twenty hours per week, and they also took two academic courses per quarter relating to their career goals (Sanchez, 1977). The combination of academic training and work experience was designed to help these talented women begin a career.

The two-semester Women's Re-Entry to Education program at San Jose City College, aimed at disadvantaged women, included personal development courses, such as career planning, study skills, health, and speech, and provided ancillary services, such as transportation, day care, counseling, and tutoring. The program was designed to prepare students to enter the job market or to continue their education (Sanchez, 1977).

AACJC also adapted to the rise of the women's movement. The Association gave council status and the potential for a board seat to the American Association of Women in Community and Junior Colleges (AAWCJC). Within two years, AAWCJC, founded in 1973 by Eileen Rossi, an instructor at City College of San Francisco, had become the largest AACJC council, with 700 members (Rossi, 1976, p. 39). In 1992 Beverly Simone, president of Madison Area Technical College in Wisconsin, became chair of the AACJC Board of Directors. She had been elected to the AACJC Board as a representative of AAWCJC. Simone was not the first woman, however, to lead the Association's Board of Directors. As early as 1938 Katherine Denworth of Massachusetts served as president, and Dorothy Bell took over as president in 1952. More recently, Helena Howe (1978), Judith Eaton (1985), and Flora Mancuso Edwards (1990) have served as Board chair.

THE ROLE OF ETHNIC MINORITIES

The role of ethnic minorities in the people's colleges was also questioned during the 1970s. Once again, many leaders were caught off guard. In the two decades since the *Brown v. Board of Education* decision, all of America's public two-year colleges had become desegregated. Two-year colleges had much higher levels of minority enrollment than universities. In 1970 minority students made up 14.4 percent of the total national community and junior college enrollment (Goodrich, Lezotte & Welch, 1972/1973, p. 28). Other data were troubling, however. Ethnic minorities accounted for only 4.5 percent of full-time community and junior college faculty and 7.1 percent of administrators (p. 30). Nearly 45 percent of the colleges had no minority-focused programs, and only a handful had a strong affirmative action program.

During the 1970s community colleges made progress on all these fronts. Much of this action resulted from requirements of the federal government and from the efforts of feminist and minority faculty members and students. The federal Civil Rights Act of 1964, which had exempted educational institutions from its employment discrimination provisions, was amended in 1972 to require colleges to eliminate discrimination in hiring. A primary tool in this effort was affirmative action, a policy of aggressively recruiting, hiring, and promoting minorities and women (Bonpua, 1973).

From the outset, affirmative action was controversial. Nonminority employees claimed that it was unconstitutional reverse discrimination. Federal courts, however, upheld the process, finding it "constitutional and valid" when used to "achieve equal employment opportunities" (p. 32). After October 1972 public and private colleges were required to maintain a written affirmative action plan. Over the next two decades affirmative action programs added thousands of new minority and female faculty to America's community colleges.

African Americans, although representing nearly 9.2 percent of all full-time community college enrollment in 1970, accounted for only 3.2 percent of faculty and 5.6 percent of administrators. Many of these professionals were employed by a few predominantly Black junior colleges (Goodrich, Lezotte & Welch, 1972/1973). AAJC also had a poor record of encouraging Black leadership. Until 1970 there were no African Americans on the AAJC Board of Directors (Smith, 1972).

The AAJC Black Caucus became the rallying point for Black leadership in the Association. The caucus was formed at a meeting of forty African American leaders held during the 1970 AAJC convention in Honolulu. Its primary leader, Malcolm Hurst, president of Malcolm X College in Chicago, had gained attention by walking out of the previous convention when an all-White chorus sang "Dixie." The Black Caucus, incensed that the AAJC nominating committee had again failed to recommend an African American Board member, during two subsequent meetings developed a strategy for overriding the committee's recommendations (p. 16). The strategy was successful, and Hurst became the first African American to serve on the AAJC Board.

At the 1971 convention the Association added three new Board positions to "accommodate the need for more minority representation" ("Annual Convention," 1971, p. 44). Once again, however, the nominating committee failed to select an African American. The Black Caucus reacted by presenting "an entire slate of Black candidates for every opening on the Board" (Smith, 1972, p. 16). In the end, Norvel Smith of Merritt College in California was elected to one of the new Board seats.

The Black Caucus also issued a position paper that included an eight-point plan for AAJC action on minority issues. This time AAJC moved quickly to implement most of the caucus's demands. The Association agreed to establish an affirmative action hiring program for its Washington staff and recruited Jesse Jackson as a speaker at the 1972 convention (Smith, 1972). Nevertheless, Smith vowed that the caucus would remain until

> the AAJC, by addressing itself to the elimination of structures and procedures that facilitate racism and discrimination, and by supporting the elimination of inequities in the support of community college programs that serve large numbers of Blacks, brings about a nation-wide system of community and junior colleges that truly democratizes public higher education (p. 17).

The Black Caucus was later reorganized as the Council on Black American Affairs (Harper, 1974), and today remains one of the strongest and most active of AACC's affiliated councils. From 1971 Black community college leaders served on the Association's Board, elected both at-large and as council representatives, and in 1976 Abel Sykes, president of Compton College in California, became the first African American Board chair.

Hispanics, the second largest ethnic minority in American two-year colleges, in 1970 accounted for about 3.7 percent of full-time enrollment. Like African Americans, they were severely underrepresented among professional staff: only 0.9 percent of administrators and 0.8 percent of faculty were of Hispanic ancestry (Goodrich, Lezotte & Welch, 1972/1973). They also began to demand a stronger voice in AAJC. In 1970 a group called the Concerned Chicano Coalition, believing the Association was concentrating all of its minority programs on African Americans and ignoring the needs of Hispanics, met with the AAJC Board (Gleazer, 1970). As a result of this meeting, the Board committed itself to involving "a variety of minority groups" in AAJC programs and projects (p. 5).

A group called El Congreso Nacional de Asuntos Colegiales was formed to help elect Hispanics to the AAJC Board. At the 1971 convention it succeeded in getting elected Walter Garcia, president of Rio Hondo College, California, to one of the three new Board seats. By 1974 the group had become an official council of the reorganized AACJC (Harper, 1974), but in 1980 lost its affiliated status for not meeting the Board-approved criteria for recognition of councils. In 1985 its successor, the National Community College Hispanic Council, was approved as an affiliated council of the Association.

AACJC, with funding provided by the US Steel Foundation, also established the Fomento program to investigate ways in which community colleges could serve the needs of Spanish-speaking citizens. The W.K. Kellogg Foundation provided Fomento with $150,480 to develop programs for Spanish-speaking administrators, counselors, and faculty ("AAJC Programs," 1973).

Native Americans commanded considerable attention from the Association as well. The AAJC office of governmental affairs worked for three years to create a community college on the Navajo reservation ("Victory on Hill," 1972), joining tribal leaders and the U.S. Office of Education in pushing the project through Congress. In December 1971 President Nixon signed a law creating Navajo Community College, allotting $5.5 million for construction and $1.2 million for annual operating expenses. AAJC also arranged a $310,500 Kellogg Foundation grant for the new college ("Kellogg Sets Fund," 1973/1974).

Like other minorities, Native Americans were severely underrepresented among community and junior college professionals. In the fall of 1970, Native American students accounted for 1.3 percent of full-time community college enrollments, and only 0.3 percent of faculty and administrators were Native Americans (Goodrich, Lezotte & Welch, 1972/1973). In 1972 the Association created an American Indian program, funded by the US Steel Foundation, designed to increase the number of Native American faculty and administrators. The Rockefeller Foundation provided $200,000 to fund fellowships through this program, allowing Native Americans to work directly with presidents and other administrators at large community colleges ("Rockefeller Grants," 1974).

SERVING THE FORGOTTEN VETERAN

After World War II the American public welcomed its veterans with open arms. After the parades and celebrations, the federal government financed a free college education for returning soldiers. The GI Bill brought unprecedented opportunities for veterans of World War II and the Korean conflict.

For Vietnam veterans, however, there were no victory parades and inadequate educational benefits (Schenkman, 1973/1974). An unmarried Vietnam veteran received a lump sum of $220 a month to cover all educational costs—on the surface, slightly more than what Korean veterans got. Yet inflation had multiplied the costs of a college education, drastically reducing the real value of GI benefits. As Love (1973) noted, "Veterans say that unless they live at home or have working wives, they just can't hack it" (p. 28).

Vietnam veterans also had other, more personal problems. At least 20,000 were receiving treatment for drug or alcohol addiction. As one veteran complained, fellow citizens thought of them as "addicts, killers, psychos, or human time bombs" (pp. 28–29). Generally, Vietnam veterans were ignored and grossly underappreciated, as a study by the Educational Testing Service confirmed:

> Because of...hostile opposition to our involvement in Vietnam, the veteran is often looked upon as a "dupe" of the system and not considered deserving any special consideration.... There was no "VE" or "VJ" day, followed by masses of returning vets. Instead, the vets returned in trickles, one or two plane loads at a time. They were dumped in a California center; and after perhaps a week of "processing" they were dispatched without fanfare back into society to make their own way (Glass & Robinson, 1976, pp. 62–63).

As a consequence of these financial and personal problems, Vietnam veterans were unlikely to enter college. Months after the last U.S. troops left Vietnam in March of 1973, less than half of Vietnam-era veterans were "taking advantage of their educational benefits" (Love, 1973, p. 28). Although the general plight of veterans remained gloomy, efforts by AACJC and individual colleges helped many veterans to reenter society.

AACJC entered into a partnership with the American Legion, the nation's largest veterans organization, whereby the legion would provide monthly regional lists of returning veterans to community colleges near the veterans' homes. The colleges contacted the veterans and offered "financial aid packaging, work study job slots, deferred tuition payments, special academic and personal counseling, and special remedial-tutorial programs" (Love, 1973, p. 29). More than 500 colleges participated in this outreach program.

AAJC also created the Program for Servicemen and Veterans, a project funded by two grants from the Carnegie Foundation: one in 1970 for $293,000 and a second in 1972 for $295,470. Under the project three regional coordinators worked with individual colleges on program planning for returning veterans and helped to establish seventy predischarge education programs and programs for disabled veterans. The project also sponsored workshops to encourage cooperation between military personnel and college administrators ("Carnegie Grants $295,000," 1972).

The Information Clearinghouse and Assistance Program, established by the Association with a $100,000 grant from the U.S. Office of Education, sponsored a series of workshops throughout the nation on how to set up collegiate veterans programs ("AACJC Sets Up Veterans' Information Clearinghouse," 1973). Veterans activist Patrick McLaughlin, then executive director of the National Association of Collegiate Veterans, headed the program.

THE STUDENTS FIND A VOICE

Community colleges were spared most of the student activism of the early 1970s. There were a few isolated demonstrations, rallies, and other protests, but generally community college campuses remained calm. In a subtler way, however, community college students were beginning to organize. Student elections became more hotly contested, and students began to attend college trustee meetings and speak out on college issues.

Students also organized on a national level. At the 1971 AAJC convention students tried unsuccessfully to elect one of their own to the Board of Directors ("Annual Convention," 1971). The following year, 250 community college students, at a conference in Washington, D.C., sponsored by the National Student Association and the Danforth Foundation, voted to start a new organization, the National Community and Junior College Student Association (NCJCSA), and elected Larry Nunley, a Vietnam veteran and father of three, as its first chair. One of the group's first actions was to send representatives to the 1972 AACJC convention to request more student representation within the association ("National J.C. Student Group," 1972). With more than two hundred NCJCSA members in attendance, the convention elected the first student member of the AACJC Board.

VOCATIONAL EDUCATION: AN OVERDUE EXPLOSION

For half a century junior college leaders had been touting the importance of vocational education. They argued that America was in danger of producing too many baccalaureate-degreed professionals and not enough trained technicians. In the 1970s these dire predictions came true.

In the late 1960s and early 1970s the number of workers with bachelor's degrees increased by nearly 8 percent a year. Soon there were not enough upper-level jobs to go around. In 1972 over 30 percent of male bachelor's and master's recipients accepted nonprofessional and nonmanagerial jobs (Brint & Karabel, 1989, p. 113). The average wage for new university graduates also dropped. This underemployment trend continued throughout the decade. The demand for technicians, allied health workers, computer operators, and other vocations, however, had risen, with many junior college vocational graduates earning higher starting salaries than their peers with a four-year degree ("Emphasis: Career Staffing Center," 1971).

These trends brought about an increased demand for vocational courses. Between 1970 and 1975 the number of vocational graduates doubled, and by the end of the decade, 62.5 percent of all two-year college graduates had received occupational degrees. Along the way two-year colleges created a new generation of vocational programs in the health, energy, and computer fields (Brint & Karabel, 1989, p. 117).

COPING WITH THE ENERGY CRISIS

In the early 1970s Americans gave little thought to energy consumption. With gasoline prices at thirty cents a gallon, the automobile industry built huge "land yachts." Families exchanged their electric fans for central air conditioning. Energy was plentiful, cheap, and seemingly inexhaustible.

In 1973 the supply lines were suddenly cut when the Organization of Petroleum Exporting Countries embargoed oil exports to the United States. Fuel prices skyrocketed and supplies dwindled. Americans waited for hours in gasoline lines. President Richard Nixon imposed a national speed limit, and many cities developed gasoline rationing systems. Even after the embargo ended, the sense of crisis remained. President Jimmy Carter declared the energy crisis the equivalent of war. As they had in other wars, two-year colleges found ways to help.

By the end of the decade 67 percent of American two-year colleges were operating energy-related programs, from teaching homeowners ways to conserve energy, to retraining builders, plumbers, electricians, facilities planners, and air conditioning technicians in energy-efficient techniques (Mahoney, 1981). A growing number of colleges offered energy-related majors and certificate programs (p. 34). Solar energy was the most popular curriculum. Degree programs relating to coal, petroleum, nuclear energy, and energy conservation were also in demand.

In all, 165 two-year colleges nationwide maintained energy-related degree programs. Among the most innovative programs were the alcohol fuel plant at Southeast Community College, Nebraska, funded by the U.S. Department of Energy; the nuclear power plant operator degree program at Chattanooga State Technical Community College, Tennessee, funded by the Tennessee Valley Authority; the energy management degree program at Edmonds Community College, Washington, in which students conducted energy audits for the local utility company; and the petroleum engineering degree program at Delgado College, Louisiana, that prepared students to work on oil rigs and pipelines (Mahoney, 1981).

EXPANDING FOUNDATION SUPPORT

Since the Kellogg grants of the 1950s, foundation funding had become a multi-million-dollar source of annual funding for community college programs. During the 1970s a host of other corporate and private foundations joined the W.K. Kellogg Foundation in its support of these programs, either channeling funds through AACJC or giving grants directly to individual colleges. These grants helped colleges experiment with new learning concepts and programs. Some have even had a lasting impact on the community college movement.

The Carnegie Corporation provided $935,000 to ten universities to develop doctor of arts degrees primarily for the training of community college teachers. This new degree had been pioneered in 1967 at Carnegie Mellon University ("Carnegie Grants $935,000," 1970). The Danforth Foundation sponsored the New Institutions Project, a three-year AAJC program. The project provided consulting services for the presidents and trustees of 200 new two-year colleges and sponsored two dozen conferences and workshops ("Danforth Project," 1971). The Mott Foundation funded the Center for Community Education, which was located in the AACJC headquarters. The center encouraged cooperation between junior colleges, public schools, and other community groups ("AACJC Center," 1975/1976). The Ford Foundation sponsored a $2 million scholarship program for minority community college graduates. These funds allowed minority students to transfer to a four-year institution after receiving their associate degree ("Ford Foundation," 1970). The Commonwealth Fund contributed $63,000 to develop vocational programs in the allied health fields (Brint & Karabel, 1989, p. 107). The U.S. Department of Justice's Law Enforcement Assistance Administration established a fourteen-month project to help raise the educational level of correctional officers ("Justice Makes Grant," 1972).

The Kellogg Foundation provided a number of grants during this period, including $700,000 for a three-year community services leadership program. This program helped develop a graduate program at the University of Michigan and a community services program at three Michigan community colleges (Raines & Myran, 1970). The foundation also awarded $478,200 to AACJC and the National Self-Help Resource Center. These funds were used to create resource centers at six community colleges to help citizens become involved in local decision making ("Kellogg Funds Resource Centers," 1978). In addition, the Kellogg Foundation funded another AAJC project to explore and develop the international dimensions of community and junior colleges ("Emphasis: International Project," 1971; Shannon, 1971b).

GROWING FEDERAL SUPPORT

Under the Nixon administration federal funding for community colleges grew exponentially, with the greatest support for vocational programs. The Education Amendment Act of 1972 provided $707 million for postsecondary vocational programs, and two years later Congress appropriated an additional $981 million (Brint & Karabel, 1989). The president, a vocal supporter of these programs, declared in a 1970 message to Congress:

> Too many people have fallen prey to the myth that a four-year liberal arts diploma is essential to a full and rewarding life, whereas in fact other forms of postsecondary education—such as a two-year community college or technical training—are far better suited to the interests of many young people (p. 109).

The new emphasis on community colleges was reflected in the staffing of the U.S. Office of Education, which in 1970 added a second two-year college specialist and then a special assistant to the commissioner of education for community and junior colleges (Diener, 1970, p. 23). In 1972 Joseph Cosand, founding president of the St. Louis Junior College District and an AAJC Board member, was appointed deputy commissioner for higher education ("Emphasis: Joseph Cosand," 1972). The following year a separate junior college unit was established, with Marie Martin, a former president in the Los Angeles Community College System, as director ("New Community College Unit," 1973). In addition to supporting community college legislation, the office funded numerous programs, mainly through Title III of the Higher Education Act, for individual colleges and AACJC. The largest of these was the Program with Developing Institutions.

The AAJC Governmental Intern Program, funded by the Office of Education and administered by the Association's office of governmental affairs, also started up in the 1970s ("Emphasis: Governmental Interns," 1971). Under this program a group of two-year college administrators was brought to Washington to learn how to "effectively deal with government" (p. 5), and after ten weeks of training worked in the offices of federal agencies and legislators.

COMMUNITY COLLEGES FOR SERVICE PERSONNEL

During the 1970s America maintained its controversial position of policing the world. Hundreds of thousands of American servicemen and -women stationed at facilities around the globe did not have the convenient opportunity to take classes at local community colleges. The community college therefore came to them.

City Colleges of Chicago pioneered the idea of community college studies for service personnel when, in the fall of 1969, the system began offering college and preparatory courses to Air Force, Army, and Navy personnel and their dependents. By the mid-1970s courses were being offered at forty American military bases in Europe (Ross, 1974). In 1976 the college district placed all of its military programs under one of its eight colleges, Chicago City-Wide College. Over the next decade the program expanded to 150 locations in ten countries and on Navy ships throughout the world. By 1985 these programs had an annual headcount of nearly 45,000 students. The college employed hundreds of instructors and field registrars at military bases worldwide. Some instructors circled the globe, shifting from one Navy ship to another (Warden, 1985). These programs were entirely self-supporting through student tuition, most of which was paid by the military tuition assistance program. For Navy servicemen and -women, however, the Navy covered all tuition costs "to help alleviate the rather arduous duty aboard ship" (p. 43).

A program called the Servicemembers Opportunity Colleges, more commonly known as SOC, created by the AAJC in 1971, helped men and women in the military earn an associate degree. Member colleges, which had to agree to special transfer practices and residency requirements for servicemembers, also awarded credit for nontraditional learning, such as the United States Armed Forces Institute (USAFI), correspondence courses, and specialized military training. By 1985, 434 institutions were participating in the SOC program, including 188 two-year colleges (p. 44).

The Community College of the Air Force began operation in the spring of 1973. The college expanded rapidly, enrolling 32,000 students in its first three years (Kaapke & Wojciechowski, 1977, p. 30). In its early days it was primarily a "brokerage house" for educational experiences (Ross, 1974, p. 10), evaluating the Air Force's 3,600 technical courses to determine which courses were acceptable "at civilian postsecondary level" (p. 36). The college converted these

253

training courses into equivalent college courses and produced a college transcript. Students could also earn credit for College Level Examination Program (CLEP) tests and USAFI courses. Following accreditation in December 1973 by the Southern Association of Colleges and Schools, Community College of the Air Force students could transfer their credits to another institution or earn a career education certificate, roughly equivalent to an associate degree.

A New Doctoral Program for Community College Leaders

The need for postgraduate training programs for community college personnel became more immediate as two-year colleges undertook new missions to serve an increasingly diverse student population. For the most part, those universities that offered doctoral programs for community college personnel operated under very traditional academic regulations. Programs tended to be highly selective, and, although some extension courses might be offered away from university campuses, in almost every case residency policies required that the student spend at least a year at the university. There was mounting criticism from community college leaders that such programs did not always serve well the community college faculty member or administrator who could not or chose not to leave his or her position for a period of time, and whose ultimate goal was to continue to work at a community college. Many community college personnel, who were themselves offering effective educational programs away from their campuses, considered university residency requirements outmoded and unnecessary.

In 1972 NOVA University, a private institution in Florida, designed and implemented a field-based doctoral program for community college faculty that, despite intense opposition from more traditional universities, became very successful. Under the leadership of program directors John Scigliano and, later, Ross Moreton and university president Abraham Fischler, and with the guidance of a prestigious national panel of community college practitioners and community college educators from several major universities, the program was tailored to the needs of two-year college faculty.

NOVA students attended weekend classes at "cluster centers" located within driving distance of their homes and jobs. Teaching faculty of the program were national lecturers, most often leading professors of community college education from other universities or nationally known community college leaders, who traveled to the cluster sites. The faculty encouraged students to undertake research projects in their areas of work, using their home institutions as laboratories. The only away-from-home requirement was attendance at two week-long summer institutes (NOVA University, Institute for Higher Education, 1976). A major accomplishment for the new program and an important factor in its success was the program's accreditation by the Southern Association of Colleges and Schools.

The program began with the opening of seven clusters scattered across the nation. Most clusters operated for several years, and new clusters began each year. At its peak in 1976, twenty-five new clusters were opened (Moreton, n.d.). By 1992 more than 1,500 community college participants had graduated from the program, and in that year the university reported that well over 100 administrators in American community colleges held NOVA doctorates.

AACJC: A Change of Strategy

The national Association went through several fundamental changes during the 1970s, many of which were in response to a strategic planning process called Project Focus. The eighteen-month process was funded by a $250,000 grant from the W.K. Kellogg Foundation ("AAJC Begins Nationwide Study," 1970).

To determine national needs, Edmund Gleazer visited political and educational leaders throughout the nation. He visited thirty colleges, interviewing dozens of faculty, staff, and administrators on each campus, and visited state capitals, talking to governors, legislators, and education officials. At each stop Gleazer asked about the educational mission of the colleges and the services they needed from a national association (Gleazer, 1971b, p. 5). At the same time, Association staff and an outside management consultant were interviewing other educational associations and authorities in the field. Based on their work, a final report for the reorganization of the Association was submitted to the AAJC membership at the 1972 convention in Dallas. The reorganization plan passed the required two-thirds vote and was adopted. The Association's name was changed to the American Association of Community and Junior Colleges. The executive director was renamed president, and other top administrators became vice president or senior vice president. The chair of the Association's Board would be elected by the Board of Directors rather than by the membership ("Amendments Are Passed," 1972). The Board of Directors was expanded to thirty members to include three seats elected at-large from member institutions, six representatives of AACJC councils, and three leading citizens. Provisions were also made for the establishment of a national assembly and for creating new AACJC councils and expanding their role to increase member participation and input into Association activities. The Kellogg Foundation agreed to provide initial funding for these groups ("Emphasis: Board," 1972).

Spurred by the new organization, the four AACJC councils grew to ten by 1974. These were the American Association of Women in Community and Junior Colleges, Congreso Nacional de Asuntos Colegiales, Council for Community Services, Council on Black American Affairs, Council on Learning (faculty), Council on Public Relations, Council on Resource Development, Council on Student Development, Council on Universities and Colleges, and National Council of State Directors (Harper, 1974).

Until Project Focus the AAJC Board had been made up almost entirely of college presidents ("Emphasis: Project Focus," 1971; Gleazer, 1971a). With the reorganization the presidents lost some control. At the same time, many presidents were losing influence at their own institutions to faculty unions, activist trustees, and expanding state control. To regain some of their prestige the presidents formed the Council of Chief Executive Administrators, reformed in 1975 as the Presidents Academy. All presidents of AACJC institutions automatically became members (McAninch, 1980). The Presidents Academy served as the networking and training organization for two-year college presidents and gave presidents a voice in the formulation of Association policy. In later years the academy established an annual summer seminar for new college presidents ("Academy Presidents," 1981).

The *Junior College Journal* also went through a change of name and staff. Beginning in the fall of 1972 it became the *Community and Junior College Journal*. Roger Yarrington left the editorship after ten years to become moderator of the national assembly. Under Yarrington the *Journal's* circulation had risen to more than 45,000, much of which was through group subscriptions paid for by member institutions. Yarrington was replaced by William A. Harper, who took the new title of vice president for communications ("Executive Staff," 1972).

The *Journal*, for that matter, was no longer the only periodical of the community college movement. The *Community Services Catalyst* was founded in 1969 by the AAJC-affiliated National Council on Community Services and Continuing Education. Other periodicals included the *Community College Social Science Quarterly*, founded in 1970; *Community College Frontiers*, 1972; *Community College Review*, 1973; and *Community/Junior College Research Quarterly*, 1976 (Clowes & Towles, 1985, p. 29). Other AACJC councils began to publish newsletters and publications of interest to their constituencies.

THE TRUSTEES ORGANIZE

Given the long history of closeness between two-year colleges and secondary schools, and the fact that in the 1960s many two-year colleges were still operating under school boards, it is not surprising that many community college trustees were active members of the National School Boards Association (NSBA). In 1965, recognizing the growth and unique problems of two-year colleges, the NSBA organized a study committee of community college trustees in order to determine the feasibility of forming a council under the umbrella of the NSBA.

Following two years of study committee reports and special workshops, the Council of Community College Boards (CCCB) was approved by the NSBA board of directors in 1967. In May 1968 J. Stuart Doyle became its executive secretary, and was succeeded in July 1970 by William H. Meardy, who would lead the trustees through organizational changes and dramatic growth. The CCCB held its first annual convention in October 1970, at which 162 trustees were in attendance.

Again reflecting the growth and increasing independence of the two-year college movement, it soon became apparent that the needs of community college trustees could not be met adequately in an organization composed primarily of school board members. In April 1972 the community college trustees voted to leave the NSBA and form an independent association, the Association of Community College Trustees (ACCT), to be governed by a fifteen-member board of directors, three for each of ACCT's five regions. In August of that year, the fledgling association moved its headquarters to Washington, D.C. In October, 603 trustees attended the new organization's annual convention in Atlanta.

Soon thereafter the American Association of Community and Junior College Boards, the trustee council of AACJC, voted to join with ACCT rather than operate as a competing organization. The nine board members of the AACJC council joined with the ACCT board to create a twenty-four-member board that continues today (Association of Community College Trustees, 1992).

The purposes of ACCT are "to strengthen lay citizen governance of community colleges" and "to help community, technical, and junior college trustees provide visionary, responsive, sensitive, and accountable education policy leadership" (Association of Community College Trustees, n.d.). The functions of the association are "trustee development, advocacy of the governing board perspective at the federal level, local board assistance, promotion of the role of community colleges, and education leadership" (Association of Community College Trustees, 1992).

In 1976 ACCT reported a membership of 516 colleges and drew 922 trustees to the annual convention. Also that year the association began an active program of publications to meet the growing interest in and need for trustee education (King, 1982), inaugurating the *Trustee Quarterly*. In 1986 ACCT membership included 720 colleges, and 1,800 trustees attended the annual convention in San Diego.

William Meardy retired from his duties as executive director in July 1988. During his term of office he had seen the struggling organization grow into a thriving national association. Under his leadership ACCT had joined with AACJC in the highly successful W.K. Kellogg Foundation-funded project Putting America Back to Work and its successor, the Sears Roebuck Foundation-funded Keeping America Working. Both projects were directed at helping community colleges learn how to work with local businesses and industries to reduce unemployment and improve local economies. Meardy oversaw the creation of the Chief Executive Search Advisory Service, one of the association's most successful ventures, and the formation with AACJC of the Joint Commission on Federal Relations.

David Viar, who had formerly worked with the trustee organization in California, became executive director in 1988 and served for two years before being lured back to California to head a statewide organization. Viar was replaced by Ray Taylor, who had been a vice chancellor in the St. Louis Community College District in Missouri.

TOWARD THE SECOND CENTURY (1980-1992)

[Community colleges are] a priceless treasure—
close to our homes and work, providing open doors
for millions of our fellow citizens...the original
higher education melting pot.

—Ronald Reagan

The new decade brought relief from four years of stagnant enrollments. In the fall of 1980 credit enrollment jumped by 7.5 percent, to 4.8 million students, with an additional four million students enrolled in noncredit courses. This resurgence was largely due to a national recession: as they had during the Great Depression, students chose two-year colleges over the more expensive four-year institutions (Gernhart, 1981).

The recession also ended the presidency of Democrat Jimmy Carter. In November 1980 Ronald Reagan won a landslide victory for the Republican party, promising to revive the American economy. The new administration jolted the economy with a tax cut and increased military spending, and within two years inflation had decreased and America was beginning its longest period of economic growth since World War II. Ironically, the recovery signaled a downturn for two-year colleges. In the fall of 1983 full-time enrollment fell to 1978 levels (Jellison, 1984) and would not fully recover until the end of the decade. Increased part-time enrollments helped ameliorate this decline.

Community college leaders had become experts in reaching out to untapped sectors of the community. To attract new students, colleges increased their advertising and public relations budgets, and offered courses at high schools, senior citizen centers, and even prisons. Many colleges experimented with newspaper and television courses. These outreach efforts brought a massive increase in part-time credit enrollment, which nearly tripled between 1970 and 1990. Many part-timers were older students, taking only one or two courses. By 1990 the average age of two-year college students had risen to twenty-eight, and more than half of all students were over twenty-four years of age (American Association of Community and Junior Colleges, 1990).

Both full-time and part-time matriculations surged in 1990, bringing enrollments near the six million mark. The nation's 1,200 two-year colleges enrolled nearly 45 percent of all students in American higher education (American Association of Community and Junior Colleges, 1988; Mahoney, 1985, 1986, 1990; Mahoney & Jimenez, 1992; Mahoney & Sallis, 1991; Palmer, 1988b; Savage, 1987).

THE WASHINGTON CONNECTION

During the 1980s two-year colleges gained increasing attention from the White House and Capitol Hill. Some of this attention was based on sheer numbers. Community colleges served more voters and children of voters than any other type of postsecondary institution, and a community college existed in almost every congressional district. Equally important, however, were the lobbying efforts of community college leaders led by AACJC and ACCT (Mensel, 1987; Mensel & Bolling, 1986/1987).

The AACJC office of governmental relations built a nationwide network of administrators and faculty to support key legislation, publishing a weekly *Network Memo* to inform colleges about pending legislation. The office was instrumental in passing the Comprehensive Veterans' Education and Rehabilitation Bill of 1980. Five years later the office threw its lobbying weight behind the Peacetime GI Bill (Mensel, 1984/1985).

The Peacetime GI Bill, designed to attract more and better recruits to the nation's new all-volunteer armed forces, drew stiff opposition from several powerful lawmakers. In a final "nerve-stretching drive," however, AACJC unleashed a "flurry of letters and calls touching almost every state" (p. 55). The resulting victory gave community colleges and their representative, AACJC, new clout on Capitol Hill.

In 1982 AACJC and ACCT formed the Joint Commission on Federal Relations with board members from both organizations. The federal relations staffs of the two organizations were brought closer together with Frank Mensel serving as AACJC vice president for federal relations and ACCT director of federal relations. This strategic alliance allowed the two groups to speak with one voice on legislation and regulations (American Association of Community and Junior Colleges, 1990; Association of Community College Trustees, 1992). That the efforts of community college administrators were now supported by influential college trustees, many with strong political bases of their own, did much to improve AACJC's prestige.

The joint commission's first success came in 1987 when Congress rewrote the formula for Pell grants. First established in 1972, the Pell grant program provided direct grants to college students, based on economic need, but unfortunately discriminated against commuting and part-time students. Commuting students had their cost-of-living allowance reduced, and less-than-half-time students were not eligible for grants. The joint commission argued that these regulations hurt students who most needed financial aid—working students and those who could not afford to leave home.

Under lobbying from the joint commission and through the nationwide support the commission was able to muster, Congress reversed these discriminatory regulations. The Higher Education Act of 1987 raised the cost-of-living allowance for commuting students to the same level as for dormitory students. It also provided Pell grants for less-than-full-time students who received no financial support from home. These changes increased the levels of financial aid for thousands of two-year college students. In 1989 the joint commission achieved further successes, including a $50 million set-aside in Title III of the Higher Education Act and a $5 million set-aside from the National Science Foundation.

Another legislative success was funding for tech-prep/associate degree (TPAD) programs. An innovation developed and promoted heavily by AACJC president Dale Parnell, TPAD formed the centerpiece of his book *The Neglected Majority* (1985). These "2 + 2" degree programs linked two-year colleges and feeder high schools, with students beginning a program in their junior year of high school and continuing through a corresponding two-year program leading to an associate degree at the community college. The Perkins Act of 1991 provided $63.4 million for TPAD programs (Keyser, 1991).

Two-year colleges also began to attract the attention of the White House. In 1984 President Ronald Reagan met with a community college delegation headed by AACJC president Dale Parnell. During the interview, Reagan described two-year colleges as "a priceless treasure—close to our homes and work, providing open doors for millions of our fellow citizens...the original higher education melting pot" (Parnell, 1984).

President George Bush came to the 1989 AACJC convention to watch First Lady Barbara Bush receive the Harry S. Truman Award, the Association's highest award given to a layperson, for her work in literacy (Reneau, 1989). It was the first time that an American president had addressed a meeting of community college leaders. Before an audience of 1,800 guests, the president praised this "American innovation" as the great success story of American education:

> Whole communities are enriched and enlightened by the cultural resources you provide, from vast libraries, to night

schools, to stages for local theatrical productions. This attitude toward education—as something more than a requirement of an industrial society, as an embellishment of life—is uniquely American. I believe that secondary and even elementary schools can learn a lot from your success.... For this and all that you are doing, you are earning the gratitude of a nation (Bush, 1989).

THE ASSOCIATION MATURES

AACJC remained the primary national advocate for community colleges (Edwards, 1989/1990), with more than 90 percent of all public two-year colleges as members. In 1981 Edmund J. Gleazer, Jr., retired after a record twenty-three years at the Association's helm. He had presided over the greatest period of growth in the history of any type of postsecondary institutions. When he took office America's two-year colleges enrolled only 585,420 students. At his retirement the total was over 4.8 million. During his term of office the Association budget grew from $52,000 to over $3.1 million ("Gleazer, Kerr," 1981/1982; "Mission 1980," 1981).

Gleazer's contribution to AACJC and to the community college movement, however, goes far beyond numbers of students and Association growth. Perhaps more than any other individual, he was responsible for articulating the unique identity of community colleges (Watson, 1981). Gleazer was able to synthesize the work and the words of his predecessors—William Rainey Harper, Leonard Koos, Doak Campbell, Jesse Bogue—into his own vision and that of many of his contemporaries. An excellent writer and speaker, he used his position as head of AACJC as a "bully pulpit" to create a language, an image, and an ethos for these new institutions. In 1958 Gleazer took over an Association representing colleges that were widely misunderstood and struggling for recognition by both the general public and the rest of higher education. Serving populations never before served and trying missions that were new to higher education, these colleges were wrestling with their own self-concept. In 1981 Gleazer left an Association representing strong, self-confident, comprehensive community colleges—colleges that were relied on and treasured by their communities and recognized as an invaluable component of the American educational system (Parnell, 1987).

On July 1, 1981, Dale Parnell took over the reins of the Association ("Parnell," 1981). At the time of his appointment Parnell was a member of the AACJC Board and president-elect of the Presidents Academy. He had a long background in public education and in the community college movement. Serving as Oregon superintendent for public instruction and maintaining a close friendship with Governor Mark Hatfield, he had been instrumental in drafting the state's community college law and in creating the state system of community colleges. He served as the founding president of Lane Community College in Eugene, Oregon. During the 1970s he served as chancellor of the San Diego Community College District and later became founding president of San Joaquin Delta Community College in Stockton, California.

Not surprisingly, given the Association's increased role as advocate for community colleges before Congress and federal agencies, a major factor in Parnell's selection was his skill and experience in the political arena. Unlike many educators who look on lobbying and the political process as a necessary evil, Parnell enjoyed it ("President Dale Parnell," 1981). He sought opportunities to showcase community and junior colleges and was more than willing to go to battle on their behalf. In the words of one observer, "Gleazer, the philosopher, has been replaced by Parnell, the street-fighter." Under his leadership the Association and its member colleges enjoyed increasing support and recognition at the national level.

AACJC moved into advanced technology services for its members (Palmer, 1988a; Cross, 1988). At the urging of Robert DeHart, the president of DeAnza College in California and a leader in the use of television in community colleges, the Association created the Community College Satellite Network (CCSN) in 1989 (Parnell, 1988). The network was designed to provide teleconferences, telecourses, and community education to member colleges. By 1991 nearly 200 colleges had signed up for the service. A nationwide system was created when six community colleges, from Virginia to California, installed up-links, allowing broadcasts to originate from their campuses (Keyser, 1991). The up-links were funded through a $584,000 grant to the Association from the U.S. Department of Commerce. The Association also sponsored ACCESS, a computer network that allowed community colleges to share information and data bases (Parnell, 1988).

Parnell was an entrepreneur, and under his leadership the Association expanded the scope and circulation of its publications program. In 1986 the *Community and Junior College Journal* was renamed the *Community, Technical, and Junior College Journal* and given a new format (Gollattscheck, 1985). The Association also published the *Community, Technical, and Junior College Times*, a biweekly newspaper with more than 10,000 subscribers, and the *AACJC Letter*, a monthly newsletter for college presidents (American Association of Community and Junior Colleges, 1990; Reinhard, 1988/1989).

The annual convention of the Association continued to grow and become a major source of income for the Association. With Parnell's entrepreneurial abilities and AACJC Vice President Connie Odems's leadership, the Association's annual convention became the largest gathering in higher education. At its peak in 1990 in Seattle, the Association's convention drew more than 4,000 attendees and involved more than 1,000 presenters and exhibitors. The following year escalating travel costs and a national economic recession that caused state budget shortfalls reduced attendance, according to Odems.

During his presidency Parnell wrote two books that helped reshape not only the Association's priorities but curricula at high schools and community colleges throughout the nation. The first of these, *The Neglected Majority*, published in 1985, became a key document in the school reform movement. In it Parnell espoused the belief that the middle 50 percent of high school students were "neglected" in that they received neither the attention given to the top 25 percent nor the special programs developed for students in the lowest 25 percent. Instead, they were allowed to drift through a general education program that did not prepare them for work or college. His solution was the tech prep/associate degree, which

267

would, for many students, remodel the upper two years of high school into technical programs planned jointly by the high school and the local community college. Graduates of the high school programs would transfer into corresponding programs at the local community college and receive an associate degree in two years. Within a few years a number of successful model programs were in existence, and federal funding had guaranteed the program's future growth. The second book, *Tech Prep/Associate Degree: A Win-Win Experience* (Hull & Parnell, 1991) furthered the movement with more examples and case studies.

With the publication of *The Neglected Majority*, AACJC launched the Community College Press, an arm of the Association geared to the publishing of major books dealing with community colleges. It was hoped that the Community College Press not only would bring revenue into the Association's budget, but would position AACJC as the recognized provider of professional literature for the two-year college field. Parnell's first book became a record-seller for a book on higher education, with more than 30,000 copies sold. By 1992 the Community College Press had published ten books and sold more than 61,000 copies, according to Bonnie Gardner, director of publications.

The Association continued its commitment to minorities through its Minority Education Initiative. This three-year program, which received $150,000 from the Association budget, was designed to assist colleges with the adoption of aggressive policies" to improve recruitment and retention of minority students and faculty. The initiative was guided by a blue-ribbon panel headed by Texas legislator Wilhelmina Delco (Keyser, 1991).

Parnell felt strongly that the Association needed to involve as many of its different constituencies as possible. Under his leadership the number of AACJC-affiliated councils grew to nineteen with other commissions and consortia raising the number of affiliated groups to thirty-one. He involved the AACJC Board of Directors more visibly in the operation of the Association and saw a dramatic increase in the number of women and ethnic minorities elected or appointed to the Board. By 1990 service on the AACJC Board had become one of the most highly prized and hotly contested positions a community college leader could seek.

Having just left a community college presidency and served on the Association's Board of Directors, Parnell was sensitive to the criticism that too many of the grant dollars the Association received remained at the national level. Under his leadership the Association concentrated on developing projects that would give individual colleges money to create innovative programs (Angel & Gares, 1981).

One of the first successes, and one that would become a model for future projects, was the Keeping America Working project. Funded with a $1 million grant from the Sears Roebuck Foundation, the project provided minigrants ($15,000 to $20,000) to colleges to improve their local economies by developing innovative partnerships with businesses and industries, local governments, high schools, organized labor, and four-year colleges and universities. Parnell's faith that providing small incentive grants would enable colleges to generate matching dollars from local communities was justified. During the four-year course of the project, 289 participating colleges received $1.2 million from the Association. These colleges generated an additional $15 million in local community support (McKenney, 1989).

Early in his administration Parnell established a long-range goal of returning to member colleges in project dollars an amount of money that exceeded the amount of money received by the Association in membership dues. Parnell finally succeeded in 1989-90. With AACJC executive vice president James Gollattscheck responsible for grant efforts, the Association received $1.3 million in institutional dues and returned $1.8 million to member colleges participating in the Association's grant-funded projects. The following year, Parnell's last as head of the Association, membership dues totaled $1.3 million and the Association returned $1.4 million.

In 1986 the AACJC Board approved Parnell's recommendation that the Association create the Commission on the Future of Community Colleges and appointed nineteen community college and university leaders, government officials, and lay citizens to the prestigious commission. The commission was charged with examining the status of America's community colleges and plotting a course for their future development. U.S. Senator Nancy Kassebaum served as honorary chair, and Ernest Boyer, president of the

Carnegie Foundation for the Advancement of Teaching, served as chair. The commission carried out its mission over an eighteen-month period, holding open hearings throughout the nation and involving thousands of citizens and representatives of colleges. The Association distributed more than 50,000 copies of the commission's final report, titled *Building Communities: A Vision for a New Century* (Ponitz, 1989).

To implement the recommendations of the Futures Commission, Parnell and Gollattscheck went to the W.K. Kellogg Foundation for funding. Once again the foundation demonstrated its faith in the community college movement with a $1.8 million grant to fund the Beacon Colleges Program. The project's five-year strategy was to select twenty-five Beacon Colleges that had already begun to implement the recommendations of the Futures Commission, and give them direct financial assistance to conduct exemplary programs suggested by the commission's research. The Beacon Colleges aided a consortium of 250 other colleges in implementing similar programs.

After sixty years of growth, the Association's institutional membership stabilized at about 1,100 colleges (Parnell & Peltason, 1984). In addition, 492 individuals, businesses, and others had become associate members. Branch campuses were also permitted to join, and by 1991 there were seventy-six branch campus members (American Association of Community and Junior Colleges, 1988; Keyser, 1991).

In the spring of 1990 Parnell announced his intention to retire as Association president on June 31, 1991, to return to Oregon and lead a new doctoral program in community college education at Oregon State University. The Chief Executive Search Advisory Service of the Association of Community College Trustees was commissioned to search for Parnell's successor. Over the next eleven months 100 candidates were considered. In April 1991 the Board chose David Pierce, chancellor of the Virginia Community College System. Having begun his career as a community college faculty member in California, Pierce had served as president of North Iowa Area Community College and as executive director of the Illinois Community College Board.

The new president took office on July 1, 1991. Like Gleazer and Parnell, Pierce had risen through the AACJC ranks and served on the Association Board; like Parnell, he had extensive experience in working with state and federal governments; and like Gleazer, Pierce held an associate degree. Gleazer had received his in 1938 from church-related Graceland College in Iowa, an institution that had in 1912, like many of its sister colleges, dropped its junior and senior years to become a junior college. Pierce was a 1958 graduate of Fullerton Junior College in California. The selection of Pierce for the prestigious position of president of AACJC was appropriate for the times. Leading the national Association as the community college movement began its second hundred years was a graduate of a public, comprehensive community college.

AT THE END OF A CENTURY

A century ago William Rainey Harper developed a plan that he claimed would revolutionize higher education. Today that prediction has come to pass (Kerr, 1985). At the end of their first century, two-year colleges are the largest segment of American higher education (Murtha, Kaufman & Warman, 1982). The associate degree has become an accepted standard of achievement. In a single century two-year colleges have opened their doors to millions of students who would otherwise have remained unserved (Cohen & Brawer, 1982; Deegan & Tillery, 1985). They have become the primary choice of racial minorities, women, and older students. The dream of Harper and all who followed for a national system of "people's colleges" has been realized, and the first century of the community college has been completed.

EPILOGUE

In this century an American institution of higher education that has come to be called the community college has developed to the extent that it may now be considered an integral part of the public education system of the United States. Every state has established one or more of these institutions designed to provide opportunity for all people in the community: those who have demonstrated academic abilities, those who have demonstrated one or more of the many other facets of human talent, those who are young, those who are mature, those who have deficiences, those who are clearly competent—in other words, the total populations of the communities in our nation. The origin of these colleges has been firmly placed in educational ideals described by Thomas Jefferson in his correspondence with Pierre-Samuel du Pont de Nemours in the late 1700s. The philosophical values implemented through community colleges reflect Jefferson's commitments and his understanding of what was necessary to encourage the development of a democracy that would work, and this twentieth-century implementation of those ideas and values came to fruition through the combined leadership of those who believed in the necessity for quality in higher education as well as those who believed in making the opportunity available to all people to develop through education during their entire lifetime.

Throughout the history of the community college movement that has been identified in this study, there has been a desire to provide individuals with an education that would enable them to become productive citizens in a democratic society. While the early support of several leading university presidents may have been, in part, motivated by their desire to focus their institutions upon the specializations required for completing a baccalaureate degree, these same presidents recognized that these "new" institutions would also provide opportunities for learning vocational skills and general education. They combined the rationalization of the elitist with the concerns of the populist. These same concerns still motivate the community college movement in the closing days of this century.

Some have claimed that the mission of the community college has been foggy, but an examination of the sweep of the history recorded in this book indicates a marvelous consistency in the institutional mission outlined at the beginning and the end of the twentieth century. It would be difficult to convince anyone that community colleges are confused about their mission when one reads the history recorded herein. Individuals may be confused, but the movement has been wonderfully consistent.

The establishment and development of community colleges has been motivated by a series of landmark publications and the events surrounding those surveys and reports. The letters of William Rainey Harper, although not generally available, outline a sound basis for community college development, and the recorded remarks of his contemporaries support this basis. The observations of Leonard Koos and Doak Campbell confirm that these institutions were developing along the bases that had been outlined. The dedication of George Zook over a number of years and the consistent support of Walter Eells kept the mission clearly in front of the practitioners. The report of the Educational Policies Commission followed by the GI Bill and the Truman Report provided a basis for community college growth and thereby the groundwork for the concerns expressed later by President Eisenhower's Committee on Education Beyond the High School. As the various states began to examine these concerns, reports from educational researchers who were seeking ways to implement the democratic educational commitments called to attention the concepts of state planning for higher education as described earlier by George Strayer and many others, and later implemented in a model state system of community colleges in Florida by James Wattenbarger and others, and encouraged by such regional agencies as the Southern Regional Education Board and the Western Interstate Commission on Higher Education, and by such national organizations as the American Council on Education and the Commission of States.

274

Educational needs were translated into educational demands, and citizen groups of various kinds called for the educational opportunities defined and recognized by these reports and researchers. Edmund Gleazer's book, *The Community College: Values Vision, and Vitality* (1980), then provided a basis for a further unfolding of the philosophy, outlined ways to meet the economic and social needs as well as the individual needs, and rounded out a series of studies that had been the major influences on this movement during the century.

Two major examples of national legislation, the Land Grant College Act of 1862 and the GI Bill of 1945, have represented great steps in moving American higher education toward the universal educational opportunity envisioned by Jefferson and by the Ordinance of 1787. These extensions of the philosophical commitments to provide equal opportunity for the growth and development of all citizens have been further implemented by the community college. The agricultural and mechanical colleges were often referred to as "people's colleges"; so were the early junior colleges (in Mississippi, for example); and when the land grant colleges turned their attention to the university portion of their mission, community colleges were ready to assume the role of serving a broader segment of the population. The century of the community colleges is the century of extended educational opportunity in consonance with the ideas that motivated the development of the land grant colleges and the opportunities provided in this century by the GI Bill.

All of these statements may seem to imply that community colleges have reached the highest ground and there is not much improvement needed. Obviously, this is not the case. Even though the foundation has been laid, even though great progress has been made, even though the median educational level is far higher than it was at the beginning of the century, the facts still indicate that much more is needed for the twenty-first century. The report of the Commission on the Future of Community Colleges, *Building Communities: A Vision for a New Century* (1988), presented more than sixty recommendations that were designed to improve the quality of community colleges. Populations as yet poorly served and age

275

groups that have been largely unserved at this post-high-school level were identified. The recommendations of the commission contained such words as "vigorously reaffirm," "aggressive outreach," "expand and improve," "more attention," "encourage," "commit," "increase," "critique"—all indicating ways to improve community colleges.

With this commitment to improve and the sound philosophical bases of the first century to build upon, the second century of the community college should be equal to or even better than the first.

The history of community colleges is not solely a history of the influences of great men or women or even of the sweeping tides of major social movements, but rather a testimony of political commitment to providing educational opportunity to the many who would not otherwise be served.

REFERENCES

AACJC Center for Community Education funded by Mott Foundation. (1975/1976). *Community and Junior College Journal, 46* (4), 39.

AACJC sets up veterans' information clearinghouse. (1973). *Community and Junior College Journal, 43* (6), 95.

AAJC begins nationwide study of community-junior colleges. (1970). *Junior College Journal, 41* (1), 56.

AAJC programs for Spanish speaking receive boost from Kellogg. (1973). *Community and Junior College Journal, 43* (7), 48.

Academy presidents share resources and ideas at workshop in Colorado. (1981). *Community and Junior College Journal, 52* (2), 46.

Albright, D. (1948). Selected references. *Junior College Journal, 19* (2), 112–115.

Alderman, L.C., Jr. (1985). Century college. *Community and Junior College Journal, 55* (8), 27–28.

Alfred, R.L., Peterson, R.O., & White, T.H. (1992). *Making community colleges more effective: Leading through student success.* Ann Arbor, MI: Community College Consortium.

Amendments are passed; name changes July 1. (1972). *Junior College Journal, 42* (7), 35.

American Association of Community and Junior Colleges. (1975). *A policy primer for community-based colleges.* Washington, DC: Author.

American Association of Community and Junior Colleges. (1978). *Forums for citizen education.* Washington, DC: Author.

American Association of Community and Junior Colleges. (1988). *A summary of selected national data pertaining to community, technical, and junior colleges.* Washington, DC: Author.

American Association of Community and Junior Colleges. (1990). *AACJC membership handbook 1990.* Washington, DC: Author.

American Association of Junior Colleges. (1921). *Proceedings.* Washington, DC: Author.

American Association of Junior Colleges. (1922a). *The American Association of Junior Colleges.* Unpublished report.

American Association of Junior Colleges. (1922b). *Report of the American Association of Junior Colleges in annual session.* Washington, DC: Author.

American Association of Junior Colleges. (1946). *Junior college directory, 1946.* Washington, DC: Author.

American Association of Junior Colleges. (1947). *Junior college directory, 1947.* Washington, DC: Author.

American Association of Junior Colleges. (1965). *1965 junior college directory.* Washington, DC: Author.

American Association of Junior Colleges. (1966). *1966 junior college directory.* Washington, DC: Author.

American Association of Junior Colleges. (1967). *AAJC: The 1960s to the decade ahead.* Washington, DC: Author.

American Association of Junior Colleges. (1969). *AAJC 1968 annual report.* Washington, DC: Author.

American Association of Junior Colleges Constitution. (1939). *Junior College Journal, 9* (8), 556–559.

American Council on Education. (1967). *An introduction to American junior colleges.* Washington, DC: Author.

Anderson, B.E. (1966). *Nursing education in community junior colleges: A four-state 5-year experience in the development of associate degree programs.* Philadelphia: Lippincott.

Andrews, J.N. (1942). The junior colleges and national defense. *Junior College Journal, 12* (7), 389–398.

Anello, M.E. (1942). 135 wartime courses. *Junior College Journal, 12* (8), 469–476.

Angel, D., & Gares, D. (1981). A bull market for foundations. *Community and Junior College Journal, 52* (3), 5–8.

Angell, J.R. (1915). The junior-college movement in high schools. *School Review, 23,* 289–302.

Annual convention draws 3,400; sees many AAJC firsts. (1971). *Junior College Journal, 41* (7), 44–46.

Association of Community College Trustees. (n.d.). *Trustee leadership for institutional excellence.* Washington, DC: Author.

Association of Community College Trustees. (1992). *ACCT history, structure.* Washington, DC: Author.

Ballard, B.J. (1942). Economic survey of Los Angeles City College. *Junior College Journal, 12* (6), 316–318.

Barker, V. (1969). A profile of accredited associate degree nursing programs. *Junior College Journal, 39* (6), 92-102.

Barton, J.W. (1928, December). *Education for life as one of the objectives of the junior college.* Paper presented at a meeting of the American Association of Junior Colleges, Fort Worth, TX.

Bastian, M.E. (1969). Impact: Missouri's community colleges. In R. Yarrington (Ed.), *Junior colleges: 50 years/50 states* (pp. 1–20). Washington, DC: American Association of Junior Colleges.

Bell, D.M. (1946). Junior college world. *Junior College Journal, 16* (8), 372–375.

Bender, L.W. (Ed.). (1990). *Spotlight on the transfer function: A national study of state policies and practices.* Washington, DC: American Association of Community and Junior Colleges.

Bender, L.W., & Hammons, J.O. (1972). Adjunct faculty: Forgotten and neglected. *Community and Junior College Journal, 43* (2), 20–22.

Bender, L.W., & Shoemaker, E.A. (1971). Miracles do happen: The Pennsylvania community colleges. *Junior College Journal, 42* (1), 10–13.

Bird, G.V. (1956). Preparation for advanced study. In N.B. Henry (Ed.), *The public junior college.* [Fifty-fifth yearbook of the National Society for the Study of Education] (pp. 77–93). Chicago: University of Chicago Press.

Black, W.A. (1945). The problems fall into fifteen categories. *Junior College Journal, 16* (2), 60–63.

Blake, L.J. (1969). A new state in Montana. In R. Yarrington (Ed.), *Junior colleges: 50 years/50 states* (pp. 210–215). Washington, DC: American Association of Junior Colleges.

Blee, M.R. (1985). Point: Is statewide exit testing for community college students a sound idea? *Community, Technical, and Junior College Journal, 56* (2), 52–53.

Blocker, C.E., Plummer, R.H., & Richardson, R.C., Jr. (1965). *The two-year college: A social synthesis.* Englewood Cliffs, NJ: Prentice-Hall.

Bogue, J.P. (1946). The midyear conference. *Junior College Journal*, 17 (1), 24.

Bogue, J.P. (1947). From the executive secretary's desk. *Junior College Journal*, 17 (5), 187–188.

Bogue, J.P. (1948). From the executive secretary's desk. *Junior College Journal*, 19 (1), 44–48.

Bogue, J.P. (1949). Report of the executive secretary. *Junior College Journal*, 19 (9), 517–525.

Bogue, J.P. (1950a). *The community college*. New York: McGraw-Hill.

Bogue, J.P. (1950b). The junior college world. *Junior College Journal*, 21 (2), 110–113.

Bogue, J.P. (1951a). The junior college world. *Junior College Journal*, 21 (7), 410–413.

Bogue, J.P. (1952a). From the executive secretary's desk. *Junior College Journal*, 22 (6), 347–350.

Bogue, J.P. (1952b). From the executive secretary's desk. *Junior College Journal*, 22 (9), 525–528.

Bogue, J.P. (1952c). From the executive secretary's desk. *Junior College Journal*, 23 (1), 56–57.

Bogue, J.P. (1954). The junior college world. *Junior College Journal*, 24 (6), 382–386.

Bogue, J.P. (1956a). Analysis of junior college growth. *Junior College Journal*, 26 (6), 354–370.

Bogue, J.P. (1956b). *Junior college directory, 1956*. Washington, DC: American Association of Junior Colleges.

Bogue, J.P. (1957). Analysis of junior college growth. *Junior College Journal*, 27 (6), 357–363.

Bogue, J.P. (1958a). Analysis of junior college growth. *Junior College Journal*, 28 (6), 352–360.

Bogue, J.P. (1958b). Executive secretary's report. *Junior College Journal*, 28 (9), 481–483.

Bogue, J.P. (1958c). Junior college directory, 1958. *Junior College Journal*, 28 (5), 277–303.

Bogue, J.P., & Sanders, S. (1948). Junior college directory, 1948. *Junior College Journal*, 18 (5), 277–304.

Bogue, J.P., & Sanders, S. (1949). Junior college directory, 1949. *Junior College Journal*, 19 (5), 280–307.

Bonos, A.B., Jr. (1948). Community colleges—the next major step in American education. *Junior College Journal, 18* (8), 425–433.

Bonpua, J.L. (1973). Remedying discrimination through affirmative action. *Community and Junior College Journal, 43* (7), 32–34.

Boozer, H.R. (1969). North Carolina is counting on community colleges. In R. Yarrington (Ed.), *Junior colleges: 50 years/50 states* (pp. 63–72). Washington, DC: American Association of Junior Colleges.

Boyce, W.T. (1949). Wanted: A family name. *Junior College Journal, 19* (8), 440–445.

Brawer, F.B. (1977). Women in community colleges: A profile. *Community College Frontiers, 5* (3), 19–22.

Brick, M. (1964). *Forum and focus for the junior college movement: The American Association of Junior Colleges.* New York: Teachers College.

Brint, S., & Karabel, J. (1989). *The diverted dream: Community colleges and the promise of educational opportunity in America 1900–1985.* New York: Oxford University Press.

Brumbaugh, A.J. (1963a). *Guidelines for the establishment of community junior colleges.* Atlanta: Southern Regional Education Board.

Brumbaugh, A.J. (1963b). *State-wide planning and coordination of higher education.* Atlanta: Southern Regional Education Board.

Brunner, K.A. (1970). Historical development of the junior college philosophy. *Junior College Journal, 40* (7), 30–34.

Buck, S.J. (Ed.). (1933). *William Watts Folwell: The autobiography and letters of a pioneer of culture.* Minneapolis: University of Minnesota Press.

Bullock, H.A. (1967). *A history of negro education in the South from 1619 to the present.* Cambridge, MA: Harvard University Press.

Bulpitt, M. (1977). Women's programs in community colleges: Who needs them? *Community College Frontiers, 5* (3), 4–7.

Bush, G.H.W. (1989). Providing quality education for all. *Community, Technical, and Junior College Journal, 59* (6), 16–17.

California State Department of Education. (1928). *The junior college in California: Bulletin G-3.* Sacramento: Author.

Campbell, D.S. (1929). *A brief study of the development of the junior college movement.* Paper presented at the annual meeting of the American Association of Junior Colleges, Atlantic City, NJ.

Campbell, D.S. (1930). *A critical study of the stated purposes of the junior college.* Nashville: George Peabody College for Teachers.

Campbell, D.S. (1931). Directory of the junior college, 1931. *Junior College Journal, 1* (4), 223–234.

Campbell, D.S. (1932). Directory of the junior college, 1932. *Junior College Journal, 2* (4), 235–248.

Campbell, D.S. (1933). Directory of the junior college, 1933. *Junior College Journal, 3* (4), 217–231.

Campbell, D.S. (1934). Directory of the junior college, 1934. *Junior College Journal, 4* (4), 205–220.

Campbell, D.S. (1935). Directory of the junior college, 1935. *Junior College Journal, 5* (4), 209–223.

Campbell, D.S. (1936a). After sixteen years. *Junior College Journal, 7* (3), 109–110.

Campbell, D.S. (1936b). Directory of the junior college, 1936. *Junior College Journal, 6* (4), 209–223.

Campbell, D.S. (1937). Directory of the junior college, 1937. *Junior College Journal, 7* (4), 209–223.

Campbell, D.S. (1938). Directory of the junior college, 1938. *Junior College Journal, 8* (4), 209–223.

Campbell, D.S. (1939). Retrospect and prospect. *Junior College Journal, 9* (8), 440–443.

Campbell, G. (1969). The community college in Canada. *Junior College Journal, 40* (3), 42–48.

Campbell, W.G. (1932). The Hillsboro four-year junior college. *Junior College Journal, 2* (5), 263–268.

Carlyon, D., & Wolf, M. (1969/1970). Delta College. *Junior College Journal, 40* (4), 22–23.

Carnegie grants $935,000 to design new doctoral degree. (1970). *Junior College Journal, 41* (1), 52.

Carnegie grants $295,000 in support of veterans programs. (1972). *Junior College Journal, 42* (9), 33.

Carpenter, W.W. (1962). Early interest of the University of Missouri in the junior college. *Junior College Journal, 32* (8), 476–484.

Carroll, J.J. (1989). A community of colleges in Micronesia. *Community, Technical, and Junior College Journal, 60* (1), 26–31.

Chapman, C.E. (1964). Ohio joins the club. *Junior College Journal, 35* (2), 8–12.

Chapman, C.E. (1970). AAJC approach: Project Focus. *Junior College Journal, 41* (2), 7–9.

Clarke, J.R., & Ammons, R.M. (1970). Identification and diagnosis of disadvantaged students. *Junior College Journal, 40* (5), 13–17.

[Classified advertising]. (1965). *Junior College Journal, 35* (5), 46–47.

Clowes, D., & Towles, D. (1985). Lessons from fifty years. *Community, Technical, and Junior College Journal, 56* (1), 28–32.

Cohen, A.M. (1970). Changing emphasis in the ERIC Clearinghouse. *Junior College Journal, 41* (1), 16–18.

Cohen, A.M., & Brawer, F.B. (1982). *The American community college.* San Francisco: Jossey-Bass.

Cohen, A.M., & Brawer, F.B. (1987). *The collegiate function of community colleges.* San Francisco: Jossey-Bass.

College head sees rise of junior school. (1922, February). *Memphis News Scimitar.*

Colleges needing teachers should contact Peace Corps. (1968). *Junior College Journal, 39* (1), 54.

Collins, C.C. (1967). *Junior college student personnel programs: What they are and what they should be.* Washington, DC: American Association of Junior Colleges.

Colvert, C.C. (1940). Junior college responsibility in total defense. *Junior College Journal, 11* (1), 3–4.

Colvert, C.C. (1956). Development of the junior college movement. In J.P. Bogue (Ed.), *American junior colleges* (4th ed.) (pp. 10–16). Washington, DC: American Council on Education.

Colvert, C.C., & Baker, M.L. (1955). Analysis of junior college growth. *Junior College Directory: 1955.* Washington, DC: American Association of Junior Colleges.

Colvert, C.C., & Littlefield, H. (1961). A brief history of the development of the American Association of Junior Colleges. *Junior College Journal, 31* (6A), 36–40.

Commission of Seven, Carnegie Foundation for the Advancement of Teaching. (1932). *State higher education in California.* Sacramento: California State Printing Office.

Commission on Legislation, American Association of Junior Colleges. (1960). *A guide to state legislation for community colleges.* Unpublished manuscript.

Commission on Legislation, American Association of Junior Colleges. (1961). *Establishing legal bases for community colleges.* Washington, DC: American Association of Junior Colleges.

Commission on the Future of Community Colleges. (1988). *Building communities: A vision for a new century.* Washington, DC: American Association of Community and Junior Colleges.

Conger, G.R., & Schultz, R.E. (1970). Leonard V. Koos: Patriarch of the junior college. *Junior College Journal, 40* (6), 26–31.

Coombs, O. (1973a). The necessity of excellence: Nairobi College. *Change, 5* (3), 38–44.

Coombs, O. (1973b). The necessity of excellence: Barber Scotia College. *Change, 5* (4), 38–43.

Coombs, O. (1973c). The necessity of excellence: Making it at Yale. *Change, 5* (5), 49–54.

Coombs, O. (1973d). The necessity of excellence: Jackson State College. *Change, 5* (8), 34–39.

Coombs, O. (1974). The necessity of excellence: Howard University. *Change, 6* (2), 36–41.

Cooper, W.J. (1928). Adult education in the junior college program. *California Quarterly of Secondary Education. 4* (1), 34–36.

Coordinating Council for Higher Education. (1965). A consideration of issues affecting California junior colleges: A staff report. Sacramento: Author.

Cosand, J.P., & Tirrell, J.E. (1964). Flying a college on the computer. *Junior College Journal, 35* (1), 5–8.

Coursault, J.S. (1915). Standardizing the junior college. *School Review, 23*, 56–62.

Cross, C. (1988). Satellite network brings AACJC into future. *Community, Technical, and Junior College Journal, 59* (2), 65–66.

D'Amico, L.A. (1960). Difference in average salaries of junior college and four-year college and university faculties. *Junior College Journal, 31* (2), 88–90.

Danforth project is completed; trustee council to come? (1971). *Junior College Journal, 42* (1), 38.

Daytona Beach creates radio counseling service. (1969). *Junior College Journal, 39* (5), 88.

Decker, R.C. (1969/1970). Cuyahoga Community College. *Junior College Journal, 40* (4), 15–18, 56–62.

Deegan, W.L., & Tillery, D. (1985). *Renewing the American community college.* San Francisco: Jossey-Bass.

Denworth, K.M. (1937). Indoctrination for a new social order? *Junior College Journal, 7* (4), 163–164.

Deutsch, M.E., Douglas, A.A., & Strayer, G.D. (1948). *A report of a survey of the needs of California in higher education.* Berkeley: University of California Press.

Diener, T.J. (1970). Junior college specialists in the U.S. Office of Education. *Junior College Journal, 41* (3), 23–26.

Diener, T.J. (1986). *Growth of an American invention.* New York: Greenwood.

Doucette, D., & Hughes, B. (Eds.). (1990). *Assessing institutional effectiveness in community colleges.* Laguna Hills, CA: League for Innovation.

Drake, S.L. (1976). *Supplemental report, 1976.* Washington, DC: American Association of Community and Junior Colleges.

Drake, S.L. (Ed.). (1977). *1977 community, junior, and technical college directory.* Washington, DC: American Association of Community and Junior Colleges.

Dunn, J.W. (1969/1970). Peralta Junior College District. *Junior College Journal, 40* (4), 43–45.

Du Pont de Nemours, P.S. (1923). *National education in the United States of America.* Newark: University of Delaware Press.

Eby, F. (1925). *The development of education in Texas.* New York: Macmillan.

Eby, F. (1937). The philosophy of the junior college. *Junior College Journal, 7* (8), 414–424.

Editorial notes: The six-year high school at work. (1906). *School Review, 14,* 609–610.

Educational Policies Commission, National Education Association. (1944). *Education for all American youth.* Washington, DC: Author, American Association of School Administrators.

Educator declares junior college essential to youth as high school. (1922, February 22). *Newark Evening News.*

Edwards, F.M. (1989/1990). A new vision for the nineties. *Community, Technical, and Junior College Journal*, 60 (3), 7.

Eells, W.C. (1931). *The junior college*. New York: Houghton Mifflin.

Eells, W.C. (1934). Two corrections. *Junior College Journal*, 4 (5), 275.

Eells, W.C. (1937a). Directory of societies. *Junior College Journal*, 7 (4), 199–201.

Eells, W.C. (1937b). Improvement of junior college libraries. *Junior College Journal*, 8 (3), 117–125.

Eells, W.C. (1937c). Significance of the junior college library. *Junior College Journal*, 8 (1), 1–2.

Eells, W.C. (1937d). *Surveys of American higher education*. New York: Carnegie Foundation for the Advancement of Teaching.

Eells, W.C. (1939a). Federal aid to junior college plants. *Junior College Journal*, 9 (6), 302–304.

Eells, W.C. (1939b). Junior college directory, 1939. *Junior College Journal*, 9 (4), 209–228.

Eells, W.C. (1939c). National junior college administrator poll. *Junior College Journal*, 10 (3), 125–126.

Eells, W.C. (1939d). Reports and discussion: War poll. *Junior College Journal*, 10 (4), 214–215.

Eells, W.C. (1940). Junior college directory, 1940. *Junior College Journal*, 10 (5), 281–300.

Eells, W.C. (1941a). *The present status of junior college terminal education* (Terminal Education Monograph No. 2). Washington, DC: American Association of Junior Colleges.

Eells, W.C. (1941b). *Why junior college terminal education?* (Terminal Education Monograph No. 3). Washington, DC: American Association of Junior Colleges.

Eells, W.C. (1942a). Annual report of the executive secretary. *Junior College Journal*, 12 (7), 378–384.

Eells, W.C. (1942b). Junior college directory, 1942. *Junior College Journal*, 12 (5), 277–301.

Eells, W.C. (1943a). Junior college directory, 1943. *Junior College Journal*, 13 (5), 245–268.

Eells, W.C. (1943b). The junior college in the postwar period. *Junior College Journal*, 14 (2), 51–52.

Eells, W.C. (1944a). From the secretary's desk. *Junior College Journal,* 15 (3), 137–138.

Eells, W.C. (1944b). Junior college directory, 1944. *Junior College Journal,* 14 (5), 215–237.

Eells, W.C. (1945). Junior college directory, 1945. *Junior College Journal,* 15 (5), 217–239.

Eells, W.C. (1951). Junior college development in Japan. *Junior College Journal,* 22 (1), 3–11.

Eells, W.C., & Winslow, P. (1941). Junior college directory, 1941. *Junior College Journal,* 11 (5), 279–300.

Eisenberg, D.U. (1980). *A national issues forum: Energy and the way we live.* Unpublished information sheet, American Association of Community and Junior Colleges.

Eldersveld, A.M. (1969). Pennsylvania opens the door. In R. Yarrington (Ed.), *Junior colleges: 50 years/50 states* (pp. 150–157). Washington, DC: American Association of Junior Colleges.

Emphasis: Project Focus ends. (1971). *Junior College Journal,* 42 (2), 3.

Emphasis: Board elects new directors. (1972). *Junior College Journal,* 42 (9), 3.

Emphasis: Career Staffing Center. (1971). *Junior College Journal,* 42 (3), 3.

Emphasis: Governmental interns. (1971). *Junior College Journal,* 41 (9), 5.

Emphasis: International project begins. (1971). *Junior College Journal,* 41 (8), 3.

Emphasis: Joseph Cosand to U.S.O.E. (1972). *Junior College Journal,* 42 (6), 5.

Engelhart, M.D. (1950). Examinations to facilitate transfer of junior college graduates to senior colleges. *Junior College Journal,* 20 (6), 332–336.

Engleman, L.E., & Eells, W.C. (1941). *The literature of junior college terminal education* (Terminal Education Monograph No. 1). Washington, DC: American Association of Junior Colleges.

Equal access to education (I). (1943). *Junior College Journal,* 14 (2), 53–57.

Erickson, C.G. (1960). *Chicago's TV college: Final report of a three year experiment of the Chicago City Junior College in offering college courses for credit via open circuit television.* Unpublished report.(ERIC Document Reproduction Service No. ED 021 442)

Erickson, C.G. (1963). Chicago's TV college. *Junior College Journal,* 33 (9), 22–24, 30–32.

Erickson, C.G. (1969). Rebirth in Illinois. In R. Yarrington (Ed.), *Junior colleges: 50 years/50 states* (pp. 180–186). Washington, DC: American Association of Junior Colleges.

Erickson, E.K. (1969/1970). Seattle Community College. *Junior College Journal,* 40 (4), 50–53.

Executive staff positions change in response to Project Focus. (1972). *Community and Junior College Journal,* 43 (1), 34.

Fariss, G.H. (1947). Committee on Legislation. *Junior College Journal,* 17 (9), 385–388.

Fawcett, J.R. (1973). Doak S. Campbell: Early junior college leader is remembered. *Community and Junior College Journal,* 44 (1), 46.

Field, G.H. (1947). Junior-college building programs. *Junior College Journal,* 17 (9), 376–380.

Fields, R.R. (1950). Recent writings. *Junior College Journal,* 21 (1), 54–57.

Fields, R.R. (1962). *The community college movement.* New York: McGraw-Hill.

Fletcher, S.M., Rue, R.N., & Young, R. (1977). Community education in community colleges: Today and tomorrow. *Community Services Catalyst,* 7, 10–15.

Flint, C.C., & Ewing, D.H. (1969/1970). Foothill Junior College District. *Junior College Journal,* 40 (4), 24–25, 66–68.

Florida State Board of Community Colleges. (1988). *Articulation.* Tallahassee, FL: Author.

Ford, N.A. (1936). The negro junior college. *Journal of Negro Education,* 5 (4), 591–594.

Ford Foundation announces minority student scholarships. (1970). *Junior College Journal,* 41 (2), 60.

Fordyce, J.W., & Bromley, A. (1969/1970). Santa Fe Junior College. *Junior College Journal,* 40 (4), 46–49, 88.

Fox, M.S. (1989). The League for Innovation in the Community College: A study of leadership. (Doctoral dissertation, University of Texas). *Dissertation Abstracts International,* 50, 1500A.

Fretwell, E.K. (1954). *Founding public junior colleges.* New York: Columbia University Bureau of Publications.

Friedan, B. (1963). *The feminine mystique.* New York: Norton.

Friedel, F. (1976). *America in the twentieth century.* New York: Knopf.

Frye, J.H. (1992). *The vision of the public junior college: 1900–1940.* New York: Greenwood.

Gannon, P.J. (1969). Fifty years of community involvement in Michigan. In R. Yarrington (Ed.), *Junior colleges: 50 years/50 states* (pp. 104–115). Washington, DC: American Association of Junior Colleges.

Gerber, D.R. (1971). William Watts Folwell and the idea of the junior college. *Junior College Journal, 41* (6), 50–53.

Gernhart, J.C. (1969). The National Council of Independent Junior Colleges. *Junior College Journal, 40* (1), 41–42.

Gernhart, J.C. (Ed.). (1981). *1981 community, junior, and technical college directory.* Washington, DC: American Association of Community and Junior Colleges.

Gilbert, F. (1979a). *Minorities and junior colleges: Data and discourse.* Washington, DC: American Association of Community and Junior Colleges. (ERIC Document Reproduction Service No. ED 171 345).

Gilbert, F. (1979b). Research report: Enrollments. *Community and Junior College Journal, 49* (5), 58.

Giles, F.T. (1961). Junior college leadership program. *Junior College Journal, 31* (6), 321–325.

Giles, F.T. (1969). Washington shows new life at forty. In R. Yarrington (Ed.), *Junior colleges: 50 years/50 states* (pp. 95–103). Washington, DC: American Association of Junior Colleges.

Gilliam, J. (1969). Junior colleges in Jordan. *Junior College Journal, 40* (2), 12–16.

Glass, J.C., Jr., & Robinson, R.A. (1976). Are community colleges reaching out to veterans? *Community College Review, 3* (4), 63–66.

Gleazer, E.J., Jr. (n.d.). *Sequence of events leading to the appeal to the W.K. Kellogg Foundation.* Washington, DC: American Association of Junior Colleges. Unpublished collection of memoranda.

Gleazer, E.J., Jr. (1960a). From the executive director's desk. *Junior College Journal. 31* (3), 166–170.

Gleazer, E.J., Jr. (1960b). From the executive director's desk. *Junior College Journal, 31* (4), 227–232.

Gleazer, E.J., Jr. (1960c). The junior college world. *Junior College Journal, 31* (2), 112–116.

Gleazer, E.J., Jr. (Ed.). (1960d). *1960 junior college directory.* Washington, DC: American Association of Junior Colleges.

Gleazer, E.J., Jr. (1961a). Annual report to the American Association of Junior Colleges. *Junior College Journal, 31* (9), 492–500.

Gleazer, E.J., Jr. (1961b). Junior college directory, 1961. *Junior College Journal, 31* (5), 267–302.

Gleazer, E.J., Jr. (1961c). Junior college growth. *Junior College Journal, 31* (6), 353–360.

Gleazer, E.J., Jr. (Ed.). (1961d). *1961 junior college directory.* Washington, DC: American Association of Junior Colleges.

Gleazer, E.J., Jr. (1961e). The junior college world. *Junior College Journal, 32* (2), 116–120.

Gleazer, E.J., Jr. (1962). *The 1962 junior college directory of the American Association of Junior Colleges.* Washington, DC: American Association of Junior Colleges.

Gleazer, E.J., Jr. (1963). *1963 junior college directory.* Washington, DC: American Association of Junior Colleges.

Gleazer, E.J., Jr. (1964). *1964 junior college directory.* Washington, DC: American Association of Junior Colleges.

Gleazer, E.J., Jr. (1970). AAJC approach: AAJC board meeting. *Junior College Journal, 41* (3), 5.

Gleazer, E.J., Jr. (1971a). AAJC approach: Growing role for councils. *Junior College Journal, 42* (3), 9.

Gleazer, E.J., Jr. (1971b). AAJC approach: Project Focus report—II. *Junior College Journal, 41* (7), 5.

Gleazer, E.J., Jr. (1972a). AACJC approach. *Community and Junior College Journal, 43* (1), 5.

Gleazer, E.J., Jr. (1972b). AAJC approach: The association name. *Junior College Journal, 42* (5), 11.

Gleazer, E.J., Jr. (1973/1974). After the boom...what now for the community colleges? *Community and Junior College Journal, 44* (4), 6–11.

Gleazer, E.J., Jr. (1974). Beyond the open door, the open college. *Community and Junior College Journal, 45* (1), 6–12.

Gleazer, E.J., Jr. (1980). *The community college: Values, vision, and vitality.* Washington, DC: American Association of Community and Junior Colleges.

Gleazer, E.J., Jr. (1991, July 10). *A participant reports his views.* Remarks at Leadership 2000, a conference sponsored by the League for Innovation in the Community College, Chicago.

Gleazer, Kerr get first ACE awards. (1981/1982). *Community and Junior College Journal, 51* (4), 43.

Godwin, W.L. (1970). *The black community and the community college: Action programs for expanding opportunity. A project report.* Atlanta: Southern Regional Education Board. (ERIC Document Reproduction Service No. ED 045 786)

Gollattscheck, J.F. (1985). From the editor: Volume fifty-six. *Community, Technical, and Junior College Journal, 56* (1), 3.

Gollattscheck, J.F., Harlacher, E.L., Roberts, E., & Wygal, B.R. (1976). *College leadership for community renewal: Beyond community-based education.* San Francisco: Jossey-Bass.

Goodspeed, T.W. (1928). *William Rainey Harper: First president of the University of Chicago.* Chicago: University of Chicago Press.

Goodrich, A.L., Lezotte, L.W., & Welch, J.A. (1972/1973). Minorities in two-year colleges: A survey. *Junior College Journal, 43* (4), 28–31.

Goodwin, G.L. (1971). The historical development of the community-junior college ideology. *Dissertation Abstracts International, 32,* 5566A. (University Microfilms No. 72–12, 178)

Graham, W.A. (1969). It may happen in Alabama, too! In R. Yarrington (Ed.), *Junior colleges: 50 years/50 states* (pp. 130–137). Washington, DC: American Association of Junior Colleges.

Green, C.B., & Cavallo, E. (1969). New junior college in Santo Domingo. *Junior College Journal, 40* (2), 29–31.

Greenleaf, W.J. (1936). *Junior colleges* (U.S. Office of Education Bulletin, 1936, No. 3). Washington, DC: U.S. Government Printing Office.

Griffith, W.S. (1976). Harper's legacy. *Community College Frontiers, 4* (3), 14–20.

Guthrie-Morse, B. (1979). The utilization of part-time faculty. *Community College Frontiers, 7* (3), 8–17.

Hannelly, R.J. (1969). The explosion in Arizona. In R. Yarrington (Ed.), *Junior colleges: 50 years/50 states* (pp. 31–36). Washington, DC: American Association of Junior Colleges.

Hansen, J.S. (1960). The college credit program for selected high school seniors at Fresno City. *Junior College Journal, 31* (4), 193–195.

Harbeson, J.W. (1939). Aviation technology at Pasadena. *Junior College Journal, 9* (8), 482–485.

Hardin, T.L. (1976). Joliet: Birth of a college. *Community College Frontiers, 4* (3), 21–23.

Harlacher, E.L. (1969). *The community dimension of the community college.* Englewood Cliffs, NJ: Prentice–Hall.

Harper, W.A. (Ed.). (1967). *1967 junior college directory.* Washington, DC: American Association of Junior Colleges.

Harper, W.A. (1968a). Dick Kosaki. *Junior College Journal, 39* (3), 18.

Harper, W.A. (Ed.). (1968b). *1968 junior college directory.* Washington, DC: American Association of Junior Colleges.

Harper, W.A. (Ed.). (1969). *1969 junior college directory.* Washington, DC: American Association of Junior Colleges.

Harper, W.A. (Ed.). (1970). *1970 junior college directory.* Washington, DC: American Association of Junior Colleges.

Harper, W.A. (1974). A brief look at the AACJC councils. *Community and Junior College Journal, 44* (8), 22.

Harper, W.A., et al. (1971). *1971 junior college directory.* Washington, DC: American Association of Junior Colleges.

Harper, W.R. (1896, April 7). [Personal correspondence to D.S. Jordan]. Chicago: University of Chicago Archives.

Harper, W.R. (1899, March 11). [Personal correspondence to D.S. Jordan]. Chicago: University of Chicago Archives.

Harper, W.R. (1900, March 3). [Personal correspondence to Mr. Ryerson]. Chicago: University of Chicago Archives.

Harper, W.R. (1902, May 29). [Personal correspondence to D.S. Jordan]. Chicago: University of Chicago Archives.

Harper, W.R. (1903). The length of the college course. In C.W. Eliot, A.F. West, W.R. Harper & N.M. Butler, *Present college questions* (pp. 79–92). New York: D. Appleton.

Heinrich, C.L. (1969). Fifty-one years in Kansas. In R. Yarrington (Ed.), *Junior colleges: 50 years/50 states* (pp. 222–229). Washington,

DC: American Association of Junior Colleges.

Helland, P.C. (1969). Minnesota turns to state junior colleges. In R. Yarrington (Ed.), *Junior colleges: 50 years/50 states* (pp. 204–209). Washington, DC: American Association of Junior Colleges.

Hicks, R.S. (1930). Report of the Junior College Committee of Wyoming. *Junior College Journal, 1* (1), 51–52.

Higdon, B.J. (Ed.). (1989). *An illustrated history of Graceland College.* Independence, MO: Herald House.

High schools superior to old colleges. (1922, February). *Memphis News Scimitar.*

Hill, M.E. (1936). Junior college developments in California. *Junior College Journal, 6* (7), 333–338.

Hill College. (1986). *Catalog.* Hillsboro, TX: Author.

Hinsdale, B.A. (1906). *History of the University of Michigan.* Ann Arbor: University of Michigan.

Hodson, G., & Crawfurd, A.P. (1969). A new law for Colorado. In R. Yarrington (Ed.), *Junior colleges: 50 years/50 states* (pp. 216–221). Washington, DC: American Association of Junior Colleges.

Hollinshead, B.S. (1936). The community junior college program. *Junior College Journal, 7* (3), 111–116.

Holt, D.H. (1969/1970). Dallas County Junior College District. *Junior College Journal, 40* (4), 19–21, 64.

Hull, D., & Parnell, D. (1991). *Tech prep/associate degree: A win-win experience.* Waco, TX: Center for Occupational Research and Development.

Hurlburt, A.S. (1969). *State master plans for community colleges.* Washington, DC: American Association of Junior Colleges.

Hutchins, R.M. (1936). *The higher learning in America.* New Haven: Yale University Press.

Huther, J.W. (1971). The open door: How open is it? *Junior College Journal, 41* (7), 24–27.

Illinois Community College Board. (1986). *A statewide follow-up study of fall 1979 transfer students from Illinois public community colleges.* Springfield, IL: Author.

Ingalls, R.C. (1937). Evaluation of semiprofessional courses. *Junior College Journal, 7* (8), 480–487.

Iriyagolla, I.M.R.A. (1969). Ceylon begins a junior college system. *Junior College Journal, 40* (2), 26–28.

Jackson, A.L. (1940). The negro junior college. *Junior College Journal,* 10 (9), 549–550.

Jacobsen, J.M. (1968). The junior college idea in South America. *Junior College Journal,* 39 (3), 9–13.

Japanese diet authorizes permanent junior colleges. (1964). *Junior College Journal,* 35 (1), 46.

Jellison, H. (Ed.). (1984). *Community, technical, and junior college directory 1984.* Washington, DC: American Association of Community and Junior Colleges.

Jenkins, H.E., Mohr, J.P., & Dodd, A.G. (1951). Report of the resolutions committee. *Junior College Journal,* 21 (9), 513–515.

Jensen, G.C. (1932). An analysis of the report of the Carnegie Foundation's survey and recommendations. *California Quarterly of Secondary Education,* 8 (1), 58–67.

Jesse Parker Bogue: A man to remember. (1961). *Junior College Journal,* 31 (6A), 22–24.

Johnson, B.L. (1964a). *Islands of innovation* (Junior College Leadership Program, Occasional Report No. 6). Los Angeles: University of California.

Johnson, B.L. (1964b). Islands of innovation. *Junior College Journal,* 34 (5), 9–14.

Johnson, B.L., & Harless, W.H. (1955). Implications of the Citizenship Education Project for the junior college. *Junior College Journal,* 25 (7), 369–375.

Johnson, W.H. (1938). Public junior colleges of Chicago. *Junior College Journal,* 8 (5), 231–234.

Journal circulation goes over 30,000. (1968). *Junior College Journal,* 39 (2), 46.

Junior college directory, 1951. (1950). *Junior College Journal,* 21 (3), 169–197.

Junior college directory, 1959. (1959). *Junior College Journal,* 29 (5), 275–302.

Junior college directory, 1960. (1960). *Junior College Journal,* 30 (5), 274–306.

The junior college world. (1936). *Junior College Journal,* 7 (2), 91–96.

The junior college world. (1939). *Junior College Journal,* 10 (2), 100–107.

Justice makes grant for new AAJC project. (1972). *Junior College Journal, 42* (6), 72.

Kaapke, L.D., & Wojciechowski, W.A. (1977). The Community College of the Air Force. *Community College Review, 4* (4), 25–31.

Kappenberg, J.N. (1990). The role of John A. Burns in the formation of Hawaii's community colleges. *The Pleiades,* 3–13.

Katsinas, S.G. (in press), George C. Wallace and the founding of Alabama's public two-year colleges. *Journal of Higher Education.*

Kellogg funds resource centers at six colleges. (1978). *Community and Junior College Journal, 49* (1), 42.

Kellogg grant to Palm Beach to start dental programs. (1965). *Junior College Journal, 36* (2), 44.

Kellogg grants $75,900 for health auxiliary programs. (1964). *Junior College Journal, 35* (3), 36.

Kellogg sets fund for Navajo youth. (1973/1974). *Community and Junior College Journal, 44* (4), 48–49.

Kempfer, H. (1950). Adult education in the community college. *Junior College Journal, 21* (1), 18–25.

Kerr, C. (1985). Foreword. In W.L. Deegan & D. Tillery, *Renewing the American community college* (pp. vii–xi). San Francisco: Jossey-Bass.

Keyser, J. (1991). From the chair: Stepping into a new year. *Community, Technical, and Junior College Journal, 61* (6), 5–6.

King, M.C. (1982, April 4–7). *Evaluation of the Boards of Trustees: A president's view.* Paper presented at the 62nd Annual Convention of the American Association of Community and Junior Colleges, St. Louis, MO.

Kintzer, F.C. (1970). Junior university college movement in Ceylon. In *International educational and cultural exchange* (pp. 76–85). Washington, DC: U.S. Advisory Commission on International Educational and Cultural Affairs, Department of State.

Kintzer, F.C. (1973). *Middleman in Higher Education.* San Francisco: Jossey-Bass.

Kintzer, F.C. (1980). *Organization and leadership of two-year colleges: Preparing for the eighties.* Gainesville: Institute of Higher Education, University of Florida.

Kintzer, F.C. (1989). Kenya's Harambee institutes of technology. *Community College Review, 17* (3), 11–17.

Kintzer, F.C., & Wattenbarger, J.L. (1985). *The articulation/transfer phenomenon: Patterns and directions.* Washington, DC: American Association of Community and Junior Colleges.

Knight, E.N. (1937). Indoctrination for a new social order? *Junior College Journal, 7* (8), 436–443.

Knoell, D. (1976). *Through the open door: A study of patterns of enrollment and performance in California's community colleges* (Report No. 76–1). Sacramento: California Postsecondary Education Commission.

Knoell, D. (1990). *Transfer, articulation, and collaboration: Twenty-five years later.* Washington, DC: American Association of Community and Junior Colleges.

Knoell, D., & Medsker, L.L. (1964). *Factors affecting performance of transfer from two- to four-year colleges: With implications for coordination and articulation* (Cooperative Research Project No. 1133). Berkeley: University of California.

Knoell, D., & Medsker, L.L. (1966). *From junior to senior college: A national study of the transfer student.* Washington, DC: American Council on Education.

Koos, L.V. (1922, March). *Continued growth of the junior college movement.* Paper presented at a meeting of the American Association of Junior Colleges, Chicago.

Koos, L.V. (1924). *The junior college.* Minneapolis: University of Minnesota.

Koos, L.V. (1925). *The junior college movement.* Boston: Ginn.

Koos, L.V. (1927). *The junior high school.* Boston: Ginn.

Koos, L.V. (1946). *Integrating high school and college: The six-four-four plan at work.* New York: Harper.

Koos, L.V. (1970). *The community college student.* Gainesville: University of Florida Press.

Kosaki, R.H. (1964). *Feasibility of community colleges in Hawaii.* Unpublished report.(ERIC Document Reproduction Service No. ED 012 601)

Kosaki, R.H. (1965). Hawaii plans for community colleges. *Junior College Journal, 36* (3), 5–7.

Lahti, R.E. (1962). Junior college education in Wyoming. *Junior College Journal, 33* (2), 93–95.

Lane, D.A., Jr. (1933). The junior college movement among negroes. *Journal of Negro Education, 2* (3), 272–283.

Lange, A.F. (1915). The junior college, with special reference to California. In *Proceedings of the National Education Association: 1915,* 119–124.

Lasell College. (1991). *Lasell College Catalog: 1991–92.* Newton, MA: Author.

League for Innovation in the Community College. (1987). *Assuring student success in the community college: The role of student professionals.* Kansas City, KS: Johnson County Community College.

Lein, D.A. (1970). And Nevada makes 50. *Junior College Journal,* 40 (6), 50–51.

Lester, R.M. (1937). The development of junior college libraries. *Junior College Journal,* 8 (1), 3–9.

Leuchtenburg, W.E. (1963). *Franklin D. Roosevelt and the New Deal.* New York: Harper & Row.

Lillard, J.B. (1929). What shall we do with the unrecommended student? *California Quarterly of Secondary Education,* 5 (1), 69–70.

Litton M.L., & Rogers, J.T. (1965). Retired military personnel: A source of additional instructors. *Junior College Journal,* 35 (8), 17–18.

Lombardi, J. (1976). The myth of no-tuition college. *Community College Review,* 4 (6), 59–63.

Long, W.R., & Sanders, S. (1946). Junior college directory, 1946. *Junior College Journal,* 16 (5), 213–235.

Long, W.R., & Sanders, S. (1947). Junior college directory, 1947. *Junior College Journal,* 17 (5), 197–224.

Love, A. (1973). Veterans: the new challenge. *Community and Junior College Journal,* 44 (1), 28–29.

M.A. degree to be offered on Harford campus next spring. (1971). *Junior College Journal,* 42 (1), 36.

MacKay, K.C. (1969). Something new in New Jersey. In R. Yarrington (Ed.), *Junior colleges: 50 years/50 states* (pp. 84–94). Washington, DC: American Association of Junior Colleges.

Mahoney, J.R. (1981). Big boom in energy programs. *Community, Technical, and Junior College Journal,* 52 (1), 32–36.

Mahoney, J.R. (Ed.). (1985). *1985 community, technical, and junior college directory.* Washington, DC: American Association of Community and Junior Colleges.

Mahoney, J.R. (Ed.). (1986). *1986 community, technical, and junior college directory.* Washington, DC: American Association of Community and Junior Colleges.

Mahoney, J.R. (Ed.). (1990). *Community, technical, and junior college statistical yearbook, 1990 edition.* Washington, DC: American Association of Community and Junior Colleges.

Mahoney, J.R., & Jimenez, E. (Eds.). (1992). *Community, technical, and junior college statistical yearbook, 1992 edition.* Washington, DC: American Association of Community and Junior Colleges.

Mahoney, J.R., & Sallis, L. (Eds.). (1991). *Community, technical, and junior college statistical yearbook, 1991 edition.* Washington, DC: American Association of Community and Junior Colleges.

Marien, M. (1972). *Beyond the Carnegie Commission: A policy study guide to space/time/credit-preference higher learning.* Syracuse: Education Policy Research Council, Syracuse University Research Corporation. (ERIC Document Reproduction Service No. ED 071 576)

Martinez, T. (1982). International connection. *Community and Junior College Journal, 52* (7), 38.

Martorana, S.V. (1954). Recent state legislation affecting junior colleges. *Junior College Journal, 24* (8), 459–471.

Martorana, S.V. (1969). Progress and plans in the empire state. In R. Yarrington (Ed.), *Junior colleges: 50 years/50 states* (pp. 169–179). Washington, DC: American Association of Junior Colleges.

Matthews, D.R., Jr. (1982). A case study of developing short-cycle postsecondary education in Venezuela: Colegios universitarios (Doctoral dissertation, University of Florida, 1982). *Dissertation Abstracts International, 44,* 336A.

Matson, J.E. (1972). A perspective on student personnel services. *Junior College Journal, 42* (6), 48–52.

McAninch, H. (1980). The maturing of the Presidents Academy. *Community and Junior College Journal, 51* (2), 18–19.

McConnell, T.R. (1962). *A general pattern for American public higher education.* New York: McGraw-Hill.

McGrath, E.J. (Ed.). (1966). *Universal higher education.* New York: McGraw-Hill.

McKenney, J. (1989). *AACJC-Sears Roebuck Foundation partnership development fund final report.* Washington, DC: American Association of Community and Junior Colleges.

McLane, C.L. (1913). The junior college or an upward extension of the high school. *School Review, 21,* 161–170.

McLeod, M.W. (1983). Constitutional provisions for community junior colleges. *Community/Junior College Quarterly of Research and Practice, 7* (2), 175–182.

Medsker, L.L. (1960). *The junior college: Progress and prospect.* New York: McGraw-Hill.

Medsker, L.L., Eells, W.C., & Hollinshead, B.S. (1942). Reports on study of terminal education. *Junior College Journal, 12* (7), 399–404.

Menefee, S. (1971). Three years of developing junior colleges. *Junior College Journal, 41* (7), 28–30.

Mensel, R.F. (1969). Federal support for two-year colleges: "A whole new ballgame." *Junior College Journal, 40* (1), 14–19.

Mensel, R.F. (1984/1985). Capital current: Peacetime GI Bill— biggest college act since Pell grants. *Community and Junior College Journal, 55* (4), 8–9.

Mensel, R.F. (1987). Capital current: New GI Bill inspires U.S. Army's new educational philosophy. *Community, Technical, and Junior College Journal, 57* (4), 10.

Mensel, R.F., & Bolling, A. (1986/1987). Capital current: New Higher Education Act: Resources for the future. *Community, Technical, and Junior College Journal, 57* (3), 10–11.

Mexicans to train at League colleges. (1980). *Community and Junior College Journal, 51* (1), 52.

Minutes and committee reports. (1938). *Junior College Journal, 8* (8), 474–484.

Mission 1980—and beyond. (1981). *Community and Junior College Journal, 51* (5), 15–30.

Monroe, C.R. (1972). *Profile of the community college: A handbook.* San Francisco: Jossey-Bass.

Moreton, R. (n.d.). [Internal memorandum relating to cluster starting dates]. Fort Lauderdale, FL: NOVA University Institute for Higher Education.

Morris, E. (1991, March 1). Historic college presidents honored in the capitol. *Tallahassee Democrat*, C1.

Morrison, D.G. (1962). Administrative salaries in junior colleges. *Junior College Journal, 32* (5), 259–263.

Morrison, D.G., & Martorana, S.V. (1961). *Criteria for the establishment of 2-year colleges* (Bulletin 1961, No. 2). Washington, DC: Office of Education.

Morrison, D.G., & Witherspoon, C.F. (1966). *Procedures for the establishment of public 2-year colleges* (Bulletin 1966, No. 14). Washington, DC: Office of Education.

Murtha, J., Kaufman, B., & Warman, J. (1982). Will success spoil community college graduates? *Community and Junior College Journal, 52* (8), 46–47.

Myran, G.A. (1969). *Community services in the community college.* Washington, DC: American Association of Junior Colleges.

Nader, S. (1969). The community college in Connecticut. *Junior College Journal, 40* (1), 31–36.

National Association of State Universities and Land Grant Colleges. (1974). *Historically black public colleges: A factbook.* Atlanta: Author, Office for the Advancement of Public Negro Colleges.

National j.c. student group formed in Washington meeting. (1972). *Junior College Journal, 42* (8), 36.

New community college unit is established at U.S.O.E. (1973). *Community and Junior College Journal, 44* (2), 47.

Newsham, L.R. (1969). Iowa sets its course. In R. Yarrington (Ed.), *Junior colleges: 50 years/50 states* (pp. 187–195). Washington, DC: American Association of Junior Colleges.

Nichols, D.D. (1975/1976). Women's programs at public community colleges. *Junior College Journal, 46* (4), 7–8.

Nickens, J. (1985). Counterpoint: Is statewide exit testing for community college students a sound idea? *Community, Technical, and Junior College Journal, 56* (2), 53.

North Carolina community college system turns 25. (1988). *Community, Technical, and Junior College Journal, 59* (2), 92.

NOVA University, Institute for Higher Education. (1976). *Ed.D. in higher education; specialization in higher education.* Fort Lauderdale, FL: Author.

O'Banion, T. (n.d.). *The League for Innovation in the Community College: A special sub-culture.* Laguna Hills, CA: The League for Innovation in the Community College.

Palinchak, R.S. (1973). *The evolution of the community college.* Metuchen, NJ: Scarecrow.

Palmer, J. (1988a). AACJC board approves satellite network, student scholars program. *Community, Technical, and Junior College Journal, 59* (2), 64.

Palmer, J. (Ed.). (1988b). *Community, technical, and junior college statistical yearbook* (1988 ed.). Washington, DC: American Association of Community and Junior Colleges.

Palmer, J. (1990). *Accountability through student tracking: A review of the literature.* Washington, DC: American Association of Community and Junior Colleges.

Parnell, D. (1984). Decision makers: President Reagan—defining the two-year college. *Community and Junior College Journal, 55* (1), 18–20.

Parnell, D. (1985). *The neglected majority.* Washington, DC: American Association of Community and Junior Colleges.

Parnell, D. (1987). Decision makers: Edmund J. Gleazer, Jr., AACJC president emeritus. *Community, Technical, and Junior College Journal, 57* (4), 12–13.

Parnell, D. (1988). From the president: A new community college satellite network. *Community, Technical, and Junior College Journal, 59* (2), 6.

Parnell, D., & Peltason, J.W. (Eds.). (1984). *American community, technical, and junior colleges.* (9th ed.). Washington, DC: American Council on Education/Macmillan.

Parnell named AACJC president. (1981). *Community and Junior College Journal, 51* (6), 40.

Pedersen, R. (1988). Small business and the early public junior college. *Community, Technical, and Junior College Journal, 59* (1), 44–46.

Pence, D.P. (1969). The Oregon story. In R. Yarrington (Ed.), *Junior colleges: 50 years/50 states* (pp. 38–53). Washington, DC: American Association of Junior Colleges.

Pesci, F.B., & Novak, R.T. (1969). Progress in Maryland. In R. Yarrington (Ed.), *Junior colleges: 50 years/50 states* (pp. 21–30). Washington, DC: American Association of Junior Colleges.

Pifer, A. (1973). *The higher education of blacks in the United States.* New York: Carnegie Corporation. (ERIC Document Reproduction Service No. ED 085 001)

Ponitz, D. (1989). A great year—Let's build on it! *Community, Technical, and Junior College Journal, 59* (6), 4.

Popejoy, T.L. (1939). Needs of youth in a democracy. *Junior College Journal, 9* (8), 518–524.

President Dale Parnell: An interview. (1981). *Community and Junior College Journal, 52* (1), 3–5.

President's Commission on Higher Education. (1947). *Higher education for American democracy* (Vols. 1–6). New York: Harper & Brothers.

President's Committee on Education Beyond the High School. (1957). *Second report to the president.* Washington, DC: U.S. Government Printing Office.

Price, H.G. (1948). Recent junior-college legislation in the various states. *Junior College Journal, 18* (8), 438–443.

Proceedings of the seventeenth educational conference of the academies and high schools affiliating or co-operating with the University of Chicago. (1904). *School Review, 12,* 1–28.

Puttman, W.C. (1954). *A survey of co-operative programs between selected state universities and public junior colleges.* Unpublished doctoral dissertation, University of North Dakota.

Raines, M.R. (1965). *Junior college student personnel programs: Appraisal and Development.* Report to the Carnegie Commission. Unpublished report. (ERIC Document Reproduction Service No. ED 043 323)

Raines, M.R., & Myran, G.A. (1970). Community services: A university-community college approach. *Junior College Journal, 41* (2), 40–49.

Rainey, H.P. (1949). New frontiers for education. *Junior College Journal, 19* (9), 501–509.

Randle, W. (1993, January 17). Diversity becomes a dollars-and-sense issue for many firms. *Washington Post,* p. H2.

Ratcliff, J.L. (1986). Should we forget William Rainey Harper? *Community College Review, 13* (4), 12–19.

Ratcliff, J.L. (1987a, November). *Anthony Caminetti, university leaders and the 1907 California junior college law.* Paper presented at the annual meeting of the Association for the Study of Higher Education, Baltimore.

Ratcliff, J.L. (1987b). First public junior colleges in an age of reform. *Journal of Higher Education, 58* (2), 151–180.

Reed, L.D. (1971). *Jesse Parker Bogue: Missionary for the two-year college.* New York: Carlton.

Reid, M.M. (1928). *List of persons attending the junior college convention held at the Hotel Jefferson, Saint Louis, Missouri.* Unpublished list.

Reinfeld, P.M. (1975). Answer: A response to women's new ideas and needs. *Community College Frontiers, 3* (3), 15–17.

Reinhard, W. (1988/1989). AACJC to publish biweekly newspaper. *Community, Technical, and Junior College Journal, 59* (3), 52.

Reneau, S. (1989). Former chief justice delivers fourth Truman lecture. *Community, Technical, and Junior College Journal, 59* (5), 46–47.

Reports and discussion: Semiprofessional courses. (1936). *Junior College Journal, 7* (2), 99–100.

Reynolds, J.W. (1958). Jesse Parker Bogue and the expanding role of junior colleges. *Junior College Journal, 28* (8), 421–422.

Reynolds, J.W. (1962). Editorial and "30." *Junior College Journal, 33* (4), 183–184.

Ricciardi, N. (1928, March). *The development of terminal courses in the junior colleges in California.* Paper presented at a meeting of the American Association of Junior Colleges, Chicago.

Richardson, O.D. (1942). Nisei evacuees—Their challenge to education. *Junior College Journal, 13* (1), 6–12.

Robbins, R. (1966). *Desegregation and the negro college in the South, and persistence in college* (Report No. DR-5-8255). Norton, MA: Wheaton College. (ERIC Document Reproduction Service No. ED 010 603)

Roberts, A.D. (1953). The guidance survey, a key to student needs and wishes. *Junior College Journal, 23* (5), 250–254.

Roberts, C.W. (1968). Fringe benefits in public junior colleges. *Junior College Journal, 39* (2), 28–35.

Rockefeller grants support to American Indian program. (1974). *Community and Junior College Journal, 44* (6), 54.

Ross, G.L. (1974). CCAF, SOC, USAFI, CLEP: Alphabet soup never tasted so good. *Community and Junior College Journal, 45* (2), 9–11.

Rossi, E.J. (1976). The women's movement: Have community colleges responded? *Community College Review, 3* (3), 36–46.

Rudolph, F. (1962). *The American college and university.* New York: Vintage.

Rutledge, L.A. (1951). *A history of the American Association of Junior Colleges, 1920–1950.* Unpublished doctoral dissertation, University of Texas, Austin.

Sachs, J. (1905). The elimination of the first two college years: A protest. *Educational Review, 30,* 488–489.

Sanchez, B.M. (1977). ERIC Clearinghouse for Junior Colleges: Women's programs in community colleges. *Community College Frontiers, 5* (3), 62–63.

Sandeen, C.A., & Goodale, T. (1976). *The transfer student: An action agenda for higher education.* Gainesville, FL: Institute of Higher Education.

Savage, D.D. (Ed.). (1987). *Community, technical, and junior college statistical yearbook, 1987/88 edition.* Washington, DC: American Association of Community and Junior Colleges.

Saylor, G. (Ed.). (1949). *Junior college studies* (Contributions to Education No. 26). Lincoln: University of Nebraska.

Says modern dance is evil to education. (1922, February). *Memphis News Scimitar.*

Schenkman, C. (1973/1974). Vietnam vets fare worse, ETS says. *Community and Junior College Journal, 44* (4), 48.

Seay, M.F. (1964). Grants for technical education. *Junior College Journal, 34* (6), 9–12.

Seashore, C.E. (1940). *The junior college movement.* New York: Holt, Rinehart & Winston.

Sexon, J.A., & Harbeson, J.W. (1946). *The new American college.* New York: Harper.

Shabat, O.E. (1969/1970). Chicago City College. *Junior College Journal, 40* (4), 12–14.

Shannon, W.G. (1971a). AAJC approach: Canadian community colleges organize. *Junior College Journal, 41* (5), 5.

Shannon, W.G. (1971b). AAJC approach: International education grant. *Junior College Journal, 41* (6), 7.

Sheldon, M.S., & Grafton, C.L. (1978). Will the "real" average age of community college students please stand? *Community College Review, 6* (2), 37–39.

Sinclair Community College. (1987). *Community, Technical, and Junior College Journal, 57* (5), 68.

Skaggs, K.G. (1962). *Principles of legislative action for community junior colleges.* Washington, DC: American Association of Junior Colleges, Commission on Legislation.

Smith, N. (1972). AAJC's Black Caucus goes into action. *Junior College Journal, 42* (6), 16–17.

Smith, W. (1991). *The magnificent twelve: Florida's black junior colleges.* Unpublished manuscript.

Snyder, A.R. (1963). A college without freshmen or sophomores. *Junior College Journal, 33* (9), 20–21.

Snyder, W.H. (1941). Philosophy of semiprofessional education. In W.C. Eells (Ed.), *Why junior college terminal education?* (256–266). Washington, DC: American Association of Junior Colleges.

Stahr, E.S., Jr. (1957). Your theme—and the president's committee. *Junior College Journal, 27* (9), 490–496.

Stanley, J.W. (1965). The oldest junior college? *Junior College Journal, 36* (3), 37–38.

Starrak, J.A., & Hughes, R.M. (1948). *The new junior college: The next step in free public education.* Ames: Iowa State College Press.

Stoddard, G.D. (1944). *Tertiary education* (The Inglis Lecture, 1944). Cambridge, MA: Harvard University Press.

Storr, R.J. (1966). *Harper's university: The beginnings.* Chicago: University of Chicago Press.

Strayer, G.D., et al. (1948). *A report of a survey of the needs of California in higher education: Submitted to the Liaison Committee of the Regents of the University of California and the State Department of Education.* Sacramento: State Department of Education.

Sweet, G.W. (1971). *Black colleges in the South: From tragedy to promise.* Atlanta: Southern Association of Colleges and Schools, Commission on Colleges. (ERIC Document Reproduction Service No. ED 053 230)

Taylor, B. (1972/1973). Funding patterns of black private junior colleges. *Junior College Journal, 43* (4), 20–21.

Taylor, W.M. (1969). Bold plans for the bay state. In R. Yarrington (Ed.), *Junior colleges: 50 years/50 states* (pp. 73–83). Washington, DC: American Association of Junior Colleges.

Texan, head of junior college association, once Fort Worth student. (1921, March 6). *Fort Worth Star-Telegram.*

Thornton, J.W., Jr. (1972). *The community junior college* (3rd ed.). New York: John Wiley and Sons.

Thurston, A.J., Zook, F.B., Neher, T., & Ingraham, J. (1972). *The chief student personnel administrator in the public two-year college* (ERIC Clearinghouse for Junior Colleges, American Association of Junior Colleges Monograph Series No. 14). Washington, DC: American Association of Junior Colleges.

Timmins, R.H. (1962). Fund raising in junior colleges. *Junior College Journal*, 33 (1), 3.

Todd, L.O. (1962). Trends in development of community junior colleges in Mississippi. In J.L. Wattenbarger & W.L. Godwin (Eds.), *The community college in the south: Progress and prospects* (pp. 72–83). Tallahassee: Southern States Work Conference.

Two legislative landmarks in one month. (1964). *Junior College Journal*, 34 (5), 4–5.

Tyler, H.T. (1969). Full partners in California's higher education. In R. Yarrington (Ed.), *Junior colleges: 50 years/50 states* (pp. 158–168). Washington, DC: American Association of Junior Colleges.

University of Chicago. (1892). *First annual report.* Chicago: Author.

University of Chicago. (1897). *Board of Affiliations' minutes.* Chicago: Author.

University of Chicago. (1898). *President's report.* Chicago: Author.

University of Chicago. (1901). *Circular of information.* Chicago: Author.

Veterans in last term under Korean G.I. Bill. (1964). *Junior College Journal*, 35 (3), 36.

Victory on Hill: Navajo wins $6.7 million funding base. (1972). *Junior College Journal*, 42 (5), 63.

Walker, C. (1970). Junior colleges—strengthening Japan's economy. *Junior College Journal*, 40 (5), 60–72.

Walker, G.H., Jr. (1950). Analysis of negro junior college growth. *Junior College Journal*, 21 (4), 221–225.

Walker, G.H., Jr. (1958). Analysis of negro junior college growth. *Junior College Journal*, 28 (6), 337–341.

Walker, J.E. (1969). *Academic performance of native and transfer students in the upper division of the University of Florida, 1966–1968.* Gainesville: University of Florida, Office of Academic Affairs.

Walker, N.W. (1926, November). *The significance of the junior college movement*. Paper presented at a meeting of the American Association of Junior Colleges, Jackson, MS.

Walter, A. (1932). A proposed system of junior colleges for the state of California. *California Quarterly of Secondary Education, 8* (1), 68–77.

Warburton, T.S. (1969/1970). Los Angeles Community College District. *Junior College Journal, 40* (4), 33–36.

Warden, M.D. (1985). We go where they go. *Community and Junior College Journal, 55* (5), 42–44.

Wartime activities. (1942a). *Junior College Journal, 12* (8), 468–476.

Wartime activities. (1942b). *Junior College Journal, 12* (9), 531–538.

Wartime activities. (1942c). *Junior College Journal, 13* (4), 211–212.

Wartime activities. (1943a). *Junior College Journal, 13* (5), 239–244.

Wartime activities. (1943b). *Junior College Journal, 14* (4), 175–177.

Wartime activities. (1944). *Junior College Journal, 14* (7), 320–322.

Watanabe, A. (1964). Genesis of the Japanese junior college. *Junior College Journal, 34* (5), 20–24.

Watson, N.E. (1981). AACJC approach: A tribute to Ed. *Community and Junior College Journal, 51* (8), 2.

Watson, N.E., & Luskin, B.J. (1969/1970). Orange Coast Junior College District. *Junior College Journal, 40* (4), 40–42, 84–86.

Wattenbarger, J.L. (1953). *A state plan for public junior colleges, with special reference to Florida*. Gainesville: University of Florida Press.

Wattenbarger, J.L. (1957). *The community college in Florida's future. The report to the state board of education by the Community College Council*. Tallahassee: Florida State Department of Education.

Wattenbarger, J.L. (Ed.). (1965). *Guidelines for improving articulation between junior and senior colleges*. Washington, DC: American Council on Education.

Wattenbarger, J.L. (1969a). Five years of progress in Florida. In R. Yarrington (Ed.), *Junior colleges: 50 years/50 states* (pp. 54–62). Washington, DC: American Association of Junior Colleges.

Wattenbarger, J.L. (1969b). The other twenty-two. In R. Yarrington (Ed.), *Junior colleges: 50 years/50 states* (pp. 276–297). Washington, DC: American Association of Junior Colleges.

Wattenbarger, J.L., & Godwin, W.L. (Eds.). (1962). *The community college in the south: Progress and prospects*. Tallahassee: Southern States Work Conference.

Wellman, F.L., & Hamel, D.B. (1969). Community college progress in Virginia. In R. Yarrington (Ed.), *Junior colleges: 50 years/50 states* (pp. 236–245). Washington, DC: American Association of Junior Colleges.

Whitney, F.L. (1928). *The junior college in America* (Colorado Teachers College Education Series No. 5). Greeley: Colorado State Teachers College.

Willingham, W.W. (1972). *The no. 2 access problem: Transfer to the upper division.* Washington, DC: American Association for Higher Education.

Wilson, G. (1962). Phi Theta Kappa—The answer. *Junior College Journal, 32* (6), 358–361.

W.K. Kellogg Foundation. (1980). *The first half century.* Battle Creek, MI: Author.

Wyman, H.B. (1935). Junior-senior college relationships. *Junior College Journal, 5* (8), 419–425.

Wyman, H.B. (1944). How Phoenix has adjusted to war needs. *Junior College Journal, 15* (2), 77–80.

Yarrington, R. (Ed.). (1969). *Junior colleges: 50 states/50 years.* Washington, DC: American Association of Junior Colleges.

Yarrington, R. (1970). Report of the 1970 AAJC International Assembly. *Junior College Journal, 40* (8), 8–16.

Zoglin, M.L. (1976). *Power and politics in the community college.* Palm Springs, CA: ETC Publications.

Zook, G.F. (1946). Changing patterns of junior college education. *Junior College Journal, 16* (9), 411–417.

Zurayk, C.K. (1963). Foreword. In Frank Bowles, *Access to higher education* (Vol. I) (pp. 9–19). New York: Columbia University Press.

INDEX

San Francisco Junior College, 123
San Jose City College, 242
Santa Barbara High School, 38
Santa Fe Junior College, 191, 195
Sarah Lawrence College, 64
Saskatchewan, 204
School Review, 30
Scigliano, John, 254
Sears Roebuck Foundation, 157, 212,
    259, 269
Seattle Community College, 192
Seattle Community College District, 195
Seay, Maurice, 83, 157–158
segregation, 55, 66, 108–109,
    197–200, 243
Servicemembers Opportunity Col-
    leges, 253
Seth Low Junior College, 64
Shabat, Oscar, 195
Shall I Attend a Junior College?, 143
Shannon, William G., 155, 238
Shell Companies Foundation, 212, 239
Sigma Iota Chi, 106
Simone, Beverly, 242
Simonsen, Edward, 195
Sinclair Community College, 12
6-4-4 system, 49–50, 56, 65, 72, 84,
    86, 121, 173
six-year high schools, SEE high
    school extensions
Skaggs, Kenneth, 226
Sloan Foundation, 212
Smith, Norvel, 244
Smith-Hughes Act, 102–103, 150
Snow College, 68
South Carolina, 67
South Dakota, 68
Southeast Community College, 250
Southern Association of Colleges and
    Schools, 42, 92, 109, 254–255
Southern Illinois University, 169
Southern Regional Education Board,
    224–225, 274

sports, 80
Springfield Junior College, 48, 64
Sri Lanka, 205
St. Joseph Junior College, 32, 58
St. Louis Junior College District, 191,
    195, 252
St. Mary's College, 92
St. Petersburg Junior College, 134
St. Philips College, 109
Stalin, Joseph, 139
standards, SEE accreditation, testing
Stanford University, 26, 32, 34, 37,
    46, 77, 81, 86, 193
State College for Women, 173
State University of Iowa, 60
State University of New York, 64,
    84, 133, 174
*State-wide Planning and Coordination of
    Higher Education*, 225
Stephens College, 32, 105, 191
Stockton Junior College, 119
Strayer, George, 128, 274
student government, 106
student services, 232–233
Sullins College, 201
Surveys of American Higher Education, 86
Sykes, Abel, 245

Tappan, Henry, 8–9, 13, 25–26, 35,
    47, 62
Taylor, Ray, 259
teacher training colleges, SEE normal
    schools
tech prep, 50, 264, 267
*Tech Prep/Associate Degree: A Win-Win
    Experience*, 268
Tennessee, 66, 146
Tennessee Polytechnic Institute, 66
Tennessee Valley Authority, 97, 250
terminal education, 39–40, 49, 83,
    97, 101–102, 110–111, 120, 143,
    146
testing, 83, 103, 130, 192, 232, 234

ABOUT THE AUTHORS

Allen A. Witt chairs the communications/humanities department at the South Campus of Broward Community College, Florida. He is a former faculty member and administrator at Lake City Community College, Florida. Witt is also an adjunct professor in the Institute of Higher Education at the University of Florida. He holds degrees from the University of Florida, the University of North Carolina-Chapel Hill, and Newberry College, South Carolina.

In addition to his numerous articles and papers on higher education issues, Witt is an authority on leadership structures. During the 1980s he headed the research department of the Metro Group, an urban leadership consulting and research firm. In this role he examined and analyzed the leadership structures of eighteen cities in the United States, Southeast Asia, and Latin America. Witt brings his unique expertise in leadership structures and higher education issues to this history of the community college movement and its leaders.

James L. Wattenbarger is a 1941 graduate of Palm Beach Community College, Florida. He has maintained his close association with community colleges almost continuously since that time. He received his bachelor's degree with high honors from the University of Florida in 1943. After serving as a navigator in the U.S. Air Corps during World War II, he returned to the University of Florida to complete his master's degree and doctorate. His doctoral dissertation became the basis for the master plan for the Florida Community College System and has been used as a model for more than 30 separate states and institutions since then.

Wattenbarger has held a variety of leadership positions in higher education. From 1955 to 1968 he was director of the Division of

Community Colleges for the state of Florida. He has been active in a number of national organizations, serving on the Board of Directors of the American Association of Community Colleges, as a member of the Commission on the Future of Community Colleges, as chair of the National Council of State Directors of Community/ Junior Colleges, and as chair of the Legislative Commission. In 1987 he was awarded AACC's Leadership Award. Wattenbarger is currently a distinguished service professor emeritus, University of Florida, after having served for 24 years as director of the Institute of Higher Education and professor of higher education.

James F. Gollattscheck has been a teacher or administrator at every level of public education from elementary school through the university. From 1970 to 1984 he was president of Valencia Community College, Florida. From 1984 to 1992 he served as vice president for communications and executive vice president of the American Association of Community Colleges. Since retiring in 1992 he has been actively involved in professional writing and consulting. Gollattscheck has published four books and has contributed chapters for various books and numerous articles for professional journals.

Gollattscheck has been an active consultant, helping community colleges and community organizations examine the quality and comprehensiveness of their institutions. Accreditation and college structure have been major emphases of his professional career. Among the many awards he has received is the Lifetime Membership Award from COMBASE. He earned graduate degrees at the University of Florida and Florida State University. Gollattscheck currently lives in Paris where he is completing a book on retiring abroad.

Joseph E. Suppiger is vice president of instruction and student services at Del Mar College, Texas. He received his bachelor's degree from Milton College, Wisconsin, his master's degree from Kansas State University, and his Ph.D. in American history from the University of Tennessee. He has written more than 45 articles related to Abraham Lincoln and Civil War activities in Tennessee in addition to serving as editor of the *Lincoln Herald*.

Suppiger taught for more than eighteen years in colleges and universities in Tennessee, South Carolina, and Texas and served as vice president of academic affairs, Limestone College, South Carolina, and president, Del Mar College, Texas. He was designated a Tennessee Colonel by Governor Lamar Alexander.

Suppiger is noted as a college administrator who encourages and supports innovative activities and structures within the community college. This is the fifth book he has written or coauthored.